LEARNING TO FLOAT

The Journey of a Woman, a Dog,
AND
Just Enough Men

Lili Wright

BANTAM BOOKS

LONDON · NEW YORK · TORONTO · SYDNEY · AUCKLAND

LEARNING TO FLOAT
A BANTAM BOOK : 0 553 81439 7

First publication in Great Britain
First published in the United States by Broadway Books,
a division of Random House, Inc.

PRINTING HISTORY
Bantam edition published 2003

1 3 5 7 9 10 8 6 4 2

Copyright © Lili Wright 2002

Set in 11/13pt Goudy by
Kestrel Data, Exeter, Devon.

Bantam Books are published by Transworld Publishers,
61–63 Uxbridge Road, London W5 5SA,
a division of The Random House Group Ltd,
in Australia by Random House Australia (Pty) Ltd,
20 Alfred Street, Milsons Point, Sydney, NSW 2061, Australia,
in New Zealand by Random House New Zealand Ltd,
18 Poland Road, Glenfield, Auckland 10, New Zealand
and in South Africa by Random House (Pty) Ltd,
Endulini, 5a Jubilee Road, Parktown 2193, South Africa.

Printed and bound in Great Britain by
Cox & Wyman Ltd, Reading, Berkshire.

Lili Wright spent ten years as a journalist in New York, New Jersey, Connecticut, Utah and Mexico. Her work has appeared in newspapers across the US, including the *New York Times* and the *Baltimore Sun*. A graduate of Columbia University's M.F.A. program, she currently teaches creative writing and journalism at DePauw University and lives in Greencastle, Indiana, with her husband and daughter.

Praise for *Learning to Float*:

'The joy of this book is the combination of fearless self-confrontation and the freedom of the open road. Lili Wright did what so many women dream of: she drove away from her relationships, had adventures, and lived to tell the tale in a funny, honest, and fascinating book'
Haven Kimmel, author of *A Girl Named Zippy* and *The Solace of Leaving Early*

'Refreshing'
Vogue

'Following Lili Wright as she floats from one seaside town to another is an invitation to break from our stodgy existences and experiment with adventure in our own lives. A must-read, for not only the thirty-something crowd but those of us way beyond'
Joan Anderson, author of *A Year by the Sea*

'Wright is a deft wordsmith'
Publishers Weekly

'With ribald candor, Lili Wright charts the treacherous territory between the desire for emotional connection and the safety of cavalier independence. *Learning to Float* is an incredibly smart, brave, and honest book about a woman trying to come to her senses'
Ken Foster, author of *The Kind I'm Likely to Get*

'Well-written. Wright vividly describes her encounters'
Kirkus Reviews

'Romantic confusion has never been as much fun as this trip down the East Coast in Lili Wright's Mazda. *Learning to Float* is witty, touching, endlessly charming, and as human as a face in a snapshot'
Luc Sante, author of *Low Life*

*For my mother who loves books
and my father who always remembers*

Contents

settle (set'l) – vi. **1)** to stop moving and stay in one place; come to rest **2)** to cast itself, as darkness, fog etc. over a landscape, or gloom or silence over a person or group; descend **3)** to become localized in a given part of the body; said of pain or disease **4)** to take up permanent residence; make one's home **5)** to move downward; sink, esp. gradually (the car *settled* in the mud).

Webster's New World Dictionary

A New Beginning

My grandfather walks out onto the deck in Maine and drags a director's chair into the sun. I am typing terrible sentences into my laptop, trying to make something happen on the page.

Grampy props his feet on the railing and looks out toward Compass Island.

'You know Nana always wanted to be a writer,' he says.

Nana, my grandmother, Grampy's wife, has been dead for ten years. She is the relative I most look like, take after. She was difficult in half a million ways.

'You're kidding,' I say. 'I never knew that.'

'Well, you remember Nanny was always good at telling stories,' says Grampy, grinning now with the memory. Nana's fake Southern accent. The cigarette she waited for a man to light. 'Of course, they weren't always true, but they sounded good.'

Mermaid

I've never seen a mermaid, but for years I felt like one.

Half pretty woman. Half cold fish.

No one knows the precise origin of the folklore, but sailors from Scandinavia to the Caribbean have sighted these bare-breasted sirens perched on ocean reefs. The most common explanation is that sailors, overcome by sun and testosterone, mistook a manatee for a beautiful woman. Manatees and women do share certain traits. Both have hair. Both sun themselves. Both breast-feed their young. And, well, that's about it.

But apparently the isolation of a long sea voyage can take its toll on a man; he learns to let his vision blur with pent-up desire. One Arctic explorer understood this well and hired the ugliest hag he could find to serve as ship cook. When the old crone began to look good to him, he knew it was time to head home.

Though the myth of the mermaid dates back to ancient Greece, she's lost none of her allure. Wherever I drove that summer, from Kennebunkport to Key Largo, mermaids perked up T-shirts and billboards and roadside menus, inevitably copping the same cartoonish pose – huge breasts, a tantalizing golden mane, a curvaceous tail that slimmed to a wedged bottom fin. Mermaid as sex symbol; it has always struck me as odd. I mean, below the belly button, the woman has nothing but scales.

Then again, perhaps it's the logistical impossibility of possessing a mermaid that makes her so desirable. She's the lover who can't be kept, the lady fish who swims away. In revenge, the scorned suitor depicts her as caricature – a big-titted monster, a high-maintenance vamp with a hand mirror and comb. Maker of storms. Tormenter of ships. Seducer of seamen. Vargas Girl meets Flipper.

Yet, for some reason, I'd always seen mermaids as kindred spirits, independent women who artfully slip between worlds. A mermaid can woo a brawny seaman and, when she tires of him, flip her tail and dive down to play with silver fishes. But the more I thought this through, and I did a lot that summer, the more I decided I had it all wrong. A mermaid is the saddest sort of hodgepodge, fulfilled in neither world. Eye on land, tail in the sea, she lingers on the cold rocks, hoping to catch the eye of a passing sailor she'll never call her own.

At the Bar

Fenwick Island, DE. It was Happy Hour and the rummy crowd at Smitty McGee's had knocked back enough half-price drinks to feel sun-flushed and loose. Around large wood tables, beaming vacationers gorged on buckets of steamers. I sat alone at the U-shaped bar, breathing in cigarettes and radon, listening to the blender grind ice cubes into slush. Finally, Christi, with a name tag, arrived with my white wine, which was served in a fish bowl and tasted like apple juice distilled through dirty nickels.

'It's huge,' I said.

'Twelve ounces,' said Christi, smiling. Christi had a tan.

Twelve ounces was fine with me – I was looking to catch a buzz. A month ago, I'd fled New York and the romantic mess I'd made there. I do my best thinking near the ocean, like dull rocks that look brighter when wet, so I'd mapped out a coastal pilgrimage from Maine to Key West. I was thirty-three and single, a woman on the emotional lam. I couldn't go home until I made some decisions, until I knew what to say to whom. But so far, I hadn't come up with any great answers.

Christi returned with a menu. I wanted oysters, but funds were running low, so I opted for a salad. Then I pulled out the Buddha book my friend Maurice had recommended, a three-inch tome I had been too impatient to read for more than a few minutes at a stretch. So far, Buddha was wandering around hoping to find a prophet who could show him the Way. It wasn't much of a plan and, in that way, reminded me of my own venture. As I was discovering, wanting to find the Way and *finding* the Way were two very different things. Siddhartha had been muddling along for a hundred pages or so, meditating, waiting for truth to reveal itself. He was more patient than Job. Meanwhile, I had meandered a thousand miles from Maine to Delaware, waiting for *anything* to reveal itself. Frankly, I was getting impatient – for him and for me.

I read a couple sentences. Buddha was focusing on eternal enlightenment; I started worrying about Stan. Stan was a cop I'd met that morning who'd offered to let me sleep in his trailer, no strings attached, no Stan attached – he'd be out of town working for a couple of days. Though originally this freebie had seemed like a real traveling coup, now that it was nearly dark, the initial trustworthiness he had conveyed seemed like a distant and perhaps unreliable first impression. The idea of sleeping in a strange man's trailer, a man whose face I could no longer clearly picture, a man who said he was a cop but who knew? . . . well, it wasn't the most secure situation. I resolved to drink myself brave or sleepy, whichever came first.

Of course, if I'd *really* been brave, I never would have called Stuart. A woman of substance should be able to sustain herself, I lectured the side of my brain willing to listen. A woman of substance should be able to sustain herself without phoning up her ex. Look at Buddha. He left behind his wife and son for *seven years* and traveled alone, and even when the Way-less monk *had* company, he ate his meals without speaking, in 'mindfulness,' trying to appreciate every precious grain of rice.

Reaching for my wine, I took a hefty gulp and tried to decide just how much mindfulness I'd need to make this house white grow precious.

18

Two men walked in and slid onto the bar stools next to me. The younger one, forty or so, ordered beers and pushed a couple of bucks Christi's way. He had a mustache, straight brown bangs, and reminded me of Sonny Bono, back in the Cher days, only with thick glasses and wafflely sneakers. Beyond him slouched an older guy, bulldoggish with long gray sideburns, neck like a frog. Under his VFW cap, he wore the empty expression of a man thinking hard about his next cold draft.

I pretended to read until the younger guy, the one sitting next to me, interrupted.

'You mind if I smoke?'

I looked up. A scar broke over the bridge of his nose like shattered glass.

'No,' I said. 'Go ahead.'

I returned to Buddha. *Then they ate in silence, mindful of each bite*.

'You visiting?' he asked.

In bars, as on airplanes, it's always risky to start up a conversation with the guy sitting next to you, particularly if you're a single woman. A single woman at a bar sticks out like the final bowling pin waiting to be taken down. Still, when traveling alone, I'd rather eat with dubious company at the bar than alone in the dining room, if only to avoid that moment when the hostess peers over your shoulder and asks, 'Just one?' as if you've never had a friend in your life.

Besides, tonight, I had nowhere to go but back to Stan's trailer and I wasn't in any hurry to get there, so conversation seemed like a fine idea. I closed Buddha, *mindfully*, looked hard into this guy's glasses to convey I was not flirting but simply passing time, and set to work opening him up, seeing what lay inside.

'Visiting,' I said. 'I'm in grad school, traveling for the summer. What about you?'

'Oh, I live here,' he said, pushing back his sleeves. 'Work as a dental technician.'

'What kind?' I asked.

After being a reporter for ten years before grad school, I could usually gather someone's life story without revealing so much as my name. It isn't hard, really. Most people are desperate to find someone who will listen. Sure enough, this guy began yammering away about his work in dental care. He smoked a Camel, snuffed it out, and lit another. My salad arrived, and I dug into iceberg lettuce, while he smoked some more, eventually wrapping up his tale.

'My name's Carl,' he said, holding out his hand. His nails were bitten to the quick.

'Lili,' I said.

'Lily?'

'No, Lee-lee. Who's your friend?'

Carl looked confused. I pointed.

'Oh, that's my dad, Ward.'

Ward looked over. I smiled and held out a neighborly hand. I felt bad the old guy had been sitting by himself all this time. His hand was shoe leathery, and he had great gray bags under his eyes.

'Nice to meet you, Ward,' I said, trying to be polite. 'How are you?'

'Fine,' he said slowly. 'Been drinking since nine a.m.'

He turned back to the TV.

Carl grinned, as if this admission were endearing.

'Is he serious?' I asked.

'He's retired,' said Carl. 'He's free to do what he wants. He's earned it.'

I sipped my wine, digesting. Did that mean Carl had been drinking since breakfast? He didn't seem drunk, though I was quickly moving that direction. The bar had become warm and pleasantly fuzzy, like a sweatshirt turned inside out.

'You married?' asked Carl.

'No,' I said. 'You?'

I was going to hold up my end of the conversation. Tit for tat.

'Separated,' said Carl, cleaning what was left of his nails with a matchbook. 'Getting divorced.'

'I'm sorry,' I said. And I was. Just one more story of love gone south. We sat quietly for a moment or two. Carl ordered more beers. The bar was filling up. A chubby woman in a red tank top dangled her arm over her froggy guy, then wiggled her hand between two buttons and rubbed his chest.

'So what went wrong?' I asked.

'With what?'

'Your marriage.'

Carl stirred his dead cigarette in the ashtray, making designs in the cinders.

'We were married nineteen years. Three kids. We had a house, a big house on the bay, a boat, forty-five horsepower. In the summer, we'd take the boat out on the bay, cruise around. The kids loved it.'

He stopped. I waited a beat or two.

'Sounds nice,' I said.

'It was nice,' he said. 'It was nice until it wasn't nice anymore.'

Carl took a defiant swig of beer, wedged his chin against the air. Foam clung to his mustache, tiny bubbles waiting to pop.

'Is your dad still married?' I said, trying to shift the subject, scrounge up a little hope.

'My mom passed away last year, but they stayed married for forty-two years.'

'That's pretty great,' I said, perking up. 'So what was his secret?'

'I don't know.' Carl waved his cigarette. 'Why don't you ask him? Hey, Pop, I told this lady you and mom were married forty-two years, and she wants to know how you did it.'

The old man craned his big head my way.

'It waren't easy.' He turned back to the TV.

I smiled like this was a fine joke, then pushed back my salad. A cocktail tomato rolled around the bowl like a head without a body. Carl lit a cigarette, motioned Christi for another round. She brought two drafts and a wine.

'Oh, wow,' I said. 'You didn't have to do that.'

Carl nodded.

I couldn't imagine drinking a second glass, mindfully or mindlessly, but I bravely set forth in that direction. Happy Hour was over and the lights had dimmed down to sexy and the tape deck was thumping like a heart in love. Young people pressed against the bar, all big teeth and cleavage.

Carl spoke up again, his voice thin and ghostly. 'I guess it was a communication problem. There wasn't much point in talking anymore. So we gave it up.'

I could hear that silence. I saw his wife, a bony woman, pretty but frayed. She was still wearing her gray work skirt and stubborn panty hose as she leaned on a vacuum cleaner in the second-floor hallway. Toys were scattered about, and you could tell by vacuum tracks molded into the carpet that she'd steered around the playthings instead of picking them up. On a wooden table under a mirror sat a mug of cold coffee, nondairy creamer congealed into a cumulus cloud. As she looked up, her mouth puckered like yesterday's rose. She took a sip, frowned, turned on the vacuum. The machine growled, sucking and wailing, filling its cavernous belly with whatever dirt it could find.

I sipped my wine, hoping old Carl was going to lighten up and tell me more about dentures, reassure me that love didn't have to come to this, but he tapped his fingers on the bar, lost in thought.

'It got so I couldn't stand the sight of her,' Carl said slowly, as if I hadn't understood the first time, as if he wanted to make things perfectly clear. 'She couldn't stand the sight of me. *We couldn't stand the sight of each other.*'

I shuddered, watched his wife shut off the vacuum, turn her back, walk into the bedroom, close the sky-blue door. No love of mine had gotten that bad, but maybe I'd left before things ran their course.

It was time to go, but I wanted to get something from this man. A lesson perhaps, some nugget or quote to remember. In my experience, you're as likely to get decent advice from a stranger as a shrink, and you don't have to wait as long or pay as much or think up all the answers yourself. But you do have to be patient because the guy often drops the gem just when you're on the verge of giving up and hunting down someone who is, as TV journalists like to say, a 'better talker.'

Carl folded his cocktail napkin, then unfolded it and refolded it, like some origami project that wasn't going well. I ripped the cuticle on my thumb, a nervous habit I never realize I'm doing until I start to bleed.

'But I don't get it,' I said, wondering if I sounded drunk and deciding no, not quite. 'That's sort of why I'm taking this trip. Marriage terrifies me. I mean, forever is a long time, and how do you know when you've met the right person? What *happened* between you and your wife?'

Carl said nothing for several moments, just watched his smoke billow and plume. I sucked down wine like a thirsty plant. Who was I kidding? I was buzzed and feeling gloriously self-destructive, bold as the woman I wanted to be. Just when I assumed Carl had forgotten my question or didn't care to answer it, he looked at me hard, angry even, bullet eyes cocked, like I was the one who'd broken his heart, like this whole fiasco called love was my fault and he was ready to get even.

'I don't know,' he said, leaning in close, challenging me with his sticky beer breath. 'You're a woman. Why don't you tell me? *Where does love go?*'

Barbie

I'd like to report that I was once a tomboy, a spitfire who played cowboys and Indians, a brave soldier who marched off to battle to protect women and children with a loaded water gun and a Cracker Jack whistle. But truth be told, I was a girlish girl. In the quiet of my room, I hosted elegant tea parties with my best plastic china and whipped up angel food cake in an Easy Bake oven – just add water and stir. I played with dolls. Not baby dolls, who wet their diapers with real water and spit up on your shoulder. No, I wanted a doll who was nobody's baby. And so my best friend Page and I spent our grade school years living vicariously through the misadventures of you-know-who, that pinup of the playground we all know as Barbie.

For hours after school, we dressed and undressed our wonder girl. The premise was always the same: Barbie was going on a big date. Ken was picking her up in his red convertible in a half hour, and Barbie needed to look good, really good. Oh, the decisions that lay before us. So many outfits, so little time. We debated the relative merits of a tulip jumper versus a strapless pantsuit, hair in a bun, hair in Indian braids, hair in pigtails with ribbons. We fished through a trunk of accessories, a tangle of Day-Glo belts and batons and princess tiaras, hoping to assemble an outfit that would stop Ken dead in his tracks. We wanted Ken speechless; we wanted Ken down on his knees. In a primping frenzy, we tugged a nylon blouse over Barbie's nippleless chest, snapped a fur-trimmed skirt around her pinched waist, fluffed her bangs, rubbed dirt off her perfect behind.

Finally, it was time to go.

'*Ding dong*,' said Page, ringing the imaginary doorbell.

'Coming,' I said, opening the imaginary front door.

'Oh, hi, Ken,' said Barbie. 'You look great.'

'Thanks, Barbie. You look great too. Do you want to go to the movies?'

'I'd love to. Let me get my purse.'

Ken drove Barbie to the movies and, before the opening credits rolled, they were making out, their bodies writhing on the popcorn-studded floor like snakes at war. Hair flew. Or rather Barbie's hair flew. Ken's was made of plastic.

'Oh, Ken,' Barbie giggled. 'You're my Dreamboat.'

'You're beautiful, Barbie,' Ken said. 'Kiss me some more.'

After about thirty seconds, kissing got boring. Kissing wasn't half as much fun as trying on clothes. So we dragged Barbie back home and got her ready for her next big date. This time, a rodeo. Ken as lonesome cowboy. On went the gingham sundress, the red cowboy boots, the leather lasso. We checked Barbie's muted reflection in the tin-foil mirror to make sure she was still beautiful. She was.

'*Ding dong*.'

Surprise! It was Ken.

He had ridden into town on a stallion named Jake. This time Barbie didn't wait for the rodeo, she attacked Ken in the doorway. They tumbled onto the shag carpet, groping, Ken on top, of course. After a few frantic seconds, I suggested the beach was nice this time of year and Barbie needed a tan.

New date. New clothes. New man.

New man?

Ken, well, sure he was nice enough, but Barbie was feeling

restless. So while Ken was at the office, she flew to the Caribbean with G.I. Joe. When the man in uniform laid down his machine gun and succumbed on the sand, she set her sights on Action Jackson, later dumping the black belt for an orange-haired troll.

Barbie understood, heaven knows how, that *getting* a man is more fun than *having* a man, and *dreaming* about a man is best of all. Even a hunk like Ken was more desirable in the abstract than he ever was in person. And that's why, eventually, Page and I gave up all pretense. Barbie never had serious relationships; she never got that close. She'd barbie one man and then she'd barbie the next. Pretty soon Barbie didn't date anyone any more. Barbie just got ready.

Ghost Crab

I've heard it said that people who are still single past thirty are complicated, and I'm not sure if that's a compliment or a curse. In my experience, the world is divided into two distinct camps: the people who have their personal lives in order but their professional lives are a mess, and those whose professional lives are in order but their personal lives are a mess. Virtually nobody gets a handle on both.

Imagine two puppies, one leash.

I was a card-carrying member of the second camp. Holding down a job had never been a problem: I'd worked for a series of newspapers, for a TV morning show, for an unscrupulous tabloid. But my romantic résumé was a mishmash of long- and short-term calamities. I nearly always had a boyfriend. Sometimes two. Sometimes one and a half. Sometimes two halves, which I counted as a whole. In my experience, it is easy to fall in love and nearly impossible to fall out. For years, I never let go of one man until I had a firm grasp of another, like a string of paper dolls joined at the hand.

'You've never loved anyone,' Stuart snapped once last spring. Stuart was a veterinarian, my most recent ex. 'You've never given anything.'

We were fighting because I'd fallen in love again, this time

27

with Peter, a dreamy writer from New York. Peter had ringlets. Peter glided his finger down the underside of my arm while I sat drinking wine one night at a bar, trying to convince myself I wasn't *really* on a date. The man did more with one finger than some guys do with a whole body, or so I imagined. A few picnics, a few confessions, I was sure Peter was The One. I'd been wrong about Stuart, listening to the wrong voices, heeding the wrong muse. There was only one problem with this sudden change of heart. After several years of long-distance dating, Stuart had just moved from Utah to New York to live with me. His brown socks were tucked in my dresser drawer. His dog was snoozing on my carpet. Just when Stuart and I had decided to move in together, my heart had flown off like a runaway kite.

I wish I could say this was an anomaly, but it felt more like déjà-vu.

While most of my friends were married – many popping out babies – I was stuck in the boyfriend stage, unable to get my heart, head, and body moving in the same direction. The men I loved most I could never marry. The men I could nearly marry I wasn't sure I loved. Or maybe I told myself I didn't love them so I wouldn't have to get married. Or maybe I told myself I couldn't marry them because I didn't know how to love.

No, I wasn't one of those desperate single women, a trophy hunter trying to bag a stag, any stag, but it was time to build a relationship that would last. I was thirty-three years old, for God's sake. When Christ was crucified at thirty-three, he'd learned to walk on water. By the time Alexander the Great succumbed to fever at thirty-three, he'd conquered the civilized world. By thirty-three, a woman should know when love is real and when it's mere delusion. By thirty-three, a woman should be ready to, as my parents would say, settle down.

But I couldn't settle down. I could barely sit down. Picture one of those ghost crabs you see at the beach on Cape Cod.

Gray legs skittering sideways along the sand, diving into a hole another creature has dug. Those crabs run so fast you're not even sure if you saw them. Naked, scared, homeless. Looking one way, scampering another.

'Who are you willing to fight for?' Roger, the Washington spin doctor, once asked me after we had broken up. 'All these men are willing to fight for you. *Who are you willing to fight for?*'

I didn't answer because I didn't know.

One night, not long after Stuart moved into my apartment, things really came to a head. It was a humid spring night, and we decided to watch the NBA playoffs in the air-conditioned cool of the neighborhood sports bar. Inside, the usual crowd had assembled: clusters of earring-studded college students sharing pitchers of bad beer. Stuart strolled to the bar to check the score.

I looked up and froze.

There was Peter, the dreamy writer, nursing a draft beer, staring at the TV screen, standing not four feet away from Stuart. The two had never met, but each knew *of* the other, and now here they were, the boyfriend, the lover, side by side, two men at the bar. Stuart rooting for the Jazz. Peter rooting for the Bulls.

My whole life shrunk into a single picture frame.

That's when everything got really slow. Slow and hushed. Like a squirrel crouched on the roadside as headlights approach, I felt the rumble of tires, danger coming on.

It was only a matter of seconds before one of them turned around. If Peter turned first, he'd call out my name, and Stuart would figure out this was the latest candidate, the affair I'd confessed a few weeks earlier, the newest in a long line of what Stuart facetiously called 'Mr Perfects.' If Stuart called me over, Peter would turn around and quickly realize this was Stuart, the boyfriend, the veterinarian without the cure. Either way, there would be introductions. Words exchanged.

It was time to make a decision. Now, while Jordan had the ball.

There was Stuart, sturdy as a shortstop, an underdog with a tinge of melancholia. There was Peter, basketball tall with glasses, hair froing up like a steel-wool pad, his expression the rescue-me innocence of a man overly steeped in charm.

Panic rose inside me like a thermometer cooking in a fat man's fist. My head was a thundering bucket of noise. Voices chanting. A Greek chorus of ruination telling me all the ways my life could go wrong. *Choose*, they chanted, *choose someone, choose something. Remember, not choosing is its own choice. What are you so afraid of? Either man is as much as you deserve, so hurry up and decide. Decide now because you're running out of time.*

But I couldn't decide. I couldn't even begin to decide. Seeing the two of them together didn't clarify a thing. Their juxtaposition brought no epiphany, no greater understanding of what was right or kind or real.

Jordan drilled a basket from behind the three-point line. Then I made my move. Without a word to Stuart, I backed out of the bar, heading not out the front door but over the patio railing; I squeezed past the potted palm, past the punk girls catsuping their fries, scissored my legs over the leather cord, almost getting high-ended midcrotch, and sprinted down the block to the corner ATM machine, my heart in my socks.

I ran away that night. Then I ran away all summer.

I got in my car and vowed not to come back until I became somebody I could stand to be with. Instead of choosing one man, I'd leave them both. Escape into the safety of strangers; escape until I could stop hurting the people I cared for the most. Motion – the only consolation for a life that's hopelessly stuck.

I'd drive. I'd take notes. I'd be a reporter with no story. I would find a story or make a story or *be* the story, and – here was the really splendid part – all these stories would add up to something, reveal something, so that by journey's end I'd discover how to have and hold the love that continued to elude me. By leaving two men, I'd learn to live with one. By taking off, I'd find a way to stay put.

Unrealistic? Impractical?

Of course. I knew that before I left. My scheme was less than half baked; it wasn't even in the oven. Taking a road trip to find direction makes as much sense as looking for love in a singles' bar, but so long as there have been bars and cars, desperate people have tried both.

Sunrise

Mount Desert Island, ME. Any fool knows that when a woman departs on a journey of self-discovery, she's supposed to leave her boyfriend at home. Particularly if the boyfriend is really an ex-boyfriend or, even shakier, a sort of ex-boyfriend. And particularly if the sort-of ex-boyfriend is the proud owner of a one-hundred-pound dog. The adventuring woman drives herself, she's not chauffeured. *The adventuring woman drives her own car.*

And yet here we were – the three of us – Stuart behind the wheel, me, sleepy gun moll at his side, and, in back, warming my ear with his gamy breath, Stuart's chocolate Labrador, Brando. It was 3:00 a.m. and we were driving to the top of Cadillac Mountain, the highest point on the Atlantic Coast, the first place in the country to see the sun come up, on this, the longest day of the year. Solstice sunrise, the opening stanza of the poetic metaphor I'd concocted for this trip of mine. Greet the sun in Maine, drive south until I ran out of land in Key West, watch the big ball slip into the sea. It was a fine plan, but already things were running amok. After all my predeparture bravado about setting out alone, I'd ended up as copilot, relegated, as my mother had always been, to squinting at road signs and fiddling with heat controls. I didn't even know my way up the mountain.

'Where are we going?' I asked.

'Up,' said Stuart. 'Way up.'

There were reasons for this awkward arrangement. There were always reasons if you rationalized hard enough. Stuart was heading to Vermont to see friends and had suggested we piggyback up the highway, he in his Ford Explorer, me in my little white Mazda. It seemed childish to insist *This is my sunrise, shoo!* The truth was, neither of us was ready to concede our relationship was kaput. Even now reconciliation seemed within reach. Maybe sleeping together would mend the broken pieces. Sex as Super Glue. But last night we'd lain in our double bed in the Cove Motel like two old logs, thinking of all we would say if we spoke, staring at the cracked ceiling in silence. And yet there was still sunrise, one final smidgen of hope.

At the summit, Stuart pulled into the parking lot, where a dozen cars had gathered. I opened my door and felt an arctic wind. It was cold, unseasonably cold, or maybe at three in the morning in Maine, June always feels like March. In my gray sweatshirt, dirty sneakers, mussed hair cinched in a fuzzy elastic, I looked like a frazzled housewife yanked from the laundry room on short notice. Stuart, meanwhile, stood snug in his Utah finery: fleece and neoprene and waterproof boots. He could have climbed Everest with all that gear; he could have climbed Everest and survived. Maybe it was his veterinarian thing, but Stuart always looked calm and prepared. He thought nothing of being beeped out of deep slumber, tying his shoes in the dark, driving to the clinic to help a Rottweiler in need. He could handle almost any situation without losing his temper. It was one of the things I loved about him; it was one of the things that drove me nuts.

With a chilled hand, I patted Brando, who leaned stiff and stoic into the wind, doing his best guard dog impression, nose thrust east, tail extended, soft ears blowing like telltales from a mast.

'We can wait in the car where it's warm if you want,' Stuart said.

'That's cheating.' I was still holding on to the illusion that this was an adventure. And as its heroine, I'd probably have to get out of the car. 'Let's walk a ways,' I said.

An elderly lady draped in foul-weather gear passed us like a silent ghost. Brando growled, scared himself, then whimpered.

'Let me put Brando back in the car,' said Stuart.

I nodded, shivering, wishing yet again that Stuart hadn't come, thinking yet again how much I'd miss him when he left tomorrow. My old boss Rose once called me the most independent-dependent person she'd ever met. It was a fair assessment. I pushed men away and then ran after them. I hung on hardest when I was trying to let go. Now that I had a mad crush on another man, now that I had confessed this affair and Stuart and I were on the verge of calling it quits, he seemed utterly essential, a treasured being I couldn't live without. Now that our three years together were ending, I could see our enormous potential, everything we'd reached for and just missed. *We'd almost gotten married.* A year ago in Utah, Stuart had pulled out a little black box and proposed. I hadn't known what to say and had stammered that I needed time to think things over (what exactly, I had no idea, just *things*), and Stuart had said it wasn't a limited-time offer and the proposal had been left hanging ever since as we waited for me to come round. But I hadn't come round. Or rather, I'd gone round and round, circling over pros and cons, chasing my tail.

Stuart reappeared. 'Where to?'

I looked ahead. Past the parking lot, giant slabs of pink granite covered the earth like a moonscape. In the distance, people huddled together in blankets. Above the rocks stretched a wide swatch of blackness where the view of

Frenchman Bay would emerge, although at this raw hour, it was hard to distinguish land from water from sky. Below this expanse sparkled a glittery cluster of lights, unmistakably Bar Harbor.

I shivered, then noticed an embankment up ahead, one of those scenic overlooks that tells you what is where.

'Let's lean up behind that wall and get out of the wind,' I said.

At the end of the point, we hunched against the backside of a rock podium that supported a large map. It felt like a child's fort, secret and safe.

Stuart smiled, the wrinkles at the corners of his green eyes forming two delicate fans. At this ridiculous hour, he had the nerve to look handsome: his brown hair clumped in tufts, an endearing 4:00 a.m. shadow. We sat in silence and watched the colors slowly shift, like pigment seeping into paper, blackish blue to midnight blue, navy blue to slate. Soon Frenchman Bay came into focus. Spruce-covered islands filed across the water, stepping-stones for a giant with a loping stride. On the far side of the bay, the Schoodic Peninsula, lavender in this first light, rolled out against the horizon.

'It's going to be a race to beat the fog,' said Stuart.

I could see what he meant. A thin strip above the horizon was clear, but just above it, a long bank of purple clouds swept across the sky.

'I hope we see something,' I said. 'Even just a little sun.'

Voices broke out overhead, tourists watching the sunrise from the lookout above.

'*Ricky, you ready man?*'

'*It hasn't hit me yet.*'

Stuart and I crouched silently, pressing ourselves against the wall. There must have been a dozen people up there. We couldn't see them; they couldn't see us, and we eavesdropped like spies.

'*Where's Althea?*'

'*The girls are worrying over lipstick and earring stuff.*'

'It's goddamn windy up here.'

'It wouldn't be a wedding if something didn't go wrong.'

A wedding?

Stuart laughed silently, his chin forming a mischievous point.

'Hey, Reverend. Thanks for coming.'

'Now who's the best man?'

'No,' I mouthed into the cold air. It couldn't be.

'A sunrise wedding,' Stuart whispered. 'It's perfect. You might want to take some notes.'

I felt myself sweat, actually sweat in the cold. This could have been us. If I'd had any guts, we'd be getting married this summer, probably somewhere in Maine, where my family has vacationed since I was a kid. Instead, Stuart and I were nothing more than voyeurs, stuck in the cheap seats, with an obstructed view.

'No, Ricky, I'm telling you, this steak could have fed three people. There was no gristle, just meat and bone.'

'Grandma, you stand there.'

I was so embarrassed I couldn't look at Stuart. What was he thinking? I hadn't the foggiest idea until he poked me. 'We should go. If anyone looks over the edge, they are going to see us.'

I shook my head. 'I'm staying.'

Fate had served up a wedding. I would be an uninvited guest. I opened my journal and scratched down a description of the sunrise (long purple cloud, sky turning orange), but what I was really thinking was maybe this wedding was an omen that Stuart and I should get married.

And why not?

Stuart was a catch. Kind, caring – a veterinarian, for God's sake. A man who cared for animals. My parents liked Stuart. My friends liked Stuart. I liked Stuart, loved Stuart. My reservations? I only had one, or two, maybe three.

First off, Stuart was short, the same height as me, shorter if I wore heels. You'd think a mature woman would appreciate

36

vertical equality, but I didn't. Perhaps I was overly sensitive having reached my full height in what felt like second grade but must have been fifth. At school dances, as 'Stairway to Heaven' wailed endlessly on, I'd be bent over some boy like a croquet wicket. These scars run deep, but you don't not marry someone because he's short, or do you? ('I'd love to spend the rest of eternity with you, but all applicants must be five foot nine.')

Another thing: Stuart didn't sing in the car. He didn't sing anywhere but I noticed it most in the car. 'Oh, dear,' fretted my friend Bonnie. 'Not even a little?' He had a lousy voice. Who cares? The point was that he should sing in the car *despite* his lousy voice. That he didn't proved he was too proud to show just how badly he could do something. The father of my old boyfriend Andy used to insist that anything worth doing was worth doing badly. While at the time I found this woefully unambitious, I was beginning to realize he had a point.

The third reason was the biggie: I wasn't sure I loved Stuart enough to marry him. *Just how much love was enough? And what kind of love?* After three years, ours was not a zowie passion, lightning in a jar, but maybe lasting marriages were built on the kind of love we now shared, a blend of respect and fondness that grew out of what Stuart called 'shared experiences,' a dreary expression that reminded me of a summer camp brochure. *'Love can burn or love can last,'* Stuart liked to say. The dichotomy troubled me. And yet, after having survived several raging fires – charred bodies carted off on stretchers – a steady warm heat had its appeal.

But marriage?

All I could picture were Cheever characters, bent over dishwater, cutting themselves with hidden knives, staring at the blood, smiling. The wife wakes up in the middle of her marriage and realizes she is living with a stranger, that her husband is just a balding man who shares the garage, the bed. That's the way marriage seemed to work. The more

37

familiar you became, the more distant you felt. *Familiar* like *family* like *famine*. How could you promise never to fall in love again? Who would want to?

'*Hey, Ricky. Is there music?*'

'*Marjorie brought a box.*'

'*Wait, wait. Here comes the bride.*'

Pachelbel's Canon warbled in on short bursts of wind. The sun, now a blinding orange ball, had risen over the hills into the narrow space just below the heavy cloud bank. It was too bright to look at, too beautiful not to try.

'*Welcome everyone,*' said the reverend. '*In my fifteen years as a minister, I have done weddings at various settings, but none as beautiful as this. As we look out on this day that God has brought . . .*'

Maybe Stuart would propose again. Here in this new sun, in this new day. Maybe he'd take my hands in his and explain why we should spend our lives together and suddenly it would all make sense and we could stop searching for someone better, different, more something, and there would be no need for a journey of self-discovery because we'd have found each other right here.

'*Althea, divest yourself of those flowers. Join hands now, please.*'

I waited.

'*You both shall share all the joys and sorrows . . .*'

And I waited.

'*Althea, will you have Ricky to be your husband, to love and to cherish . . .*'

Perhaps it was up to me to get the ball rolling. I looked over at Stuart and tried to think of what to say, but instead noticed his nose was dripping and his eyes were lined with tears. Maybe he was overcome with emotion. It didn't seem likely. Stuart never cried. He took to the couch, now and then, lay in the gloom with his Scotch on the rocks melting and the Cowboy Junkies simmering and Brando consoling, but he did not cry. The only time I'd seen him break down was after the movie *Forrest Gump*. He said he felt like Forrest, always following around a girl who had somewhere better to be. He told me this, and I felt terrible.

I offered him a balled-up tissue.

'Are you crying?' I asked hopefully.

'Cry?' Stuart said, making his usual joke. 'Never. Just cold.'

He took the tissue and blew his nose. The drip returned. I pointed. He blew again. The top edge of the sun slid behind a cloud bank.

'*A ring is a symbol of your eternal love. Now, I understand both of you had your rings inscribed. Could each of you share those words with us now. Althea?*'

'*I thought about us starting a new life together so mine says "A New Beginning."*'

That's what *we* need, I thought, A New Beginning.

'*And you, Ricky?*'

'*Well, I had them write "I love you, Pumpkin."*'

Stuart chortled. I met his laugh. We had to laugh because this wasn't us, because Stuart wasn't crying and I couldn't think of what to say and that meant I was going to have to leave on a journey of self-discovery and lose him for good and I didn't want that, but instead of trying to explain this I whispered: 'I wait and I wait, and you never call me Pumpkin.'

'Oh, my little zucchini squash,' Stuart whispered back, 'you know how I feel about you.'

Stuart always thought I should know how he felt about me. I always wanted him to say it. I wanted him to say it *now*.

'*I now pronounce you man and wife. Ricky, you may kiss the bride.*'

Wild whooping broke out overhead, cheers carried on the wind. A voice cried out over the commotion.

'*Ohhhhhhh, yes! Ricky got a little tongue.*'

Stuart kissed my cold cheek. I looked at him, wondering if somehow we'd been married by proxy, if maybe Ricky and

Althea were movie stand-ins, actors pretending to be us while we got into character.

'Are you ready to go?' Stuart gently asked.

All at once, I felt stupid. Of course Stuart wasn't going to propose. After the way I'd treated him, he didn't dare believe in us anymore. We were only intimate from memory, from some old reflex. It was like being on land after a long day of sailing, how you can still feel the ocean rock, reminding you where you've been. And if he did propose, what would I say? That I didn't know. *After all this time, I still didn't know*.

I picked up a pebble, hurled it, watched it smack from rock to rock.

Clouds overwhelmed the sky. It was just another gray Maine day now, as if this brief moment of light had never happened at all.

'What are we supposed to do now?' I asked.

'Breakfast,' Stuart said. 'Blueberry pancakes.'

'How is that going to help?'

'We won't be hungry.'

Now that the wedding was over and the sun was gone, there was nothing to do but pick ourselves off the rocks, trudge back to the car, circle back down Cadillac Mountain with the heater blasting and my head pounding and Brando wagging happily because we were all back together, the three of us. We pulled into a pancake house for a half stack of buckwheat with blueberries. Poured maple syrup into sticky puddles. Waited for the butter to melt. I'd been on the road for all of three hours and already I wanted to go home.

'I feel sick,' I said, twisting my fork.

Stuart jammed a four-story bite into his mouth, then raised a sardonic eyebrow.

'It could be worse,' he said. 'At least you're not married.'

Traveling

We never took family vacations when I was a kid. While my friends and their families were discovering America, jaunting through Europe, barreling around the Bahamas on mopeds, the Wright family stayed put.

There were reasons for this. The first was that we spent every summer in Maine, and my parents could not imagine any place on the planet half as nice. Money posed another obstacle. The public schools weren't great in the Connecticut town where I grew up, so my older brother, Chip, and I both went to private day school and later boarding school. After my parents shelled out for two hefty tuitions, there wasn't much left over for posh ski trips to Aspen. But the paramount reason we didn't travel was not Maine or money but this: When I was in first or second grade, my dad developed claustrophobia.

That's what he called it, 'claustrophobia,' but actually it was more like agoraphobia, or some kind of all-over fear. He got anxious in crowded places, windowless rooms, social gatherings from which he could not easily escape. In public places, he had panic attacks, sudden bouts of dizziness and anxiety when he felt overwhelmed or trapped. He didn't like being around too many people. People in particular he

ed – his fraternity brothers, the fish man, the cashier at
  farm stand – with these people, he listened and joked. But
  ie lost stomach for the public, the dumb throng, the pushy
women in the deli line, the cars on the highway, the cocktail
idiots, the yeah-yeah carpool kids who on rainy days drew
hearts and swears in the mist of our station wagon windows
and chanted 'Bad, Bad Leroy Brown' in his ear, off key, chorus
only, in an endless rattle of noise. Noise. Noise was too much.
Parties were too much. My mother playing piano was too
much.

Though my father was troubled – afraid of his fears, afraid
to trace them back wherever they led – he never sought
professional help. Psychiatrists were suspect characters,
smarmy opportunists who got rich convincing healthy people
they were sick in the head. Instead, Dad refrained from doing
things that made him uncomfortable, and over the years, this
list continued to grow. He didn't go to movies or eat in
restaurants, wouldn't fly in a plane. One day he quit his job at
the bank and never went back. He dabbled in real estate but
couldn't stay in the game without capital, which we didn't
have. Mom went to law school and supported us, while Dad
stayed home and cared for me and Chip – a role reversal
virtually unheard of in the seventies, at least in our private-
school circle, a world where fathers commuted to the
insurance office and mothers played paddle tennis at the
country club.

I never understood what was wrong with my dad. It was
seldom discussed. When friends asked what my father did for
a living, I said he worked in real estate. (This wasn't *really* a
lie, I told myself, it was the last thing he did and he might,
conceivably, go back to it.) My dad worked real estate all
through my years in high school and college until he was old
enough to take early retirement, which, in a way, is exactly
what he did.

We never learned what caused his anxiety. Was it psy-
chological? Chemical? To this day, Dad blames Manhattan.

Years ago, one sweltering August afternoon while he was in business school, the subway broke down, and he was stuck for hours in an airless car, pressed next to strangers, sweating in the dark. The same summer he lived in a steamy railroad apartment. Every night, he'd drag a mattress next to the lone window, trying to find a little air. Dad says he was never the same, although I suspect his troubles started much earlier. His mother, Virginia, Nana to me, divorced when he was a toddler. The split was so bitter my father only saw his natural father twice more in his life. Nana later married Grampy, who adopted Dad and raised him as his own son, but it was not the most secure childhood. While Nana went to graduate school during the war, she dropped off her little boy with her sister or mother for weeks, months, years at a time. Later, Dad had trouble learning. Teachers instructed him to write with his right hand, not his left. When he read, words jumped around the page, letters flopped side to side. Parents disappearing, home in flux, difficulties in school, they did a number on my dad. I suspect this is why he craves control at all costs. He wants to know what is going to happen next. His mantra is 'I hate surprises' (even good ones), and he means it.

As a child, I didn't understand any of this. All I knew was that at any time, Dad might shatter, like a delicate vase on the edge of a mantel. As if to confirm this, he started carrying a cane to the supermarket. He'd bring the wooden stick with him in case he ever felt boxed in or lost or got stuck in the canned soup aisle, unable to move. I hated that cane and all it stood for, hated how it followed us wherever we went, reminding us how, any time we left the house, something might go terribly wrong.

Since then, Dad has filled his days with finances and car maintenance and groceries and worry. He worries about many things, particularly me, about my jobs and my love affairs. He worries about my credit rating, my lost credit card, the tires on my car, the paint on my car, the rust that is spreading, that I won't find what I was looking for in the refrigerator so he'd better have a look, that I won't stack the dishwasher to optimal capacity, that I'll never get one of those journalism prizes (*What are they called? A Pulitzer*), that I'll get lost on the highway, that I'll forget my estimated tax payment, that I'll marry a man I don't love, that I'll marry a dolt, that I'll never marry, that I'll lose my apartment, my job, my patience, my way, my traveler's checks, my proof of insurance, my car keys, my chance to have a baby. Sometimes he jokes about his worries – 'Well, you know I have to have something to worry about' – but more often worry festers like a untreated wound. Drinking eases his nerves, but he doesn't want to do too much of that, another worry, so instead he tries to 'keep things simple.' Basic people. Basic days. Basic civility. When ATM machines and home computers and voice mail and the Internet came along, Dad said no thanks, he was keeping things simple. But the world doesn't wait around for those who want less. Life got complicated and left my father behind.

How a father with claustrophobia raised a daughter with wanderlust, how an agoraphobic raised a reporter, is beyond me; I just know that it happened. I like to think I take after my grandmothers. There's no doubt I look like Nana, so much so that when the doctors presented my mother with her newborn daughter, she peeked into the swaddling and saw, with more than a little trepidation, that she'd given birth to her mother-in-law. On more than one occasion, when I would make some particularly cutting remark, Dad would accuse me of 'turning into Nana.' This was intended as a threat, but turning into Nana didn't scare me. From what I could tell, grandmothers – my two grandmothers – were having all the fun. They were the storytellers in our family; they were the travelers.

As a kid, I used to brag to my mother that I would be the best grandmother ever. Mom would look at me, perplexed.

'Aren't you missing something?' she asked. 'What about being the best *mother*?'

I shrugged indifferently. Motherhood held little appeal.

44

While I depended on my mother's steady love, she had none of the dash and swagger of a grandmother. Grandmothers had all the freedom and power, the stories and the cigarettes. Grandmothers had luggage. Grandmothers could move.

For Nana, travel was an act of reinvention. She liked to be pampered, to pretend she was one of the 'upper ups.' Onto the *QE II* she swished, first class all the way with her set of matching monogrammed luggage. Before you could wave a white hankie adieu, she was sitting at the captain's table, Scotch in hand, flirting. Once, in Italy, she was mistaken for a glamorous American movie star. She confessed in a loud whisper that, yes, she was the leading lady, traveling under an assumed name to escape her devoted fans. Another time, prior to boarding a European cruise, she had Grampy change their dollars into pounds so she could pass herself off as British.

My other grandmother, my mother's mother, Betsy, dressed in peacock colors, drank all the alcohol she wanted, and traveled to India, to Africa, in one or two nylon dresses. Like Nana, Grandmother was a raconteur with no qualms about flexing the facts. (Not until he applied for a passport for his honeymoon did my uncle learn he was not born on Valentine's Day, as he had always been told, but a day earlier. My aunt's birthday was nudged a day forward so it would land on Halloween.) Grandmother studied the travel section of the *Times* and kept a folder of places she wanted to visit. When Grandfather announced he had a spare week or weekend from work, she produced an itinerary and packed their bags. Not many bags, mind you. Grandmother believed in traveling light. With great chortles, she would recount how Grandfather rescued – literally saved – some silly American woman who was stranded with her bags at the Gare du Nord because she couldn't carry her luggage and couldn't find a porter.

'Never pack more than you can carry,' she'd tell me. 'You can't count on a man coming to save you.'

While my grandmothers were adventurers, neither traveled as much as she wanted. They were hampered by the usual constraints – time, money, children, husbands with careers, husbands who didn't share their passions. Their inability to pick up and go was a source of grinding frustration. And now the travel gene had jumped a generation, like a skipping stone with a particularly long bounce. Only when traveling did I feel truly alive. Traveling, falling in love, it was the same sort of high. That both were ultimately unsustainable only made me crave them more.

Forget keeping things simple. Bring on the surprises.

Though the little voices cautioned it was getting time to settle, settle in, settle for, settle down, I muzzled these mutterings. One more love affair before marriage. One more trip before stagnation. One more adventure before I turn in my car keys and close the front door.

The Parking Lot

Rockland, ME. Brando slouched on the hot pavement, doing his very best to look forlorn. Leash slack, shoulders heavy, he watched Stuart with wistful eyes, laying the guilt on thick. The flurry of duffel bags and tents and bicycles, the transferring of gear from the blue truck to the white car, signaled something irregular was afoot, a move, a change, a break in the old routine. Someone was going somewhere; someone was being left behind. Brando wanted to make damn sure the latter someone wasn't him.

The day after the wedding on Cadillac Mountain, Althea and Ricky flew to Cancun for their honeymoon (or so I imagined), and Stuart and I drove to the Rockland Ferry Terminal to break up.

Rockland is a small port town about halfway up the Maine coast. It's where you catch the ferry to North Haven, the island where Nana and Grampy have two shingled summer houses and a swath of land on Penobscot Bay. But this time, I wasn't going to North Haven. Stuart and I had merely stopped in the terminal parking lot to repack, to separate his things from mine. Stuart was driving on to Vermont. I was heading south to who knows where.

The weather was all wrong for a good-bye. The sky was a

cloudless blue, the air sailboat crisp. I watched Stuart futz around with a bungee cord, sizing up empty spaces and finding inventive ways to fill them. He was a master packer, good with his hands, the first man I had dated who could actually fix things: toaster ovens, bike flats, whatever was smoking under the hood.

'I'm going to leave you this,' said Stuart, holding up his empty cooler. 'You're going to need it.'

Brando whimpered.

'It's okay,' I said, scratching behind his ears. 'You're coming with me.'

It was an odd arrangement, leaving the boyfriend and taking his dog. But we'd decided Brando would be happier on the road than holed up in my studio apartment in New York with Stuart, who was starting a yearlong medical fellowship, who'd be looking for his own apartment, moving out of mine. Besides, Stuart thought Brando would be good protection for me on the road.

My father was doubtful.

'I've met Brando,' he said dryly, when I had called to tell him about my plan, 'and he's not exactly the kind of dog who is going to protect your virginity.'

A silver-haired couple in Bermuda shorts strolled by with a canvas sail bag and a carton filled with liquor bottles. Summer people, with sail hats and wrinkled knees. Bostonians, I imagined, married forty years and still starting the summer with a pit stop at the New Hampshire border for tax-free booze.

'Brando and I are sad,' I called out to Stuart. 'We need ice cream cones.'

Stuart turned to me, his eyes taking in me and his dog and my car and the ferry dock and the vacationers and the lone seagull gliding thin through the summer sky and the smoke-stacks of the fish-processing factory, pumping out a noxious smell.

'It's going to be okay,' Stuart said. 'This is what you wanted.'

He slammed my trunk, then walked toward me. I reached

around to hug him. He felt fragile in my arms, as if there were once more of him, as if this were all that was left.

'Be careful,' Stuart said, his words drifting over my shoulder. 'Call me from the road. Be good to Brando. Have him call me from the road.'

'I love you,' I said. I wanted him to understand this, even if I didn't quite.

Stuart pulled away.

'I love you,' he said. 'Now go.'

Stuart took Brando's leash off the post and handed it to me, then walked back to his truck in his worn suede moccasins, the ones I'd threatened to throw away. He shut the front door, turned the ignition.

I ran after him.

Love was so confusing, who you needed, who you wanted, who you wanted now but not forever, who you wanted forever but not now. When I got to his window, I found I had nothing to say.

'Drive carefully,' I said.

'I will,' said Stuart. His voice had a cardboard quality, the tone he used when he was trying to remain composed. 'You too. Be safe.'

He stared through his windshield, cracking his jaw, refusing to look at me. Then his voice broke. 'How do you think I feel saying good-bye to my two favorite people?'

'I'm sorry,' I said. 'We'll be back.'

'Do you expect me to wait forever?'

Stuart would not cry. He would drive away before he cried. He reached for the stick shift. 'Let me go.'

The truck swung in reverse, then headed up the hill, leaving me and Brando standing in the parking lot. I waved. I'm not sure Stuart saw it, but I waved. Brando pranced nervously, licking his jowls, not taking his eyes off the place Stuart had been and now wasn't. I looked there too, willing the blue truck to turn around and come back, but it didn't. And we waited and it didn't. He had left me, us.

'C'mon, big dog,' I whispered.

I pulled Brando's leash. He whined, fidgeted, wouldn't budge. I reached into my pocket for a low-fat dog biscuit, hoping he wouldn't fall for this trick, hoping Brando was so in love with Stuart that he'd sit forever in the parking lot and wait, but his whiskers twitched at the smell of chicken. He turned and snatched the biscuit from my hand. I felt like the evil stepmother, winning over children with cheap candy bars.

The two of us padded back to the car. Brando hopped in the backseat. He sat upright, curious, trying to figure out this sudden turn of events. I closed the door, careful not to catch his tail, backed the car around in a half circle, headed up the road, driving over the same stretch of pavement we'd decided to no longer watch.

A quiet lane led out of town, a row of white houses, orderly and complete. I fumbled for the radio, racing through channels to find a love song, finally landing on an old tune whose words I knew by heart. *He's so fine, he used to be mine. Yeah, yeah, yeah, yeah.* Merging onto Route 1, I rolled past the strip malls, parking lots baking in the sun. *How I love my baby, he's so fine, so good lookin', he's so fine . . .*

At the red light, I looked around. Some guy in the next car had his window down and was giving me the once-over. Sometimes I get embarrassed when people catch me singing, particularly when I'm crying at the same time. But today, here, in the first moments of my New Beginning, I didn't give a shit.

Swimming Lessons

Beach toys in hand, Page and I raced over the hot sand toward the ocean, the crashing surf filling our ears. At an open stretch of sand, we threw down our towels, our toys. Page ran into the water, and I stopped and stared with something like awe.

It was the first time I'd ever seen waves.

The only beach I knew was our cove up in Maine, where the ocean laps to shore, so clear and calm that no matter how deep you wade, you can always see your cold feet beneath you and study your reflection on its welcoming face. But this was Cape Cod, where Page's family had a summer house. This was a *real* beach with sandbox sand, not pebbles, with a lifeguard perched in a white lookout chair, with teenagers tanning in a line, listening to Top 40 songs, beating back time with their toes, with mothers circled toward the sun, sipping Tab and passing the communal potato chip bag. The waves here looked like ones I'd seen in picture books, only bigger and madder, as if each wave had something important to say and we'd all better listen. They were beautiful, and they scared me.

Looking up and down the beach, I could see all the other kids knew what to do. They dove into the surf or rode on top of it or sank to the bottom to hide, but I had no idea how to swim in water like this.

'C'mon, it's great,' Page shouted with a wave. She'd swum out past where the waves crested and was bobbing about, sleek as a fish. 'C'mon.'

I waded hesitantly into the water, holding my shoulders, pretending I was cold to buy a little time. When the water reached my chest, an enormous wave approached, curled its upper lip, and ate me whole in one swallow. Suddenly I was scraping along the sand, trapped underwater, hair choking my face, wondering where I was going, whether this was how people drowned. I couldn't move. I couldn't breathe. Everything hurt.

All at once, the wave heaved me onto the shore, as if, having taught its lesson, it had grown sullen and bored. As I staggered to my feet, my legs wobbled and my nostrils burned. I burped up peanut butter, potato chips. Digging sand out of my swimsuit, I tried not to cry.

Page called for me again.

'You've got to come farther out,' she yelled. 'It's great.'

'It's great *here*,' I yelled back, smiling, splashing water around like a kid to convey everything was just grand right where I was.

I should have swum out farther, of course, but I didn't know that then. I had no idea that beyond the breakers, the ocean rocks you in the most gentle way and you can float on your back in its rhythm and look up at the pillowy clouds and feel as coddled as driftwood, smoothing out over time. That sort of pleasure was inconceivable from where I stood. All I saw were the waves.

So I stayed where I thought it was safe.

Too scared to go deeper, too proud to turn back, I waded up to my chest, legs bracing against the undertow, and waited there for the next swell to come take me down.

Grampy walks out onto the deck in Maine and drags a director's chair into the sun. I have just changed my font to Zapf Dingbats, making what little I have written illegible. Much to my surprise, it looks better this way.

'Lili, I forgot to show you.' Grampy holds up what looks like a plastic tennis racquet. 'Have you seen one of these? It's a Japanese invention, an electric fly swatter. You turn it on and an electric current runs through the wire. Those Japs, they think of everything.'

Grampy, a retired biochemistry professor, likes nothing more than a new gizmo: healing magnets, garlic strippers, the anticancer contraption he keeps in his basement known as 'The Zapper.'

'It looks like quite a machine,' I say.

'So, Lili, when you write your Pulitzer Prize-winning novel *Grampy and Me*, you don't have to make it all factual. You start with the fact you're stuck on this island with this old fuddy-duddy guy, that sort of thing. You begin with a few facts and change things a bit. Take a dozen people and turn them into three or four strange types. It's called poetic license.'

'Do you know any writers?' I ask.

'I knew Alan Jay Lerner. He was more of a songwriter. Anyway, we played football together at Choate. He went through nine wives.'

I sit up in my chair. 'Who has time for nine wives?'

'Well,' says Grampy. 'I guess he didn't have time for eight of them.'

Natural Selection

Lot 59, Pine Grove Campground, Hampton Beach, NH. While I struggled to set up the tent, Brando marked the perimeter of our campsite with short blasts of carefully targeted piss. With a toothy grin, he jogged from picnic table to trash can to pine sapling, blessing each with his finest holy water. No matter how often I'd watched this ritual, it never failed to amaze me. The inefficiency, the machismo, the homage to all objects remotely phallic . . . it was just so male. I was used to girl dogs, sensible females like the English setter we grew up with, who would pick a soft patch of grass, hunch modestly, relieve herself, get on with her life. But for Brando, every whiz was a Whitmanesque celebration of self. Even when the well ran dry, he'd go through the motions, showing the range of his ambitions, his potency, his musk.

We had made it to New Hampshire. Earlier that morning, I'd pulled off 1–95 at a town called Hampton Beach. I knew nothing about the place, but I wanted to swim in every state I visited, and it seemed likely that a town called Hampton Beach would offer such an opportunity. Hampton Beach turned out to be hectic, steeped in concrete, one of those beach towns with millions of parking meters and no place to park. The sky was overcast, the air half dead. Brando looked hot and bored, and since dogs weren't allowed on the beach, I decided to bag the swim and instead mark my stay in New Hampshire with a rite of passage: I'd spend my first night camping alone.

Now I realize, for most people, sleeping alone in a tent hardly constitutes an act of great daring. My Utah friends wouldn't even classify it as an adventure, especially if you're talking campground camping, where everyone's stacked up like cordwood and you spend all night cuddled up next to some goateed dude blasting Black Sabbath. But *any* camping was an adventure to me. The closest my family came to nature was mowing the lawn, and the only times I had slept *en plein air* was with male suitors. Out west, men invite women camping when they are trying to finagle them into the sack. Asking a girl to unroll her mummy bag is less forward than inviting her to bed. Camping is so healthy, so downright natural. *Why, look at all the stars*. Once you've both drunk yourselves silly on cheap red wine, the man is primed to make his move, and the woman is primed to accept it. Even the tawdriest male specimen looks appealing when you're marooned in the desert with nothing but wailing coyotes and a bag of blue tortilla chips. Besides, any woman worth her salt understands the implicit suggestion behind a Utah man's 'camping' invitation. Should the woman accept this mission, it's because she's ready to look up and see stars.

Another metal stake bent in two. This was my first tent assembly and despite Stuart's predeparture lesson (he had tried not to be condescending, really, he'd tried), I was having a hard time wobbling the stakes into the ground. I picked up a rock and started banging the stake straight again, feeling like Wilma Flintstone, without the pearls, without Fred. I jammed the last stake in and picked up a tent pole, creepy contraptions that always remind me of dislocated limbs. After clicking the joints in place, I hunted for the loops to slide them through, and that's when I realized I'd staked the entire tent in upside down.

Oh, it's all part of the experience, I muttered, ripping out stakes. *This* is where the good stuff begins. Hardship. Endurance. Why, every great journey of self-discovery begins with a tent. The pilgrim sleeps on the hard ground, gazes up at the Milky Way, puts her worries into cosmic perspective. She hunts, she gathers. Her arm muscles chisel. As the sausage browns and the coffee percolates, she finds Meaning in a sparrow's song, in the way sunlight caresses the tender veins of an oak leaf. *Blah blah blah*. I wasn't camping for the experience; I was camping to save money. Between food, gas, and lodging, the couple thousand dollars I'd squirreled away could easily evaporate before I reached New Jersey.

With the stakes happily nestled in new holes, I fed the poles through the nylon loops, fastening them in the eyelets at the base of the dome. Over went the rain fly. Up went the awning. Soon my pup tent was standing, all four feet of it.

I sat at the picnic table, admiring my handiwork, wondering what to do next. What exactly do you *do* camping if you don't get high or have sex? I picked the dirt from my nails, touched my toes, smoked a cigarette to create some kind of mood – a get-out-of-Dodge mood, an *Easy Rider* mood, sexy and knowing, half hoping a cute ranger would come along and create a diversion. When no one bit, I changed strategies, opted for waiflike, waited for a nice mother to offer a lemon square, an apple.

Still no takers.

There must have been two hundred people crammed into this woods, but each campsite was an island, disinterested in what lay beyond its shore. The smell of hamburgers and toasting buns filled me with lonesome yearnings. A gang of children raced by on bicycles, plastic fringe blowing back in a breeze of their own making, sneaker laces fluttering dangerously near the chains. Across the dirt road at a neighboring compound, a family readied dinner. Big Daddy going crazy with the lighter fluid. *Squirt. Squirt.* Girl sipping soda through a straw. Boy noshing cookies. Tired Mom cutting carrots into sticks, her voice meting out law and order.

What did I say, Michael, what did I just say?

He started it.

Did not.

Families always made me feel alone, like a 'single person,' a term I'd always resented. Families are so insular, so pre-occupied with one another, so devoted to vegetables and bedtimes and watching their step – sensible priorities we single people had the freedom to ignore. I took out my notebook and wrote *He started it. Did not*, wondering if this meant something. *She started it. Did not. She started without him. She could never start without him.* This was getting me nowhere. I debated calling Peter, imagining his voice in my ear, but instead settled for the consummate distraction: food.

'C'mon, Brando.'

The brown dog harumphed into the backseat, and as we drove through the campground, a small boy on a bike chased us down the dirt road. I jammed the accelerator, sending up a smoke bomb of dust. The boy squinted, then turned his rubber wheel for home.

Families – I blew hot and cold on the whole idea. The first time I asked Stuart if he wanted children, he replied with a half yawn, a gesture I later identified as an unconscious sign of nervousness, that 'It might be important some day.'

'*Might be important?*' I snorted. 'Boy, that's enthusiasm.'

While I teased Stuart for being dispassionate about the miracle of life, I harbored my own ocean of doubts. Could I give enough to a child? Could I care for a little being even more independent-dependent than me? So much of my identity was caught up in being on the run. I tried to imagine slowing down to tuck away animal crackers, extra diapers, a pacifier, and all the other sweet-smelling accoutrements babies need before they are carried outdoors. The drool, the mustard poops, the nasal aspirators honking up snot, the fussfuss, the googoo, the dada, the mama – everything happening in syrupy twos. The *thereness* of babies, wherever you left them, *there* they were. Even when they grew up, moved out, they were still *there*, even when they weren't. Children were like a computer virus you couldn't delete; they ate up your memory, devoured your RAM.

And why did all my dreams about babies turn into ghoulish nightmares? In one dream, I gave birth to a puppy dog who bore a startling resemblance to Brando. Another night I delivered Satan's son, an orange-eyed, fanged-tooth love child I conceived after the devil had come and, well, possessed me. Once I breast-fed a newborn who gazed up from my snowy bosom and began talking in full sentences; it (babies were always its, not hes or shes) turned out to be a grown man under a spell. Then there was the time I discovered my little it in the refrigerator, frozen solid next to four sticks of butter.

Maybe I wasn't the mothering type. The whole idea of breast-feeding revolted me. My girlfriends swore it felt warm and womanly, but I didn't relish one of my favorite erogenous zones being turned into a lunch counter.

'Oh, no,' friends cooed, 'just wait until the endorphins kick in. Just wait. Remember. It's different when they are *yours*.'

I wanted children. I wanted children because I didn't want to miss out on one of life's great – if not greatest – experiences. Creating another person. Watching a baby discover its world. This was the real stuff of life. Besides, after hundreds of periods and thousands of birth control pills, it seemed a shame never to put my equipment to use, to *get* something after all that pain. But maybe I was more suited to being a father than a mother, one of those 1950s' dads who loosens his tie, reads a teddy bear storybook, and tucks Junior into bed. Being a father, being *that* kind of father, was the sort of low-impact parenting I could handle. But to be a mother, you had to wade into deep waters. Practically drown.

And yet other women did it, loved it. My friend Bonnie once dreamed her little boy had fallen out of her apartment window and that she had jumped after him because life wasn't worth living without little Harris.

'You just have no idea how much you can love a child,' she said. 'I used to think I couldn't love anyone more than Rosy.'

Rosy was her dog.

'So Bob is number three?' I asked. Bob was her husband.

'No, Bob is number two,' said Bonnie with a sigh. 'On a good day.'

The supermarket was cold as a meat locker, bright as radiation. You can feel pretty small in those mega-grocery stores, surrounded by so much choice. Stuck in the cracker aisle, I stared at the low-fat crackers and the low-salt crackers and the original crackers with salt and fat and the breadsticks with sesame seeds or poppy seeds or garlic or everything all together and one brand was on sale but the bigger package might be cheaper if you could only do the math. Possibility, packaging, they were wearing me down.

I landed at the Garden Bowl Salad Bar with its iceberg lettuce, defrosted peas, tiny ears of corn from a can. A nurse in a stained white uniform was scooping watermelon chunks. Her name tag said 'Lois.' Farther down a mechanic, his face worn from sun and cigarettes, was doing some damage to the potato salad. I picked up a plastic clamshell container and blindly shoveled. A minute later, I browsed the wine aisle. This must be how alcoholics get their start: in for cottage cheese, out with Gallo in a box.

By the time we got back to camp, it was dark. The mosquitoes were so monstrous, so utterly immune to bug spray, that I ate huddled inside the tent. Leaving my shoes outside, I crawled in with my salad, wine, book, and this new gizmo I'd bought called a Jakstrap, a modern version of the coal miner's lamp. An elastic band slips over your head, and there's a slot for a skinny flashlight. Sitting cross-legged, flashlight beaming, I felt like a one-feathered Indian, a chief without a tribe. Dinner hadn't traveled well; the hard-boiled egg had rolled into the melon and the melon tumbled into the pasta salad. I pulled out my Swiss Army knife, admiring its bright red economy, and uncorked the wine. After swigging from the bottle, I wiped my mouth across my hand, trying to feel butch with my tent, my Jakstrap, my dog—

That's when I remembered Brando.

'Brando,' I called out. Not a sound. 'Braaando.'

He must have taken off. Brando was good at that. He liked to chase women. When he smelled a choice bitch on the breeze, he'd roam for miles in a pheromone haze. Terrified his dog was lost or run over, Stuart would drive panicked squares around the city, hunting for a familiar brown tail. That night or the next day, the telephone would ring. The prodigal son was returned. He'd cower on the carpet in mock repent as Stuart scolded, 'Bad dog, baaaaad dog.' Castration had somewhat curbed these romantic urges, only now Brando was fat. Like his namesake, the dog had merely substituted one appetite for another.

Pushing my salad to the side, I decided to let Brando get his yahs-yahs out before hunting him down. I started to read Maurice's Buddha book. For years, Maurice found his spiritual fulfillment at the men's department at Barney's, the beautiful suits, the beautiful boys, but lately he'd become fascinated with Bloomsbury, devouring books by and about Virginia Woolf, Lytton Strachey, and particularly Vita Sackville-West. In moments of crisis or indecision, Maurice would ask: 'What would Vita do?' The answer was usually *Vita wouldn't give a shit*, which he found infinitely reassuring.

Buddha, meanwhile, was learning how to breathe, a key to attaining a superior level of awareness.

'*Knowledge is gained from direct experience and direct attainment, not from mental arguments,*' explained a monk named Alara. '*To attain different states of meditation, it is necessary to rid yourself of all thoughts of past and future. You must focus on nothing but liberation.*'

My flashlight flickered and died. For a long moment, I sat

in the dark. Then I staggered out to the car to look for the emergency flashlight my father had stashed in the glove compartment, *just in case*. My dad is the king of *just in case*, and it was amazing, though I was loath to admit it, just how often *just in case* came to pass. As I was fishing around, I rubbed my eyelid and my contact lens disappeared and everything went blurry and I started feeling around the dashboard like a blind woman searching for Braille.

Just then, I heard footsteps. A figure came walking down the path. A man, from the looks of his shoulders, his muscular calves. I froze up, tried to squint him into focus, but he was pure silhouette. He marched purposefully, as if he knew what he wanted and whatever it was, he was sure he'd find it over by me. I gripped my plastic flashlight like a bully stick, *just in case*. When he had nearly reached my front fender, he called out from the night.

'Hey, do you have a chocolate lab named Brando?'

'Yes, yes, I do.'

'He's here. He's a good dog. He was wandering over at the other end of the campsite, looking for food, I guess. We gave him a cheeseburger, but I didn't want the camp folks to find him.'

Brando slunk toward me, dog tags jingling.

'Thanks,' I said, dropping my shoulders. 'Thanks so much.'

I grabbed the flashlight, threw out the other lens. One seeing eye was worse than two blind ones. Standing over Brando, I wagged my finger.

'Bad dog. *Baaaaaad dog.*'

Brando sank to the ground in a great show of self-loathing. I tried to be a strict disciplinarian, but it was hopeless. When Brando felt bad, I felt bad, even though I was pretty sure he was faking. I patted his head, he licked my fingers, we made up.

It was time for bed, not because I was tired, but because I'd had enough of this day. Too lazy to hunt down the bathrooms, I spat foamy puddles of toothpaste into the dirt and squatted behind a thin bush, shorts round my ankles, teetering, like a cow primed for tipping. Pee splattered onto my bare toes, drying on top of the pollen and bug spray and sweat, like a fourth and final coat of shellac.

The next question was whether to sleep with Brando. Stuart slept with Brando, but Stuart slept with anybody. While it would be comforting to curl up next to Brando's warm body, I didn't relish sleeping inches away from his slurping jowls, his redolent farts. Now, now, I lectured myself, these are the endearing foibles we learn to accept in our loved ones. I opened the tent flap. Brando walked daintily inside. Zipping the mosquito netting behind him, I motioned him to the right – I *always* sleep on the left. We stared at each other in the soft flashlight glow.

'Lie down.'

Brando stepped to the low end of the tent, then got his head stuck and couldn't figure out how to turn around. Brando was handsome, but not the brightest bulb.

'Back. Back, back, back.'

Brando shuffled back, squeezed his head around, staggering over my legs and finally sitting, his burly head pressing against the roof. As I got undressed, he studied my breasts, and I couldn't help wondering if he were Stuart in disguise. His odor was ripe and manly. I sniffed under my arm. My odor was ripe and manly. A mosquito buzzed by, and I murdered the bastard. Brando looked confused. When I pulled on my cotton nightshirt, the dog lost interest entirely, collapsing on the air mattress and sighing like a man who has seen the future and understands how little to expect. Within minutes, my guard dog was snoring.

I lay down but couldn't sleep. I felt naked, exposed. After living in New York, it felt strange to be sleeping with nothing but nylon between me and so many strangers, like wrapping yourself in a shower curtain and dozing in Central Park. Bugs slapped against the walls as I breathed in old smells of Stuart, the sweet grass and sweat. Where was he tonight? Did he miss me? I missed him, though not in a terrible, empty, every-thing's-over way. As I see it, a relationship isn't over until you know you could never, no matter what you did, win the guy back. Stuart and I hadn't reached that point, at least I didn't think we had, and I comforted myself with this tenuous loophole.

I started thinking about Brando marking our campsite; it reminded me of the arguments Stuart and I used to have about male behavior. Stuart once told me that whenever a man meets a woman his first thought is: *Does he want to sleep with her?*

'*Any* woman?' I asked.

It was morning, and we were lying in bed.

'Any woman. It's like a switch. You ask yourself, yes or no?'

'*Every* woman?' I asked. 'At work, wherever?'

Stuart nodded. 'Pretty much.'

If the answer is yes, Stuart continued, proud to play tour guide of the male psyche, then the man asks himself whether he *could* sleep with her. If the answer is yes, he calculates how much work it would take; he considers the ramifications, social, sexual, and so on.

'That is most annoying thing I've ever heard,' I said.

Unfazed, Stuart waxed nostalgic about an animal behavior class he took at Middlebury College (apparently, an ideal laboratory for the study of animal behavior). According to Darwin's theory of natural selection, women are genetically predisposed to being choosy; men just want to spread seed. Why? Because women can only have a fixed number of offspring – one a year, max – while men can procreate from puberty to their deathbeds. Women need men who provide; they hold out for solid, upstanding sperm. Men just want to get laid.

'Men are pathetic,' I said.

Stuart shrugged. 'It's been working for thousands of years.'

'You are just looking for a genetic rationalization to philander.'

63

'Men *have* a genetic rationalization to philander. Of course, they don't have to *act* on those impulses, but the impulses are still there.'

'How civilized of them,' I snorted.

'Why do you get so angry about this? What's the big deal?' Stuart threw up a hand, to show how little a deal it was. 'Sometimes sex is just sex.'

'I only have sex when I'm in love,' I said. The reason for this had little to do with virtue, but I wasn't going to point this out.

'But you're *always* in love,' Stuart said.

There was no refuting that.

'Well, you would have sex with anything that walked.' I was being ridiculous, but I didn't care. 'You have no feelings.'

'I have *plenty* of feelings,' Stuart protested. He pressed his hand to his heart as if it were a safe deposit box filled with valuables. 'I don't fall in love as easily as you do, so I have sex with women I like but don't necessarily want to spend the rest of my life with. What? I shouldn't have sex until I fall in love? It could be . . . *weeks*.'

Stuart grinned.

After losing several such arguments, I started reading up on animal reproduction. God's little creatures did nothing to bolster my case. Male frogs are so horny they jump other male frogs by mistake. Male snakes fornicate with the dead.

Later, I made the mistake of asking Stuart how many lovers he'd had. Several days later, as we were driving to a party in Park City, he announced he'd crunched the numbers. I didn't feel so special when I learned I was number forty-two.

'*Forty-two?*' I said, aghast, deflated. 'My God. How can you even remember forty-two women?'

'I remember them all.'

I did my own math. It didn't take long.

'Well, I remember all nine men I've slept with,' I said, rolling down my window for air. 'I loved every one of them.'

'Even the tennis clown?'

'*Even the tennis clown.*'

The clown in question went by his stage name, Soleil. We met the last month of my junior year abroad in France. Soleil used to play professional tennis but when his career fizzled, he turned to comedy. Dressed in an oversized pink madras blazer and a floppy bow tie, Soleil performed a slapstick routine on the courts before major competitive matches. To warm up the audience, he juggled tennis racquets, spouted French puns, made winning shots between his legs. Not long after we met, he took me on tour with him. With a case of champagne in the trunk, we drove one hundred and ten miles an hour through the countryside in his white convertible Rabbit. After each performance, I waited for him to sign autographs, proud to be dating a celebrity.

Here was my complete list:

1. My high school sweetheart
2. Rawl, a waiter on Nantucket
3. Soleil, the French tennis clown
4. A college boy
5. Dodge, a Wall Street banker from Greenwich
6. Andy, the house painter
7. Roger, a ski bum turned Washington spin doctor
8. Louis, a botanist from Costa Rica
9. Stuart

I was proud of my list. Suitably eclectic. Not a creep in the bunch.

'Nine is a dinner party,' I said. 'Forty-two is a football team.'

'I never should have told you,' said Stuart, regripping the wheel. 'I should never tell you anything. You just use it against me. You are never going to forget this, are you?'

'How could I?' I glared at him. 'You don't forget a number like forty-two.'

I looked out the window into the woods, trying to imagine forty-two pine trees. Forty-two pine trees was a forest.

'Listen, forty-two may sound like a lot, but if you asked most men in their early thirties how many women they've slept with, after what – fifteen years of dating – their numbers would be up there too.'

'Their numbers would be up there too?' I repeated in disgust. 'What is this, a batting average?'

Stuart smiled. 'You might say runs batted in.'

We had this argument over and over again. It wasn't that I thought Darwin's ideas were wrong; I just didn't think they were fair. Why should men have all the fun? Maybe I had penis envy. *Nah.* I didn't want a penis, I wanted penis prerogatives. I wanted to have a big bold bag full of seed and not care where I spread it. Of course, plenty of women are promiscuous, but I wasn't. Couldn't be. Thought I shouldn't be.

Okay, I guess I had been modestly promiscuous with Peter. My stomach rippled with pleasure. What was *he* doing tonight? Then I spent a few minutes trying to assess in an objective, reporterly fashion whether Peter and I were on to something real. It was hard to say. But this one afternoon, when we were lying on his bed, I'd had this skinny glimpse of certainty, so fleeting, so hard to trust. I said something about it being sunny out and Peter started bellowing 'Sunshine on My Shoulders' and I'd laughed, begging him to stop, hoping he wouldn't. By the second wretched verse, I was sure that hearing his voice parade around my room was a reason to marry.

If not this, then what?

But the Greek chorus smothered this rebellion. After considering Peter's career path (uncertain), his future earnings (dubious), his emotional makeup (writer = sensitive = volatile as me), I decided the relationship would never work. Or not that it would never work, but that it *might not* work, or that it might work *better* with Stuart, someone more *reliable*.

A man who knows the lyrics to 'Sunshine on My Shoulders' – and sings them loudly, arms thrusting to the ceiling like a busty opera singer – is not a man to be trusted over the long haul. And that's what marriage is. A long haul. One to be approached with realism. Not John Denver.

I told this to my friend Margaret, who sighed knowingly. There are two kinds of men, she said: Boyfriends and Husbands. Boyfriends are sexy and playful, but ultimately unreliable. Husbands are kind and sensible and occasionally dull.

Every woman has to choose.

One of Margaret's girlfriends was engaged to a Husband named Glen. He was stable, kind but no zowie guy. Then she met Barclay, a Boyfriend, the 'best sex ever.' The woman panicked. Should she call off the wedding? After a week of sleepless nights, she went for the Husband.

'Why?' I asked. Clearly this woman had lost her mind.

Margaret explained: 'Because she said to herself, "If there was ever a fire, I know Glen would find a way to save me. Barclay would be off somewhere smoking pot."'

The moral was clear. I nodded at the grave implications of choosing a Boyfriend, trying to convince myself that when my time came I would choose the Husband with his fire extinguisher. What if the same theory held true for women? Was I a Girlfriend or a Wife? *Hmmm*. I guess I started out a Girlfriend, clever and flirty, until I was confident the man was sufficiently wooed that I could reveal my true wifey nature. Seduce in a black dress, then whammo, probe the credit rating. I was the worst sort of phony: a Wife in Girlfriend clothing.

No, that wasn't quite right. I vacillated between Girlfriend and Wife depending on whom I was dating. When I dated Husbands, I was a Girlfriend; with Boyfriends, I played Wife. After all, *somebody* had to be the responsible one. Either way, I was dissatisfied. I resented the Boyfriends for making me grow up; I was bored by Husbands who weren't sufficiently carefree. What I really wanted was to be a perpetual Girl-friend, dabble in Wifehood, experiment in Motherhood, have a brilliant, illustrious career in *something*, all without having to worry about money or taxes or lawn care.

Let's face it: I needed a Boyfriend *and* a Husband. And maybe a Wife, to boot.

Letting go a long huff, I rearranged the cotton sweater I was using as a pillow. Husband, Boyfriend, whatever it was going to be, it was time to get all this settled; it was time to put the puzzle pieces in place. God, my mother was the worst with puzzles. She wouldn't let us look at the picture on the box; that was cheating. You had to fit the pieces together and *then* discover what the hell you were trying to make. Were the blue pieces ocean or sky? Were the silver chunks a car door or a shadow? It took almost forever. Fiddling and shifting, trying again.

'You have to figure it out for yourself,' my mother said, slapping my hand when I peeked at the box. '*That's the fun.*'

It had been fun then, but it wasn't fun now. I needed to make a picture, and I needed to make it soon. Sitting up, I uncorked the red wine, took a swallow, then rubbed Brando's ears, grateful for company.

'Are we having fun yet?' I whispered.

Brando opened one droopy eye, then let it fall shut. I lay back down and tried to sleep but couldn't stop thinking about my list, my nine old boyfriends. They didn't feel like exes, they felt current, alive. Didn't someone say that we're all a product of the relationships we've had? Someone did; and if no one did, someone should have. I'd spent more time with these men than I had with my parents, my friends. More than the jobs I'd held or the places I'd lived, these relationships were my life history.

All at once, I knew what I had to do: To figure out *now*, I needed to understand *then*, all nine *thens*, or at least the major ones. I'd start with Nantucket; I'd *go* to Nantucket. Everything that came after began on that island. Love began.

Sex and its consequences began. I needed to go back and remember it all.

This was my trip: traveling, remembering. *This was the way out.*

I got so excited, I couldn't sleep. My mind churned bright streamers of hope. I rolled onto one side, then rolled back again. I must have wasted a good hour playing nighttime rotisserie until the click-clicking of bugs and the bleep of tree frogs and the snatches of conversation soothed me into a slumber deep enough that not until morning did I realize I'd slept the entire night with the Jakstrap wrapped around my head.

A Journey of Exes

Jane Tarbox

Jane Tarbox was from the Midwest, but by the time I knew her, when we worked together at a Bowery newspaper, my second job after college, New York had drained the niceness out of her a long time ago. Jane Tarbox dressed in black, only black, summer spring fall and winter black, and she sculpted her bleached crew cut into porcupine-like spikes. Her eyeglasses were the shape and color of stop signs. Her pale skin was faintly creased, like paper that wouldn't unfold.

Every year, Jane Tarbox got older. From where I sat, an elbow away, I could actually hear her age . . . thirty-one . . . thirty-two . . . thirty-three . . . the years tolled by like a foghorn calling over sharp rocks.

All day long, I listened to Jane Tarbox complain. After pasting up another grocery-store ad, she'd roll her eyes and tell me Lady Chatterly, her decrepit parrot with colon cancer, was crapping up her apartment again, or the seven-foot beveled mirror she'd ordered had arrived with a crack the shape of Italy, or the exorbitant merino wool pants she'd bought last month no longer fit over her uncooperative thighs.

Jane Tarbox dreamed of being a portrait photographer to

the rich and discriminating, but she'd never found a way out of her day job.

'It's a good thing I got that art degree,' Jane Tarbox hissed. 'So I could draw shadows on dancing bottles of Joy.'

If Jane Tarbox's professional life had slumped, her personal life lay comatose, a helium balloon collapsed at her feet. Her cautionary love story was retold in whispers behind her back: For ten years, Jane Tarbox had dated a reporter named Lobo Lerner. She had given all of her twenties, the prime dating years, to a man who went to a bar one night and fell in love with someone else. In three months, Lobo was engaged. Three more, married. A few more, the newlyweds strolled their coo-baby bundle through the office for everyone to admire.

Jane Tarbox kept quiet about this, this and other things. All around her, younger women were getting the things you were supposed to assemble after you'd gotten tired of running around New York: a husband, children, a loft where you didn't have to sweat the rent. Jane Tarbox dreamed of a thin Frenchman with impeccable taste. He smoked Gauloise cigarettes; he wore polished shoes. But Guy de Rochambeau hadn't shown up yet, and frankly, Jane Tarbox was tired of waiting.

'There are no men out there,' she'd sneer. 'And if there were, they wouldn't be interested in me.'

Every day around three, Jane Tarbox would go out for a fresh cup of coffee and something chocolate. Sometimes, she'd bring me back a frosted brownie so she wouldn't have to eat alone.

'I shouldn't be doing this,' she'd say, sipping her coffee, leaving lipstick kisses on her Greek deli cup. 'My skin is going to break out.'

'You've been working hard,' I'd say. 'You deserve it.'

'Not really,' Jane Tarbox replied. 'But it doesn't matter if I get a rash. No one looks at me anyway . . . *Just kidding.*'

I was only twenty-four back then. I wore a kelly green work

dress with a matching cardboard belt and my tan stayed tan year-round and my backhand had topspin and I didn't know much but even I could see that Jane Tarbox had blown it. If you wanted to get married – and I did, some day – you couldn't wait around forever. Women had expiration dates; Jane Tarbox's was overdue.

I felt sorry for Jane Tarbox, but it was her own damn fault. She'd let her life run away from her, like a rubber ball loose on a hill. She could have found a Frenchman, she could have found *someone* if she weren't so bitter, so stymied by expectation. It was mean to say, but *Thank God that wasn't me*. I still had plenty of time and choices and I was dating a cute boy named Dodge who was smart and athletic and close to perfect in every way and we'd get married when we were ready so there was no way I was going to end up single and thirty-one . . . thirty-two . . . thirty-three . . . eating brownies, waiting to break out.

Grampy walks out onto the deck in Maine and drags a director's chair into the sun. He is wearing his Maine clothes, which means they are in varying stages of decay. The toes of his tennis sneakers are riddled with holes. His khaki trousers barely reach his ankles. Tucked in the breast pocket of his frayed shirt are two pencils, a bit of string, an unpaid phone bill, and a wooden clothespin.

'This is the life.' He sighs as he sits down and crosses his hands over his belly. 'Casual living, that's what we like. None of that regimented crap. Spend half the day in your underwear.'

Grampy eyes my computer. 'So, Lili, are you going to write a sexy novel? They're the ones that sell these days.'

Grampy is the only person in my family who ever talks about sex.

'I don't know,' I say. 'I guess most books have some sex.'

Grampy nods approvingly. 'Nowadays, you have to have kinky sex or no one is interested.'

Fantasy Island

Nantucket Island, MA. So I went to Nantucket. It wasn't hard to arrange. My friend John had rented a house there for the summer with a bunch of his finance buddies. They flew up every weekend, but during the week, the place sat empty. In Hyannis, I boarded Brando in a kennel, then paid an old woman to let me park in her yard for a few days. After politely listening to her rail against Rose Kennedy, I made my excuses and rolled my bike onto the boat. The whole ride over, all three hours of it, I felt jittery. It didn't matter that Rawl didn't live here anymore; I still had that feeling you get when you visit an old boyfriend after many years, how you know even before you go that it could be a big mistake, that some memories are better stuffed upstairs in the attic.

In 1982, I spent the summer before college on Nantucket with two girlfriends from boarding school. The three of us shared a two-room apartment at the Four Corners, an inter-section of five roads not far from downtown. Our bedroom had the style and coherence of the Salvation Army – three beds, narrow as hospital bunks, three sticky dressers, two closets, each with sliding reed doors, broken, one monstrous lamp with a tangerine base and burned shade. The kitchen floor tipped queasily toward one corner like a boat frozen midswell. There was a doll-size oven, a grunting fridge, a card table, four chairs, a cabinet full of dented pots and mismatched forks. It was the first time I'd paid my own rent, actually supported myself, and though we had no washing machine or dishwasher, no TV or phone, our sagging apartment felt glamorous simply because it was ours.

The three of us got along famously. Sylvia, a year older and already in college, smoked Marlboro Lights and framed her enormous blue eyes with charcoal eyeliner. I tried to mimic her smart expressions, like 'I don't know squat' and 'Oh, boo.' Wendy was bohemian, a jogger, a journal writer who ate Wheaties with chopsticks and who taught me the best way to eat salad was to dump it in your soup. When I wasn't working, I mooned around the kitchen in a fifty-cent used Lilly Pulitzer dress, which I wore without a bra. When it swayed, you could see a bit of my breast through the armhole, which made me feel sexy in a smoldering housewife-next-door kind of way.

The only bone of contention among the three of us was the refrigerator. Vegetable concoctions dozed on the back shelf until the stir-fry zucchini grew a silvery mold. Notes of apology were taped to the last bite of cold spaghetti. No one could be bothered to buy staples. When the toilet paper ran out, we used Kleenex. When the Kleenex ran out, we used paper towels. When the paper towels ran out, we remembered to pee at work, until I took to stealing rolls of toilet paper from the town docks, an idea we considered nothing short of brilliant.

I got a job bussing tables at the Oyster Shell Cafe, a seafood restaurant near the ferry dock. Working breakfast and lunch left my nights free to do what people do best on Nantucket: party. It was nearly impossible to stay home. Our house sat on the main road out to Thirty Acres and the Muse, the two nightclubs with live music. Every night boozy noise and snatches of careening conversation bubbled up through our gritty bamboo curtains, beckoning us to come out and play.

The partying began each day at Happy Hour. Most bars had drink specials, and we quickly learned which served free hors d'oeuvres. At art openings, we scarfed crudité and sipped plastic-cup wine while checking out yet another batch of overwrought Nantucket landscapes – the shingles, the roses, the fog. Around eleven we'd hitch a ride to the clubs and bluff our way past the bouncer by flirting or climbing over the fence or borrowing an ID, real or fake, from someone who looked like us, which most people, male or female, sort of did.

Inside, the clubs were packed, sweaty, and drunken. Some cover band would proudly be pounding out Rolling Stones tunes as if they had written 'Brown Sugar' themselves. It was too loud to talk so we'd communicate with eyebrows and winks while stirring Cape Codders with tanned fingers hoping for some male attention, which was pretty much there for the taking. We flirted with Tim, the Dartmouth Dead Head in the ripped jeans (so cute), or Doug, the house painter from Louisiana (so cute), or Butch, the landscaper who smirked as if he already had his hands down your pants and was turning you on (what an asshole). It was animal, but at eighteen, we were eager to join the zoo.

When the house lights came up, we squinted, finally getting a good look at the boys we'd wooed. Unimpressed or, more often, overwhelmed by a seduction we didn't dare consummate, we three blondes clamored into a taxi and headed home, hoping we didn't end up in Mr Flannigan's cab. Mr Flannigan was a skinny scab of a man whose station wagon reeked of French fries and kitty litter. He'd stare at you hungrily in the rearview mirror, grinding his stubbly jaw and making crude advances.

'Never had a blonde. Kind of like to ride one.'

Safe in our kitchen, we feasted on leftover broccoli, giggling at how we'd dumped Claude the Lifeguard with the old bathroom-disappearing trick. Not having a telephone was another great way to lose unwanted suitors. When a guy asked for your number, you'd say, 'We don't have a phone. Let me take your number.' Then, of course, we'd never call. Cute boys were told to tack a note to the front door, an old-fashioned gesture awash with romance.

These nights, sitting around the kitchen table with Sylvia and Wendy, I was utterly content. It felt as though my whole life had been leading up to this. The lonely moments of childhood, the awkwardness of adolescence were miles behind me. I was tan in a black miniskirt. My pink bikini had a ruffle. For the first time, men were attracted to me, and I was drunk on their attentions. Though I'd recently lost my virginity with my high school sweetheart, sex was still new. Dating was new. In the warm summer nights on this crescent of land thirty miles from the real world, life seemed as if it would roll on forever, a magic carpet ready to take me anywhere I wanted to go. There was so much time. The good stuff had finally begun.

My second week of work I met Rawl – Rawlwood Johnson from Louisville, Kentucky, a Southern good ol' boy who prided himself on his gentlemanly charm, his God-given drawl and swagger. He was a waiter at the restaurant where I worked. Rawl was always humming some Temptations tune, swiveling his narrow hips, hand cocked behind his long blond hair, like a drag queen working the crowd. I didn't pay much attention until someone joked that Rawl had a crush on me. After that, I blushed whenever I was near him, tried to move more gracefully through space.

Rawl was a night waiter, though he grudgingly worked the breakfast shift. He'd straggle in late, unshaven, hair wet, and make a beeline for the clam chowder warming in a double boiler, easing his hangover by lapping soup from a white coffee mug. His freckled hands shook around his spoon.

'Hey, Cookie,' he'd call in to the kitchen. 'Y'all have any aspirin? I'm dying.'

Rawl's signature flannel shirt hung off his shoulders like a sheet on a scarecrow. He didn't walk so much as shuffle. It was amazing that customers ever got their Eggs Benedict – or 'Eggs Benny' as Rawl called them – because he was usually off somewhere scrounging up a mint to mask his morning breath or eating bacon scraps off a cleared plate or sticking a straw in a customer's freshly made piña colada, capping the top and letting sweet slush droozle into his mouth or mine.

When the breakfast rush hit, he picked up the pace.

'Lil,' Rawl would say, squinting flirtatiously. 'You gotta help me. I'm in the weeds.'

This was my first restaurant job, and I took my duties seriously. As the lone busgirl, I felt incredibly important, the linchpin that kept the whole intricate machine pumping. I wiped down white patio tables, memorized daily specials, remembered to sprinkle cinnamon on the coffee grounds before snapping the red percolate switch.

Refill at 23. Creamer for the corner deuce. Harvest French Toast is 86ed. Take the burned toast back. Take the over-easy eggs back. Fork, knife, spoon, fork, knife, spoon. The leather lady wants her cranberry muffin heated. Heated with butter. And honey, honey on the side. And tea, bag on the side. Do we have those eggs that aren't really eggs, the British woman wants them scrambled, almost wet, no butter, with a sticky bun, and if we don't have sticky buns, a bagel, and if we don't have bagels, a scone, and if we don't have scones, just forget the whole thing.

In the middle of it all was Rawl, brown eyes winking, hip slung as he scratched down orders on his green Guest Checks, seducing women with his Southern *yes ma'ams*, reminding grumpy diners that it was another beautiful day in paradise.

'*I'm lying, I'm dying.*'

Before you could say 'more coffee,' plump women in turquoise were being coy over link sausages, ordering one more mimosa light on the OJ, leaving Rawl 30 percent with an if-only smile. Back at the wait station, Rawl fanned dollar bills before my eyes. 'Pick a card, any card.'

'I've always been good at cards,' I said, swiping the lone five.

Rawl was the cutest guy I'd ever seen. He was twenty-six years old. I was eighteen.

The ferry arrived after dark. Nantucket harbor glistened with golden lights like a galaxy of fallen stars. *Jesus Christ, I'm back.* I tried to make out the old places. The twin church steeples, one round and Unitarian, one pointed and Congregational. There, at the end of a pier, was the Skipper, the restaurant where singing waiters belted out show tunes to a Russian-dressing crowd. And there – my stomach squeezed – the Oyster Shell Cafe, the white picket fence, the two-tops and four-tops, the very patio where I fell crazy in love with Rawl.

The terminal was mobbed, but I found a taxi with a bike rack.

'I'm going to Hummock Pond Road,' I told the driver, a college kid named Bud. 'A place called Full House, right on the beach.'

Bud said he knew where it was, more or less. We bounced over the cobblestones, me peeking out windows at the blur of downtown, the shimmering restaurant lights, the tourists, milling, holding hands through another summer night.

'You here for the month?' Bud asked.

'I wish,' I answered. 'No, just a few days. A friend of mine rented a house with friends. He said I could come stay during the week. Have the place to myself.'

We drove along some road where large beach houses were separated by long stretches of darkness.

'This is the turnoff for Hummock Pond Road,' Bud said. 'I think I remember which one it is.'

The van's lights burned through the night, illuminating millions of starstruck bugs. We passed long, lonely patches of field, then a series of houses, looming rectangles against the sky, like giant sheets hung to dry.

'This is it,' he said, pulling into the driveway of a large house.

'This *couldn't* be it,' I said. 'The lights are on.'

We got out, motor running. A little girl's face peered through the curtained window. A woman, Italian-looking, opened the door.

'Is this Full House?' I asked.

She nodded.

'I'm John Gunther's friend,' I said hesitantly. 'I am spending the week here.'

'I'm Randy Jackomine's sister. We're here for the week.'

'*Really?*' I said, trying to sound calm. 'That's funny. John said I would have the place to myself. He sort of reserved it. I was going to try to do some writing . . .'

'Well, we're here. There are eleven of us. Four adults and seven children.'

Seven children. Oh my God. There was no ferry back to Hyannis, and I didn't want to plunk down a hundred bucks a night for a hotel room.

'Is there room for one more? I won't make a lot of noise.'

'We will,' she said. 'But we'll put you somewhere.'

I grabbed my duffel. Bud rolled my bike against the house.

'If it gets bad,' he whispered, 'you can stay on my couch.'

The living room was huge and startlingly bright. There were wicker couches and rocking chairs and children's clothes bunched up in odd places, under an end table, dripping off the banister, and a scattering of toys and girls, just girls, three or four of them, pretty in that skinny girl way, bird legs and long hair and lollipop lips, and another woman, fake blondish, a cheerleader turned forty. I blinked.

'Well,' said the woman. 'I'm Lisa.' She held out her hand.

'Lili,' I said. 'Nice to meet you.

'Oh, this is my friend Ramsey,' said Lisa, introducing me to the cheerleader. 'She's got *her* three kids. I've got my three, plus one friend. Why don't you take that room,' she said, pointing past the TV.

'Great,' I said, relieved to have a room to myself.

After making requisite small talk, I announced I was going

to unpack and closed my door, wondering if this was rude. I needed some time alone to lower my expectations. The bedroom was small but clean with a separate bath. When I went to pee, my underwear was stained, red like an accusation. What impeccable timing: Arrive, get your period. For so many years, I'd been relieved to see blood each month, but now, more and more, periods depressed me. Another good uterine lining gone to waste. I didn't want a baby yet, but bleeding was such a glaring reminder that I wasn't having one.

I ransacked my backpack for supplies, then inserted and adhered all manner of feminine protection, swallowed three Advil, and collapsed on the bed with a grunt. There's nothing like a Maxipad to make you feel piglike. Fat and stuck.

A car pulled up to the house.

'*They're back*,' Lisa called out, a motherly pronouncement of the obvious.

'*The boys are back*,' shrieked a little girl. '*Boys, boys, boys.*'

The screen door slammed.

'*We're back!*' called a male voice.

'*Tom*,' said Lisa softly. '*There's a girl staying here this week with us. Her name is Lili.*'

'*What girl?*' Tom growled.

'*She's a writer.*'

'*Is she going to write about us?*'

'*Sam, sit down or you're going to fall over backward.*'

The phone rang. The other husband answered it. '*Hello . . . Hey, it's Uncle Louie. Everyone say hi to Louie.*'

'*Hiiiiii, Uncle Louieeeeeee.*'

'*Listen, guys, guys. It's a little crowded. There are twelve of us now. But we're all going to beach it and have a good time.*'

'*Sam, where's your underwear?*'

'*This stupid TV only gets channel two. What a gyp.*'

'*Eat up, Tim.*'

'*I don't like crust.*'

'*What are you, Mr Negative? Most kids kill for crust.*'

Crash. A child's wail. '*I told you you were going to fall over backward.*'

The TV spat up mouthfuls of static. '*Sam, what are you watching?*'

'*Da-aaad.*' It was a childlike diphthong, initial dissonance falling into a sour pool. '*We want to watch Clueless.*'

'*Clueless? Isn't that a girls' movie?*'

I tried to pretend I was invisible, that my room was a wooden dinghy ready to cut loose from the mother ship. This wasn't the spiritual retreat I had in mind. A woman on a journey of self-discovery doesn't share a house with seven children. And she certainly doesn't get her period. Oh, a more maternal woman would have found the kids darling, broken out a board game, sung like Julie Andrews, played flashlight tag until a lamp broke or someone started to cry. Instead, I hid behind my thin door, bloated and grouchy, hoping me and my perfumed sanitary napkin would make it through the night.

Two weeks after I'd started work at the Oyster Shell, Rawl asked me out. The other waiters joked that he was 'robbing the cradle,' but I didn't care. It was my first real date. Rawl pinned a note to our front door saying I had two choices: We could dine by candlelight or visit other galaxies.

Naturally, I chose the galaxies.

We got there by eating mushrooms. I didn't know much about drugs except that smoking pot made me woolly tongued and stupid, but I figured what the hell, I'd try something new. Fear was an abstract idea, like death or the year 2000. If mushrooms were creepy, I wouldn't do them again. It was that easy. Yes now, no later. Besides, no matter how high I got, eventually I'd have to come down.

Around six, Rawl bounced up the stairs in blue seersucker pants, his jaw freshly shaven and smelling of Old Spice. At the kitchen table, he opened a can of Coke, then a plastic baggy. I thought mushrooms would be lavender, whimsically shaped like fairy food, but each cap was wizened and brown, like the shrunken head of a tiny child.

'They're all *natural*, Lil,' Rawl said with a salesman's grin, his thigh fidgeting with excitement. 'Me and this guy Pogie from Baton Rouge used to go pick 'em off cow patties in Kentucky. The thing is, they're not like acid. The Indians eat them to see God.' He passed his hands over his face like a magician preparing a trick. 'The Maker in tech-no-color.'

He divided the stash into two unequal piles.

'Not too much for you, but you want some of the blue stems. They're what gets you off. Now, they're a bitch to get down, but you got to chew them. Here, drown out the taste with Coca-Cola. Lil, you are going to love this. Trip the light fantastic.'

He fluttered his hands like a showgirl in a kickline. '*Razz-a-ma-tazz.*'

The mushrooms tasted like old attic. Globs gummed up in my teeth. With a fingernail, I picked out gooey chunks, dutifully washing them down in the bubble and burn of warm Coke. When the deed was done, we climbed in a borrowed car and drove to the Walwinet Inn, a grand hotel overlooking the sea. Rawl said it was the best place on Nantucket to see the sun go down.

'*What a day for a daydream,*' sang Rawl. '*Custom made for a daydreaming boy . . .*'

The hotel appeared. We parked and walked in back. Walwinet's backyard was enormous, a huge plain of grass shaved to a crew cut. A Myers and OJ arrived, and I held it in my hand, the ice cubes jangling like wind chimes. Rum sweetened my mouth sticky. I kept waiting for the trip to start, but all I felt was energy pumping through my veins, and my body felt distant, irrelevant, like I was a head propped on air. The view was stupendous. The sky, a powdery pink with great purple splinters, the sun, a radiant peach. Wind roared past my ears with great whooshes of breath. Fingering my black cotton dress, I admired how each string was woven, over and under, the waft, the wave, the woove, the woof. My tan legs looked hard yet soft, hairless and sleek. I noticed the grass. Tiny shoots of hope. I remembered my mouth. I remembered my date.

Where was Rawl?

Oh, there he was, up ahead, moseying off somewhere, playing by himself, walking down an imaginary balance beam, palms turned out like miniature umbrellas. The salty wind filled my short dress, blowing inside and outside, furling around my waist and hips and thighs like a thick loving tongue. Now the whole damn sky was up to something. Shattering orange clouds rising in every direction. Purple rubber bands stretched to near snap.

Life was so beautiful.

Rawl was so beautiful.

The pulp in my Myers and OJ was so beautiful.

We drove to Siasconset, an old fishing village on the eastern side of the island. When the car stopped, Rawl leaned over the gear box and whispered: 'Lili, this is the most romantic restaurant on the planet.'

'The planet?'

'*I'm lying. I'm dying.*'

Peeking around great boxwood hedges, I saw Rawl was right. It was called the Summer House, and it was a dream. A white crushed shell path wound through flower beds to a farmhouse with a long, lazy porch. Around the garden were tiny cottages, Munchkin-size, crawling with pink roses and Christmas lights. Up ahead, the porch was glowing and candles flick flickered inside and the hum of dinner chatter wound its way through the open screens. As we crunched down the white path, a piano serenaded us with 'Satin Doll' and the smell of garlic and wine and cigarettes beckoned us closer.

Rawl bounded up the stairs and held open the screen door.

'*Entrez, mademoiselle,*' he said, with a bow and wink. 'Ladies first.'

Inside, the bartender smiled, as if he'd been expecting us. Over his head, wineglasses hung upside down as if clinging on for dear life. The bar area had a fireplace and a green floor and flowery cushions sprouting out of wicker chairs, and the whole place looked like a garden transplanted indoors.

Rawl doffed an imaginary top hat to the piano player, an old guy in a snappy tuxedo.

'Maestro,' said Rawl. 'Want you to meet a friend of mine. Sal, this is Lili.'

Sal nodded politely and didn't stop playing all those black and white keys, never once looking at his hands. We sat by the fire, a bit of winter in summer, watching its perfect orange flames flash blue and snippets of green. Over in the dining room, tuxedoed waiters bent and clucked over customers, offering great steaming plates of food, like doctors presenting newborn babies. The wine guy sashayed around all rococo, popping champagne and overturning corks to sniff. The happy voices and the pink flower chairs and the tickling piano – it was paradise. It was the Garden of Eden.

Wine came. Great goblets of white wine. I couldn't imagine putting anything into my body; I was already complete. One sip and the wine would dribble down my chin, like pouring water in a bottle already full.

I'd forgotten about Rawl again: But there he was now, soft and sexy in the firelight. He looked utterly relaxed, his flannel sleeves rolled to the elbow, shoelaces untied, his legs casually crossed, top leg bouncing to the music, and his face warmed with a shit-eating grin.

He mouthed, 'You all right?'

I couldn't speak but smiled. My wine was still in my hand. I set it down onto the table because I couldn't hold it and watch everything. Not both together. I looked at my hands. The half-moons in my fingernails glowed like sunrise. My fingertips were remarkable, all those faint looping lines – I'd made those, they were mine and they circled toward the center like a secret waiting to be told.

Behind me, a middle-aged couple started dancing. They were handsome and chummy. She, in a pink cocktail dress and wedged espadrilles. He, in Madras shorts and a polka-dot bow tie and navy blazer. She was motherly around the hips like married women are supposed to be and they were doing the swing and you could see that after all these years they were still in love. *Really in love.* It was so great to see people, *old* people, still in love. Wherever Bow Tie turned Pink Dress, she spun around after him. Even when their arms got all mixed up with twists, it worked out perfectly in the end. That's who I wanted to be someday. An old couple still dancing.

I had to pee but wasn't sure my legs would work. Pressing on each wicker arm, I pushed and found myself standing. Rawl pointed past the bar. I tried to look normal. *Smile at the bartender. Look for a W. Take the door handle. Pull. Slide into the opening between wall and door. Here we are. Just one stall. Empty. Open. Lock. Pee. Wipe. Flush.*

When I looked into the huge wall mirror to comb my hair, I froze, unable to believe what I saw.

I was beautiful. Gorgeous.

My nose had thinned, my cheeks were angular. My hair was no longer dirty blonde but platinum, gleaming and thick. When I combed it back, every comb tooth left an individual groove. Instead of poking my skin or frowning, I stared at this reflection of myself, this ravishing, cat-eyed woman.

She could have anybody. She could be anything.

Maybe I wasn't tripping at all.

I didn't want to leave the bathroom because this woman might disappear forever and I was falling in love, but you can't stand forever in the ladies' room staring at yourself because people will wonder what you're up to and Rawl was waiting for me at the bar and he'd promised to take me to the secret forest where the wood fairies lived and then, later that night, we'd stumble back to the Four Corners and collapse on my single bed with our clothes on and hold each other until all the spinning colors finally went dark and the bed cushioned our bodies like sand at the beach.

I opened the bathroom door, walked past the bartender, worrying I wouldn't be able to find Rawl, that he might have up and disappeared, but there he was by the fire, tucking his hair behind his ear, grinning that grin.

He stood and swept his arm gallantly toward my lily-splashed throne, as if all this wonder were his doing.

'Welcome to Fantasy Island.' He sounded like Ricardo Montalban, only Southern.

And I said, 'Da plane. Da plane.'

In Full House, the first bowl of cold cereal was poured at 6:30 a.m., so I got an early start on the day. Mid-morning, I rode my bike into town. Walking around the cobblestone streets was like stumbling into a familiar dream. The old captains' homes, the flower boxes, the hydrangeas, the old elms along Main Street, the compass mural showing Nantucket as the epicenter of the universe and listing the mileage to a few lesser places you might want to go: Paris 3,746 miles, Bermuda 690 miles, Hong Kong 10,453 miles. The old status symbols: women carrying their lightship baskets, handwoven cane baskets with scrimshaw tops used as summer purses, men wearing their Nantucket Reds, brick-colored khakis that after many washings fade to dusty pink.

What would the Quakers think of their island now? It was hard to imagine Nantucket had been cultivated by a community so devout it frowned on music and dancing. By the 1800s, hardworking Quakers had turned this fourteen-mile island into the greatest whaling harbor in the world. But as the whaling industry faded, so did Nantucket. For years, the island, which the Wampanoag Indians called Nantucket, meaning 'far away island,' stood all but abandoned until the coming of the second great cash cow: the tourist.

Nantucket was touristy when I knew it, but it now felt overrun. Everything had gotten even more upscale. The women downtown were done up in gold. They drove Range Rovers with cell phones, mouths pinched as they stressed about shopping. I remembered Nantucket as more ragtag, a place to lollygag on a bench with a drippy ice cream cone, some leashless dog slobbering over to make friends. Nantucket used to feel like an imaginary, forgotten place. Now it seemed like a resort where people *pretended* to forget, an island decorated to look like an island, something Martha Stewart would create, or re-create in the image of what had once been there for real.

At the Jared Coffin House, I took a seat on the patio, right where Rawl and I had always hung out. Looking around at the umbrellas, the customers and their lemonades, I tried to figure out just how long ago fifteen years felt like; it felt distant but connected, an earlier book in a series, a story I'd have to reread to recall in detail.

My waitress was blonde and ponytail cute, and I wondered if she was hung over. For old times' sake, I ordered a Budweiser, no glass, and a pack of Marlboro Lights. I took a long slug of beer and then picked at the wilting label. My father had been horrified when I announced in college that I drank Bud, and now I could see why. I lit my Marlboro, inhaled, waited for the head rush. I don't smoke much but every now and then I like a cigarette, especially when I'm drinking; it's such a quick and tidy rebellion.

It was on this very patio that I learned to smoke. Rawl taught me how, like so many other things. At first I resisted, but eventually I partook now and then to be cordial, an accommodation that filled Rawl with pride.

'Lil doesn't smoke,' he'd confide to friends. 'But she'll share a tube with you.'

When people gave Rawl grief about how young I was, he'd brag I was the smart one. Truth was, there wasn't much to be smart about. Life on Nantucket was an endless party, a festooned carriage without brakes. Mushrooms. Pot. Cocaine.

Percocet. No matter how high you were, someone else was higher. The debauchery crescendoed at the annual Wapatula Party, a come-one, come-all beach drunkfest where everyone dumped a bottle – tequila, Old Milwaukee, grain alcohol, whatever – into a massive vat where it was ladled out to bombed-out partiers. Unsure of the toxicity of the communal brew, many guests arrived tripping, just to be sure they got off.

After work, Rawl and I holed up in candlelit bars, shooting the shit. We drank Madrases, Sea Breezes, Bloody Marys, Tom Collinses, White Russians, Kamikazes, Salty Dogs, Cape Codders, Iced Teas, Tequila Sunrises, Frozen Mud Slides, Stingers straight up, Gimlets, Margaritas, Mimosas, Courvoisiers, Camparis, rum punches, Pousse-Cafés, Grand Marniers, Fuzzy Navels, Sloe Comfortable Screws, Sex Between the Sheets, Sex on the Beach, Tanqueray and Tonics, Seven and Sevens, Tabs with lemon, rum and Cokes, and, for hangovers, the hair of the dog, beer with Worcestershire sauce over ice.

Rawl always had a friend at the bar; our tab seldom topped ten bucks.

We first had sex a week or two after that first date. Rawl liked to joke about the gay boys driving to the beach for 'a quickie,' their heads popping from the dunes like rabbits, but the truth was we weren't all that different. One night, we climbed on his moped and rode out to Seaside Beach. Rawl howled in the moonlight, let his unbuttoned shirt whip in the warm wind. We spread a short towel on a patch of sand. I looked up at a million dusty stars. Sex on the beach, the act, not the drink, was another first, though, like many bold maneuvers, better in theory than practice. Rawl always looked amazed when we made love, like he couldn't believe we were really going to set the whole pretty house on fire.

As summer passed, we developed a reputation around town for falling asleep on the hoods of parked cars. We'd lean back to gaze at the moon and drift off only to wake up to Officer

Friendly shining a flashlight in our faces and telling us to get on home.

'Yes-sir,' Rawl'd say. 'Just dozing. Nice night, izinit?'

We fell asleep on benches and curbs because we were exhausted. We worked even harder than we played. Rawl worked double shifts; I picked up Happy Hour. Many nights I was so delirious I waited tables in my sleep. In this nightmare night shift, tables and menus swirled about as angry customers clamored for their daiquiris, their checks, their oyster crackers. Their soup was cold. Their ice had melted. No matter how hard I ran, I could never keep everyone happy.

On our rare days off, Rawl brought me to beautiful places where we practiced the fine art of doing absolutely nothing. One morning after a plate of fried eggs, Rawl took me to a secluded dock, and we lay on the wood planks, letting the sun warm our faces.

'*Sitting on the dock of the bay, watching the TIII-IIIIDE roll away,*' sang Rawl. '*Sitting on the dock of the day, wasting TIIIMMME.*'

I lay my head on his growling stomach, listening to the ocean slurp up against the pilings. Rawl had settled into his favorite topic, how he wanted to open his own restaurant on Nantucket.

'Lil, all I got to do is get a place,' Rawl began. He spread his blond locks out to bake in the sun; they looked like a halo. 'Stoofie can be the chef. His cream sauce puts the *cha* in your *cha-cha-cha*. Arnball runs the dining room. Arnball Henderson ran After Fives in Memphis. Kept the gay boys in line. We decorate like the Summer House, all pink flowers and shit.'

'What'll we do in the winters?' I asked. Ever practical.

'Winters?' said Rawl. 'Well, little Lil. We go to the Virgin Islands. Ohhhh, God, you would love it down there. We're talking paradise. *Live in a fucking hammock.* Make a little afternoon delight. Sip a cocktail. Do you think you could handle it?'

'You know, Rawl,' I said, squeezing his hand. 'I think I could handle it.'

The way Rawl saw it, investment bankers had it all wrong. They worked like dogs to buy the Nantucket dream house that they had no time to enjoy because they were slaving away to bring home the bones. Meanwhile, here we were, two carefree waitrons living on this gorgeous rock, waving the bankers off on the noon boat. Let them have the cash-*ishe*. We had Nantucket. The important thing was to live for beauty. To take the CEO's money with a smile.

As I lay on the dock, blinded by the July sun, I realized my parents had totally blown it. They didn't live for beauty. They were too worried about taxes and carburetors and mold. They'd never pile into the car and drive to a dock and just sit there. If they went somewhere, *they went for a reason*. They didn't drink Mai Tais and make out. Old people could drink Mai Tais and make out, but my parents didn't, and it was a roaring shame. But there was no way to suggest this to your parents. They had to figure these things out for themselves. Only maybe I would rent them a hotel room on Nantucket. Sit them in front of the fireplace at the Summer House. Drag them to sea water. Make them drink.

Rawl was still talking about his restaurant. It seemed doubtful he'd ever get the money together to open his own place, but I wasn't going to pop his balloon. Let him dream on. That's what I loved about Rawl; he was everything I was raised not to be. My father's pragmatism, my mother's propriety, I threw them in a closet, slammed the door, ran off barefoot in the moonlight.

Of course, the reprieve was only temporary. Reality skulked with the coat hangers, plotting its revenge. '*The Moving Finger writes; and, having writ, Moves on; nor all your piety nor wit Shall lure it back to cancel half a line.*' It was one of Rawl's favorite sayings, most of which made me laugh, but this moving-finger business gave me the creeps. I pictured a gloved hand signing a blank page with a quill pen in black ink. Still, I didn't really understand what it meant – *the moving finger writes* – consequence being inconceivable to an eighteen-year-old, consequence being inconceivable on Nantucket.

The days kept getting shorter as summer pushed its way to fall.

That September, I was starting my freshman year of college in Providence. Rawl decided to move to Boston, an hour away. We would make it work, somehow. My last week on the island, I sank deep into each moment, the roses, the church bell, Rawl's hand on my thigh, the wavy lines across his forehead. All those bars. All those aproned bartenders drying snifters with hip rags. The smell of salty peanuts and wedges of lime.

'Let's order oysters,' Rawl said. 'Put some lead in my pencil. Now, Lili, promise me you won't change. Promise me you won't let those college boys get to you.'

'Promise me you won't smoke too much pot,' I countered.

Pot was the one thing we fought about. I thought pot made Rawl stupid. Rawl thought pot made him smart. I'd say he just felt smart because he was too stoned to know the difference. Rawl would say pot helped him relax. Then I'd say he seemed to be doing fine in that department without the pot.

Rawl took out a cigarette, tucked it behind his ear like a pencil.

'Promise me you'll always wear mismatched socks,' he said.

I held up two fingers. 'Scout's honor.'

'I'm serious about the socks.' Rawl shook his head with a cackle. 'That's my Lili. She's an Ivy League girl, but her socks don't match.'

'*Woman*,' I said. 'An Ivy League woman.'

'Such a fucking liberal Yankee.'

'Oh, boo.'

August came. I stood on the upper deck of the ferry and looked down at Rawl, hip tilted to one side, face in cupped hand, flannel shirt tied around his narrow waist, blond hair tucked behind his ears. I wanted to jump. I wanted to jump and swim back to him. Everything I had and everything I believed in was standing in the parking lot. Rawl wiped his eyes. The ferry horn sounded. I waved. The ferry pulled away. Rawl waved one sad hand. I wondered if I jumped, if I would die from the impact of hitting the water. Maybe if I wore a life preserver I'd make it. Maybe once I got to Hyannis I could take the next boat back. I waved, but Rawl had no face now. He was just a white shirt. When he turned away, he was nothing at all.

Our Full House flowethed over. Kids were everywhere with their sandals and water guns and uneaten crusts. Early one morning, I took a long walk on the beach. The sky was pale and sleepy, the mist still thick. Five-foot waves slammed on the cool sand. A ways down the beach, a naked man appeared out of the fog. He was stocky, covered with hair, like one of those ape men you see in evolution charts with long arms and a primitive slouch. I kept staring at him, making sure he was real. Yes, he was definitely there. A naked man with a penis. A swimmer, I suppose, skinny dipping before the beach crowd descended. As he came closer, I looked away, pretending to be fascinated by some seagull so the guy wouldn't think I was checking him out, which, of course, was what I was doing. Funny how naked men look helpless, harmless, genitals bouncing like floppy fruit. It's incredible how that bundle of organs drives the modern world. Reproduction. Continuation of the species. For the want of a penis I am a woman. I know lots of women think penises are beautiful creatures, but I've never been wowed. They feel good to be sure, and their enthusiasm is admirable, but the penis as art, as erotica, doesn't do much for me. Maybe I should have been more gung-ho about the velvet hammer. Maybe that was the problem. There was still so much about sex I didn't understand. In my book, sex is as mysterious as God, maybe more so. No, definitely more so, because sex *seems* simple and isn't. What could be more basic than your own body, and yet the chemistry of pleasure is pure voodoo.

It reminds me of a Degas photograph I once saw. Somehow Degas solarized his film during development so his image – a dancer, of course – is partially positive, partially negative. The background, through some chemical mishap, is this astounding orange, like the final cosmic blast before the world goes dark. In the middle of this orange fire, the girl dances. And she's there and not there; she's herself and her shadow. This seems close to the otherworldly place where sex resides, the place I spent years trying to find.

My sex education was sketchy at best. My parents kept mum on the subject. Chip was four years older but he wasn't talking. After my first sex education class in grade school, I struggled to assimilate the strange new words. *Va-jine-ah. Eee-jack-you-la-tion.*

'But I don't understand why anyone would want to *do* that,' I said to my mother after school as she washed dishes in her blue rubber gloves. It made as much sense to me as sticking your elbow up some boy's nose, your toe in his ear. 'I mean, what if it never *occurred* to you?'

Our teacher had managed to explain sexual intercourse without a single mention of pleasure or desire. Just a filmstrip about *eee-jack-you-la-tion* and swimming sperm and a cartoon showing a dozing baby dangling from his umbilical cord. Lust made parents nervous. It was so, well, uncontrollable. So in Connecticut, grown-ups had sexual intercourse to make babies, an explanation that made us children feel warm and wanted, as if our parents had endured sex just for us.

At home, the closest Chip and I came to hearing about sex was when my father would say so-and-so 'really got his rocks off,' and my mother would wince. Or my father would mention some actress was 'shacking up' with so-and-so, and my mother would look pained.

In the breach, I learned about sex from Rawl. While my

girlfriends spent their freshman year of college trying to lose their virginity, I slipped down the hill and took the bus to Boston. Rawl taught me about oral sex and anal sex and what a sixty-nine was and how to do it. He told me stories about people who pee on each other, a 'yellow shower' or something. When Rawl came after me wearing my undies around his neck or wanting to drizzle honey on my breasts, I didn't object. You were supposed to like sex – all sex – or you were frigid, which I certainly didn't want to be, so I went with whatever came, wishing I could lighten up, be more adventurous, wondering why I didn't want to push the limits, poke and root around all those orifices, describe every sensation, experiment, indulge. But I didn't. I liked when sex was clean and loving, playful but kind. I liked the after-parts. The exhaustion, the hush, folding together like soufflé, whites blending into yolk.

No matter what we did, I never had an orgasm. I never even came close.

This concerned Rawl, and sometime that winter, he started devising inventive ways to fix me. He'd toss out suggestions as we lay in bed at night. Maybe I needed a bong hit. Maybe I needed to see a shrink for some minor-league head games. Or a prostitute, a sex professional who could orchestrate some world-class pyrotechnics.

'The prostitute would have to be a woman, so I won't be jealous,' Rawl said.

'Maybe that'd work,' I'd say, half asleep. 'Who knows?'

It seemed like Rawl wanted this orgasm more than I did. He wanted me to have one for me, but he also wanted me to have one for *him*, because being with a woman he couldn't satisfy made him feel like he was a lousy lover. As I'd never had an orgasm, I didn't know what I was missing. Talking about how I was broken only made me feel worse.

Sometimes, Rawl would joke to friends that I was cold.

Humiliated, I said nothing.

Eventually, Rawl hatched a foolproof scheme. A threesome. Twice the stimulation. Twice the manpower on the job. Me, queen bee, lying back and soaking it up. Only Rawl would be jealous if I was with another man, but maybe it would be okay if it was Seymour, his good friend from Louisville. *Keep it all in the family*. When I reached the brink, Seymour would retreat and Rawl would finish me off, like an interior decorator who arrives in time to put the last pillow in place.

'Well,' I said, 'we can try.'

So one night in Boston, the three of us went to bed. The light was dimmed. Rawl lay on my right, Seymour on my left.

Two slices of white bread, I thought, a girl sandwich.

The men didn't want to touch each other. Boys who are from south of the Mason Dixon line don't do that. Rawl kissed me. Seymour felt a breast. Rawl pawed the other breast. Two wolves. One carcass. I lay on my back, watching the spectacle, feeling nothing at all. This had nothing to do with me. Seymour hoisted himself over me. He inserted his penis. I tried to decide if he felt different from Rawl. Thinner maybe. Less bulk.

Orgy – such a plump, playful word. I pictured Romans cavorting, polished bodies writhing in silk and pearls, passing grapes on the steps between Corinthian columns, letting red wine dribble down their chins. Saturnalia. Bacchanalia. A happy confusion of limbs. Lusty greed and greedy lust. Everybody happy all at the same time, living for pleasure.

But this wasn't that. This sex was cold and silent; frozen frames of film snipped from their neighbor with an indifferent blade. Seymour pulled out. Rawl went in. Woman as gas tank.

Seymour watched. I watched Seymour watch. Rawl lay back down. Apparently, it wasn't working. Nothing was happening or working. We were all still here.

'How do you feel?' Rawl whispered.

'Fine,' I said.

'Good?'

'Fine.'

No one had an orgasm that night. No one had the heart.

Later, back in our room, I lay alone with Rawl, cold tears lining my eyelids like lace. It was the first and last of Rawl's sexual experiments. For the rest of the time we were together, he just kept quiet about sex and he came and I didn't and neither of us expected I would. I didn't care if I ever had an orgasm. Some broken things are better left unfixed.

The whole time I was back on Nantucket, I kept expecting to run into someone I knew. When I struck up a conversation with a British landscaper, we ran through a game of do-you-know-so-and-so, and finally found a name in common: Cooper.

Cooper was an island celebrity. He'd worked all the high-stakes bars around town; wherever the Irishman went, the party was sure to follow. Cooper tended bar at the Oyster Shell when I worked there. He'd always been kind. The afternoon when I dropped an entire tray of strawberry daiquiris with 151-proof rum floaters, Cooper cleaned my tray and started up the blender without a mean word.

The guy told me Cooper was working at the Salty Dog, an old chowder house that apparently now was the happening place to be. And the next afternoon, I slid onto a stool and studied the bartender. He didn't look like the Cooper I remembered and yet he didn't *not* look like him. Round face, pink skin, brown hair like fringe, thick mustache.

Two loud guys in baseball caps next to me were tossing back draft beer, talking about the fog. One guy was complaining that he couldn't fly to Atlantic City because of the poor visibility, and he was going to lose his mind if he didn't get off this rock.

'Excuse me,' I said, pointing to the bartender. 'What's his name?'

'Cooper,' said one.

I started to make out my memory in his face. Of course, it was Cooper. It had been fifteen years. Hearing his name,

Cooper came over, leaned his elbows on the lacquered bar. I'd forgotten how Cooper could be so attentive, as if your frozen melon colada were the most important thing on the planet.

'What can I do you for, my dear?' he asked gently.

'White wine, please.'

'White wine for the lady,' he said.

In the corner table, three girls were yakking it up. Tan round faces. Tank tops. Cutoffs. Cocktails bright as beach balls. They appeared tipsy, joking and smoking, tilting in captain's chairs, lost at sea.

At my elbow, the two bar guys were chatting up Cooper.

'I already had the room booked,' the Gambler said. 'Had the money in my pocket ready to lose. Then, *boom*, the fog rolls in, and Jimmy says he's not flying. I say, "Jimmy don't do this to me, man. I took the weekend off." But he says no chance. So where's a decent place around here to get a steak?'

'Club Car?' suggested Cooper.

The Gambler made a face.

'Rose and Crown?'

'Nah.'

'Hey, did you hear about this guy who lost his arm today?' Cooper asked. 'Riding a motorcycle. Driver slammed into him.'

'How's the steak at Arno's?' asked the Gambler, skipping over the biker with the severed arm.

I rolled my eyes. How do so many careless people end up in one place?

A blond woman from the corner called out, 'Hey, Cooper. 'Nother round for the birthday girl.'

Cooper looked over, smiled. 'Ever had a Flaming Screamer?'

'Uh-uh,' said the girl, fixing her bra strap.

'Well, then.' Cooper grabbed two bottles in each hand. Four spouts emptied into a canister.

The birthday girl blustered over, face flushed. 'You're the greatest, Cooper.'

101

The bartender emptied his concoction into a parfait glass with two straws. 'Race you.'

The girl took the second straw and said, 'No, *I'll* race *you*.'

Then Cooper said, '*Ready – set – go.*'

When they reached the gurgly bottom of the glass, they threw back their straws and kissed.

'*Haaaaappy Birthday*,' yelled Cooper, ringing the order-up bell *dingdingding*. He spun around once and asked me, 'More wine?'

'Sure. Please.'

It was only five o' clock, and I was buzzed, buzzed enough to have the courage to ask.

'Cooper,' I started. 'Cooper, do you remember me? We used to work together years ago at the Oyster Shell.'

He came close, squinted. So many summers. So many girls.

'Margie's place,' he says, rolling through his mental Rolodex, 'on Easy Street?'

I'd forgotten I once worked on Easy Street.

'When was that, 1983, 1982? Hmmm.' He looked into my face. 'You look familiar . . .'

'Lili,' I said. 'Rawl Johnson's old girlfriend.' Rawl Johnson's girlfriend, now old.

Cooper smiled with recognition, or maybe he was faking it to make me feel good.

'Lili. Of course. Unbelievable. What brings you here, love?'

The three girls came over in search of vodka shooters. Their arms were fresh and smooth, like mine had been back when I was too young to notice or care, and for a moment I envied them. To be young again on Nantucket. To be that young anywhere.

When the shooters arrived, each girl held up a tiny shot glass, curved like a woman.

One of her friends chimed in. 'A toast – to the birthday girl.'

'Nooooooo,' said birthday girl, swatting the air. 'I said I have a toast. Get your glasses. Stef, get your glass. Ready. Cooper, come here. You gotta hear this.'

The three girls leaned their heads together, teammates readying for the fight song. The birthday girl chanted:

Here's to the men we love
Here's to the men who love us
And if the men we love don't love us
Fuck them. Here's to us.

The Greek doctor was losing his temper. His English was hard to decipher, and Rawl was near tears asking again and again, Are you sure? Maybe we needed some other kind of test. I didn't see any point in arguing. My crotch stung. You can't argue the facts.

We had traveled to Greece for vacation to celebrate spring break. It was our third year together. I was spending my junior year in France and Rawl had flown to see me and we'd taken the ferry between the Greek islands until we arrived at Paros. It was supposed to be a dream vacation, but we'd ended up in a medical clinic. The doctor nodded and gestured and scribbled out a prescription and I studied the Greek letters printed on medical posters, such a funny alphabet, cryptic characters I wanted to meet.

The doctor had just told me I had herpes.

Rawl didn't seem to have it, but he might have it and not know it and then again he might not. I didn't know much about herpes, just enough to know I didn't want to have it. I knew it had no cure, that you got it, and could give it by having sex.

I looked over at Rawl. He was in a panic. Couldn't it be something else?

The Greek doctor threw up his arms and said he was sorry and handed me a packet of pills. We stumbled outside into the heat, past white shops trimmed in blue. A shawled grandma selling puppets waved her brown claw toward me, holding up a poncho she wanted me to buy.

Rawl spun around and snarled: 'You slept with some Frenchie, didn't you? Just tell me if you did. I can take it.'

'No,' I said. 'I didn't.'

'So where did it come from?'

'I don't know. Maybe I got it in those baths in Baden-Baden,' I offered, trying to be helpful. 'Maybe from a toilet seat or something.'

'Don't you understand what this means?'

I shook my head. I had no idea what this meant. I was just twenty-one and still waiting for my first orgasm.

'Nobody fucking wants you if you've got herpes. Do you understand?' Rawl leaned into his words. 'Nobody wants you.'

He was crying. He walked ahead of me, spinning around when he had something to add.

'Maybe you don't have it,' I said. 'Maybe it's just me and we'll be careful and it will always be my thing, not yours.'

'Maybe the doctor doesn't know what the fuck he's doing,' Rawl said. 'Maybe it's the clap. Or syphilis. I'd settle for syphilis.'

Rawl looked up to the sky and bartered. 'Please, God, not the herpe. Anything but the herpe.'

Later that night, Rawl calmed down. He stopped blaming me and started blaming the Fickle Hand of Fate. As he slept, I lay awake, wondering if I was a different person now, if now no one would want me. Maybe Rawl wouldn't want me either. The sores stung but worse than that, they felt shameful, as if I'd done something to deserve them, but I couldn't think what. I'd just have to keep it a secret; I was good at that. Bury the truth deep underground. Perhaps I should give up sex altogether, if such a thing were possible. All at once, I felt older, as if I were no longer the person I once was, and there was no way to get that other me back.

I thought back to the moped ride we'd taken that morning. On a curvy stretch of highway, we'd stopped to watch goats wander the cliffs. At first I thought the animals were wild, free to roam about at will, but when we slowed the motor, I heard brass bells clanging around their necks. As Rawl fired the throttle, the goats cocked their heads to watch us, two human curiosities on wheels, escaping round the bend.

Cooper was pouring cocktails five and six at a time. The bar was loud with all the birthday girls. I was drunk and my cigarette was making me dizzy. Head rush. Happy Hour. It was everybody's birthday. Rawl and I broke up not long after Greece. I met a French tennis clown who could juggle five spinning racquets and I drove away with him in a VW Rabbit going one hundred and ten miles an hour. *I'm lying, I'm dying.* Those birthday girls with the vodka shooters, they were Sylvia and Wendy and me. Every summer, girls come to Nantucket. Some leave broken, though they may not know it yet. *Because the moving finger writes.* One summer we three blondes wore miniskirts to the Muse. I was eighteen and my bikini had a ruffle. *Never had a blonde, kind of like to ride one.* One summer, I ate cold cereal with chopsticks and for three months my socks never matched. *We don't have a phone. Let me take your number.* Once, fifteen years ago on a faraway island, I was the kind of girl who could fall asleep on a curb looking up at the stars. I fell asleep all over that island. *If only piety or wit could lure back or cancel half a line.*

The Gambler invited me to dinner.

I shook my head. Thanks but I don't think so.

He said, 'It won't cost you anything. What's to lose?'

I just smiled. There was always more to lose.

I asked Cooper for the check.

Cooper shook his head with a wink. 'Your money isn't good here, love.'

On Nantucket, pretty girls drink for free.

The next day I left Nantucket on the noon boat. The ferry was packed, but the dock stood empty except for men in uniform who ran the boat. It seemed odd no one had come to see us off, as if no one on board merited a hug farewell. This was the boat I'd taken when I left the island that summer. I tried to picture Rawl standing in the parking lot, hip slung, Marlboros tucked in his pocket, waving me good-bye with one sad hand. That was fifteen years ago, half a lifetime from now. As the ferry pressed out to sea, as the tourists snapped photos and children reached for low-flying gulls, I gazed over the railing, mesmerized by the dance of the waves, wondering if ever again I'd love a man enough to want to jump.

The First Proposal

The college boy unzipped his fly to show me his penis. There was a rash along the shaft, a cluster of tiny scabs and bumps that looked like an embroidery of cross stitches. This was what sex had brought, what moved from me to him when I was working hard not to think or be, when I very nearly disappeared but never quite. We were twenty-one years old.

This was college. This was college after Rawl.

I asked if it hurt and he said it stung, itched, but the worst part was it wouldn't go away and it was hard to keep your dick hidden when you're living in a fraternity and sharing a boxcar with three other guys and everyone struts around in the buff. I asked if he'd gone to health services for cream and he said yes and it hadn't helped and he looked like he was going to cry. We stared at the penis, willing it to be better, willing things to be different from the way they were.

Sadness pressed down on me, a second kind of gravity. This was my fault and he was taking it hard and I had wanted to break up and now I couldn't. Or could I? He was looking at me with something like hate, not because of what I'd given him but because I might leave him like this.

'Who am I going to date?' He pulled back the wrinkles of

his penis to get a closer look. 'You think a nice girl is going to want to spend her life with this?'

I tried to imagine I was a nice girl and what I would think if he showed me his penis with the cross stitches, but I couldn't make even the first part of this scenario come into focus.

'If she loves you, she won't care.' This was the most encouraging thing I could think to say. I wondered if it were true.

'How would anyone know me well enough to love me? They're going to take one look at this and say no thanks. There are plenty of other guys out there. What have I got to offer?'

It was a good question. What did anyone have to offer, when you came right down to it?

'But you're *you*.' I sounded like a motivational poster, a photograph of daybreak, a white bunny nibbling grass. '*She'll like you*.'

'Oh yeah, I forgot,' he said, playing the fool. 'She's going to like *me*. Look at this thing, it's grim. Do you know what this means? I'm never going to get married or have a family. I'm going to end up alone.'

This took me aback; I'd never known men worried about ending up alone. I looked into his face. Welts had swelled under each eye, bruises from a tiny fist. There was no way to make things right, so I told myself that he knew the risks. He *had* known the risks and we'd had sex in cars and hotel rooms and wherever we dared, and sex was getting to be great fun again and now this, and I wish he'd just deal with it, like I had to when I got it, and Rawl blamed me and I knew I'd never had it and so we blamed German toilet seats and the Fickle Hand of Fate. But this was different. This was all my fault. The weight of this responsibility made me fume.

It wasn't fair. College was not supposed to be like this.

The way college was supposed to be was just down the hallway, where the stereo was cranking Bob Marley and the frat boys were prowling, pounding walls, craving that first beer but resisting, because the worst thing you could do on a Friday night was to peak too soon.

'Do you want to get married?'

I threw this out there as a dare, then studied my shoes. Black patent leather wingtips I wore with skirts, like a school girl, only naughty.

'*Married?*'

'I don't know,' I said. 'What do you want me to do? You say we should stay together. Are we going to stay together forever?'

'Look.' He put his hands on his knees, grateful for something solid. 'All I am saying is that you said we were in this together, and now you're walking away. It's so easy for you. You always find someone else. How do you think I feel?'

I tried to imagine how he felt. It was harder for him. A woman with herpes feels soiled. A man with herpes feels impotent, and an impotent man can barely pull his pants on in the morning and walk out the door. It's not that men *think* with their dicks, like the old joke goes. They *feel* with their dicks, which is worse. The dick is the divining rod that leads a man to precious metals; without it, he is just another scavenger, lost in the sand.

'I know how you feel,' I said, even though I'd just realized I didn't. 'The same thing happened to me. It will get better soon. Mine's mostly gone away.'

'It never goes way.' He threw each word like a rock. '*Unlike you, this is never going away.*'

He tucked his penis back into his boxers and stalked to the bathroom to wash his hands. I flopped on his bunk bed, stared at a poster of grinning Grateful Dead skeletons, and grinned back. A tear slid down my temple, gunning for my ear, and I thought maybe we *should* get married. Married because of this.

Grampy walks out onto the deck in Maine and drags a director's chair into the sun. I am doodling on a yellow legal pad, unable to write a thing.

'So, Grampy, where did you and Nana first meet?' I ask.

'Well, it was at a graduate dance at Cornell. I looked across the room and saw her. She had these big blue eyes, and she looked so demure. I thought, there's a cute cookie, so I asked her to dance.'

'So that was it?'

'Well, no.' Grampy shakes his head. 'Nanny always had fourteen or fifteen suitors after her. I asked my roommate – boy, was he a ladies' man – what a cad. Anyway, I asked him what should I do. He said I should monopolize her time. So that's what I did. I kept asking her to do things.'

'Like what?'

'Oh, we went to concerts or plays.'

'Did you bring her flowers?'

'No,' says Grampy, sounding disappointed with himself. 'Back then, I didn't know women liked flowers. But one time when she was sick, I bought her a box of oranges. You know, vitamin C. None of the other fellows did that. I guess that made an impression.'

Being Nice
with the Nice

Greenwich, CT. I drove to Greenwich in search of Dodge Dominguez, the banker who came after the college boy who came after Rawl. I was on a manhunt now. A journey of exes. Never mind Dodge now lived in San Francisco (an Internet start-up, with stock options, talk of an IPO, of course, of course). Whoever Dodge was *now* was irrelevant. What mattered was who he'd been *then*, who *I'd* been then with him. The key was to go back, to use yesterday's fuck-ups to make something new work, like a car dealer salvaging a crackup for parts. The present was a diving board, a springy platform from which I could plunge into the past.

Dodge and I dated for five years. *Five years*. One sixth of my life. It was my longest relationship, my closest look at marriage, not that we'd almost *gotten* married, we hadn't, but I'd *felt* married. We were settled. We had a routine. We lived in Manhattan, worked hard during the week, then spent weekends with Dodge's parents in Greenwich. Those Friday afternoon train rides were surreal. Squeezed next to the rich people in suits, we'd race through the concrete projects of Harlem, past the layers of illegible graffiti, past the vast forgotten areas of concrete and soot. Dodge fit in; Dodge was a rich person in a suit. Well, he was too young to be too rich, but he was rich-in-training. My mom says the closer you work to money, the more money you make.

Dodge worked on Wall Street.

I worked on the Bowery.

I worked for a community newspaper that sold for a quarter. I typed my stories on a manual typewriter; my paychecks bounced. On slow days, entrepreneurs from the men's shelter would shuffle into our office hawking a case of stolen Raisin Bran or a gently used pair of size 13 sneakers. I couldn't have been any farther from money if I worked in Bangladesh.

But this wasn't a story about money; it was a story about love. Money shouldn't have been a part of it, but it was. Connecticut is the richest state in the country, and Fairfield County is the richest county in the state, and the crown jewel of the county is Greenwich, the last stop in Connecticut before the New York border, the gateway to New England, the bucolic retreat of celebrities and sports stars and silk-tied scoundrels. People in Greenwich own horses and boats. The average home sells for $2 million.

I pulled off I-95 at the Greenwich exit, drove past the train station, and circled to the top of Greenwich Avenue, the heart of downtown, a one-way, one-mile stretch of boutiques and boulangeries and crock shops and frock shops and fine leather stores. There are places in the country where you pay more for things, but not many. I slid into a parking place, slipped on Brando's leash, fed the meter a few quarters, then strolled down the hill, past the Volvos and Saabs jousting for parking, past the beleaguered traffic cop trying to control traffic with his muscular forearm and bully whistle, past the perfumerie smelling of honey and gold, past the shoppers, wives my age tottering off to Saks in their mules and power headbands, past a mother at the corner carping at her little boy: 'Is it such a terrible thing to hold my hand? Well, is it?'

I could have been her. Or her or her.

112

It was like putting on your old prom dress, turning circles for the mirror, trying to fathom who you'd be now if you'd stuck with your date.

My skin prickled with rebelliousness. I let Brando sniff up garbage; I let him pee on the corner of a dress shop. I felt like I was being watched. I *wanted* to be watched. I wanted strangers to see that I'd opted out of Greenwich and had no regrets. I wanted people to see I was on to something much cooler; what – I had only the haziest idea. Something edgy and immortal, something you had to scrape the bottom to find. You couldn't go near the bottom with someone like Dodge. Dodge was like cream, always floating on top.

Though his father was Argentinian and his mother was French, Dodge Dominguez was an all-American boy: mannered, cheerful, hipbone thin, thick brown hair, a prominent nose that burned in the sun. A graceful athlete, Dodge could throw a Frisbee for miles. With one smooth release of his arm, the plastic disc glided flawlessly through the air, never curving or wobbling, never doubting its lofty trajectory, just confidently soaring onward, onward, until it arrived perfectly into the waiting player's eager, outstretched hand.

Dodge's parents were nothing like mine. His father, Salvador, an international financier, made boatloads of money, and his mother, Noelle, knew just how to spend it. Dodge and I toodled past winding stone walls in his mother's red convertible Saab and tanned by the glittery light of their pool. At night, his parents threw dinner parties for their friends, businessmen in lumber or tin, and their handsome wives, who made polite conversation. Though I poked fun at these sunny Republican circles, I was having my Greenwich and eating it too. I played tennis at the country club, even as I rolled my eyes at the ladies lunching in pearls. I privately tut-tutted Noelle's lavish wardrobe, her double-decker walk-in closet packed to the gills, even as I accepted her hand-me-downs. Dodge's family welcomed me with open loving arms, and I fell into them, thrilled to wrap myself in the gilded life I had long admired and resented from afar.

Well, maybe afar is overstating it, but certainly out of reach. Though my family is from Connecticut, I didn't grow up in Greenwich swank. My parents settled outside Hartford, the depleted insurance capital, which rolls up every day at five o'clock, when the office workers flee to the suburbs as if propelled by centrifugal force. I grew up thinking we were poor. We weren't poor. We were 'slugging it out,' as my father likes to say, trying to stretch a middle-class income in an upper-middle-class world, like a tape measure reaching around a fat man's waist. My private-school friends lived in Tudor houses. They had maids with aprons, black women who rattled around the house with vacuums and rags, sucking up dust, polishing mahogany, rescuing Parchisi pieces that had rolled under the armoire.

'We didn't have the bucks,' my father says. 'I was just sweating it out at the bank, trying to feed four mouths. These guys all had trust funds. Oliver Roderick would take me aside and slap my back and say, "Kit, why don't you join the golf club? We'll sponsor you." Hell, the entrance fee was more than my annual salary at the bank. We didn't realize the crowd we'd fallen into. People in Hartford had money. We didn't have money. We didn't have *that* kind of money.'

The kind of money we had was old money. Really old. My great-great-grandfather had earned a fortune banking in Chicago before the onset of that epidemic known as income tax. Some people might call us WASPs, but that connotes a sense of ease I never felt. We're Yankees, Connecticut Yankees, or, as Grampy likes to say, Swamp Yankees, a pejorative for tight New Englanders who purchase cheap land, presumably near the swamp. Yankees are practical, prudish, and proud. We're modest, hardworking, tax-paying – and here's the big one – thrifty. Yankees like us don't throw anything away. We reuse tin foil, recycle yogurt containers, save chipped beef jars to use as spare glasses. We wear underwear until it shreds, then use the shreds as rags. My mother will buy a dress she doesn't like much because it's on sale. (According to this complex calculus, a half-price dress is worth buying if it looks half as a good as a full-price dress.)

The great irony is that my grandparents, my mother's parents, lived in Greenwich. Back in 1960, Grandmother and Grandfather built a modest brick house on inherited land overlooking Long Island Sound. Ever practical, Grandmother covered the walls with pegboard and the floor with linoleum. She shopped at the Greenwich Thrift Shop to prove she could get by on what other people threw away. While my grandparents lived in Greenwich, they resisted the *new* Greenwich: newer cars, bigger houses, faster money. Grandmother could only laugh when the young couple next door tore down an enormous Victorian to build something roomier, when her neighbors' son, a millionaire equestrian, was thrown in jail for poisoning his racehorse to collect insurance.

My grandfather, Del, a corporate attorney, personified discipline and restraint. At thirty-nine, he volunteered to serve in the navy during World War II, stranding Grandmother with three small children; he rose to the rank of lieutenant commander. When I knew him, he was always working, law work or yard work. His sole indulgences: a daily bowl of ice cream and a lukewarm bath. Every Sunday, he polished everybody's shoes, lining them up like schoolchildren he'd told to sit still. As a girl, I was sure he liked my shoes best because they were small and red, a welcome break from the black pointy pairs. Legends about Grandfather – about his work ethic, his sense of decorum and duty – were retold and exaggerated and retold again. Of all of them, this one killed me and it's true: Each Christmas when he was a boy, he and his three sisters were told to pick their favorite toy and then made to give it to the poor.

So although Dodge and I had Greenwich in common, we

came from different worlds. When the Dominguezs didn't feel like cooking, they ordered in sushi. When Grandmother didn't feel like cooking, she boiled an egg. My family seldom left home; the Dominguezs hung a map of the world in their kitchen and stabbed each country they visited with a flagged thumbtack. There were legions of flags. Flags in Bolivia and Argentina and Thailand and Hong Kong and Bora Bora. Not even the South Pole was spared. Come summer, the Dominguezs traveled to the Riviera to go windsurfing. Come summer, the Wrights went to Maine to do yard work.

Yard work, perhaps my most enduring memory of childhood. No sooner had we unpacked the station wagon in Maine than the battle began: four small people in a death-do-us-part war against alders and raspberries and mosquitoes and juniper and wild roses and black flies and bunches of prickly shoots and bushes known collectively as brush. Roused from our books or card games, Chip and I mowed, clipped, sickled, raked, bagged, wheelbarrowed, and felt terribly sorry for ourselves. Nobody felt sorry for us. Our friends were too busy racing bumper cars on the Cape or floating downwind on the family yawl saying *ta-ta* and *right-o*. Or so we imagined.

Of course, summer wasn't all work. I went to camp. I hated camp. I felt lonelier among all those camp kids than I ever did alone. In these circles, athletics were important. Physical bravado was important. To win at games, to jump off the high-dive, to swing a bat – these things conferred status, and these were things I didn't do well. I imagined myself a pitiful waif, a shy ragamuffin, polishing a peephole in the frost to watch the clever children, the athletes, the breezy kids, who navigated their charmed lives in ways I could only envy.

So Dodge was my entree into the good life. And oh, how good it was. Always a joke. Always a party. A fund-raising scavenger hunt around Manhattan in stretch limousines, a dinner dance on the battleship *Intrepid*, and a Sunday tradition of low-key croquet parties in New Canaan, where my best friend, Charlotte, made hors d'oeuvres from *Gourmet*

Magazine and the boys quoted Monty Python. For the first several years, we air-kissed our friends hello, on one cheek and later, to signal our growing sophistication, on both cheeks. As the sun fell across the steady lawns of New Canaan, the men played Frisbee, and the women gossiped about who would marry first.

Charlotte and I got hot into feminism. We were learning to have opinions. Charlotte nicknamed her boyfriend Anderson 'the Fascist' because he supported supply-side economics and worked for a market research firm that studied consumer sales of pudding pops. Charlotte managed a dance studio in Manhattan, where she coddled neurotic gay men and anorexic pixies with extravagant complexes and empty bank accounts.

'Women have been denied acccss to the top echelons of corporate America,' said Charlotte, flexing her chin like a drill sergeant in the middle of Anderson's kitchen. 'Look at the Fortune 500 companies. Look at Congress! Look at the Senate, for God's sake.'

Charlotte would shake her needlepoint in a rage.

Charlotte was into needlepoint back then. She was stitching Anderson a pillow with the Brown University coat of arms on it. She was also into triathlons. Or more accurately, she was into beating Anderson at triathlons.

'When the good old boys tap their successors, who are they going to pick?' Charlotte would exhort. 'A *woman*? Fat chance. Their golf buddies. *Their drinking buddies*. Some Uncle John clone.'

Uncle John, Anderson's Uncle John, was a millionaire. Uncle John owned a large white house in New Canaan with a semicircular drive with pea pebbles that crackled under your tires. Behind the imposing colonial, past the English lavender beds and boxwood hedges, through the wainscoted gate, down the grassy slope, past the swimming pool lined with mossy slate, past the pink geraniums in cherub-shape planters, was a cottage, the old servants' quarters, and this is where Anderson lived. When we weren't at Dodge's in

Greenwich, we hung out at Anderson's cottage, where we made great hay of Uncle John – his daughter's little drinking problem, his wife's beefy facade – even as we played touch football on his lawn and frolicked in his heated pool.

'*Society will not change until women break through the glass ceiling*,' said Charlotte, building up steam.

'Give her a bugle, she's off again,' said Anderson.

'*Society will not change until women join together and rise out of the pink-collar ghetto.*'

I pictured a circle of naked women, pink cheeks, pink collars, rising into the heavens with briefcases.

'Stand back,' Anderson warned. 'Give her room. She's winding up for a crescendo.'

'Men *do* have all the power,' I said, ever loyal to Charlotte, ever loyal to womankind, to pink collars, pink cheeks. 'Look at our presidents. Look at the Senate. Look at our doctors and lawyers and *Wall Street*.'

'Power schmower,' Anderson said. 'Dodge, Captain of Industry, pass me a Rolling Rock.'

'Rolling Rock, coming right up,' said Dodge, doing his best Yogi Bear impression. 'And how about another pic-i-nic basket?'

I remember the banter, and yet I can hardly remember a thing Dodge and I talked about in private. *What did I say? What did he say? Where did all that life go?* We were affectionate, I know. We hugged in his parents' spotless kitchen, while his little sisters rolled their eyes. Somehow we got into baking bread, fretting over the rising loaves like they were babies in an incubator. Looking back, we were most tender in the shower. Behind a plastic curtain emblazoned with a map of the world, we washed each other clean, soaping buttocks, sudsing feet.

Between the tennis and the jogging and the friends, we seldom had time for sex. Somehow we always forgot how much we enjoyed sex until we were having it and then we wondered why we didn't pencil it in more often.

'Did you come?' he'd whisper.

I'd whisper back 'Yes' or 'I think so.'

This didn't feel like a lie but rather a harmless exaggeration. Having decided I was no good at sex, like I'm no good at softball, a white lie seemed preferable to the humiliation of having Dodge try to fix me, the pushing, the prodding, the expectation, the necessity of bringing out power tools. I shared Dodge's orgasm. Though I wasn't technically satisfied, I was emotionally satisfied, happy in the afterglow, proud to be the sensual being that aroused his desire and fulfillment.

The truth was I was glad to be having any sex at all. I'd believed Rawl when he had said *nobody wants you* and was grateful that Dodge was willing to risk transmission to be with me. The strange part was my outbreaks were so rare during those years, I half forgot I had the virus. Maybe this is proof I was happy. Maybe this is proof I was numb. One thing I do know is that you can't fool herpes. Over the years, I grew to understand this, even respect it. Herpes can read nerve endings; it can sniff out buried dread. It knows you better than you know yourself. You can pretend that *everything is just fine* until you wake up one morning with a stinging reminder of who lives under your skin. Herpes is like God that way. Invisible, omniscient, everlasting.

But my years with Dodge just rolled along, with few outbreaks and little angst. We never fought. I didn't cry, except in the movies or with a book. What was there to cry about? Dodge seldom got close enough to hurt my feelings. He wasn't particularly curious about my inner workings, the secret fears that shape intimacy and confession. I had just come into his life as so many good things had – effortlessly. In turn, I was content to be with someone who didn't pry, relieved to be too busy *doing* to think or feel much. Maybe this is the great gift of being in your twenties. So much activity, so little reflection.

*   *   *

Cracks began to form. Fissures in the china.

I got tired of playing grown-up. I got tired of listening to rich people defend trickle-down economics. (I envisioned honey dripping off a tabletop, a hive of famished people buzzing underneath, trying to catch the sweet gold on their tongues.) It bugged me how Dodge had so much and yet always wanted more. It wasn't enough the sun was shining. He wanted to wind-surf. He wanted to sail. He started taking flying lessons at a hundred dollars an hour. He always had to be moving through things, going faster. My parents felt this. One afternoon Dodge and I stopped into Hartford on our way to a black-tie wedding, the red convertible freshly cleaned; my parents shook their heads at the person their dirt-road daughter in braids had become.

'I like Dodge,' my mother said. 'I just worry what would happen if someone took his toys away.'

Dodge never got sick of hanging out with his parents and their friends. When the last shiny couple had climbed into their BMW, Dodge would stand beneath the lilac tree, shake his head, and smile in genuine affection.

'The Bradershaws, the Robertsons.' He'd sigh. 'They're such sweet people.'

And they were. But I was more interested in the crazies and the loons. Failure was more interesting than success could ever be. How did my family fit into this world? Grandmother with her gallon sherry bottle at her feet. My father who was scared to fly. My friend Maurice with his personal trainer, his healer, his off-again, on-again therapist; Maurice, a sexual late bloomer, who had just experienced his first penis and found it, well, rubbery.

'It's not the penis,' our friend Rose coached him. 'It's the man attached.'

'Oh,' said Maurice.

And yet, I genuinely liked the Dominguezs, despite all their Greenwich money and charm. Something about Mr Dominguez's punctiliousness, his pressed shirts, his silk pocket square, was endearing; he really believed he could bring order to the world. Returning from some eighteen-hour flight, jet-lagged, exhausted, he'd put down his suitcases and start Soft Scrubbing the kitchen counter, the kitchen counter that was already immaculately white.

I'd get all dreamy listening to Noelle's stories of when she and Salvador first met, how they could barely communicate, how they had no furniture, just a candle and a trunk. Secretly, I wished Dodge and I had started out like this. (It never struck me as odd that I imagined not being able to communicate would be romantic, that the less we understood each other, the more we'd be in love.) But Dodge was already merging and acquiring. He was working on a deal that was part of a hostile takeover that was linked to arbitrage that involved Ivan Boesky. There was no going back to candles and trunks.

Every week, I grew more restless. When the Sunday paper arrived, I'd pore through the Help Wanted ads, imagining who I could become if I sent out one more résumé: Concierge, Zoo Manager, Staff Writer for *Hustler*. Sprawled on the Persian rug, I'd gaze at the gray deck steps leading down to the pool, where the lawn boy had weedwhacked the grass to perfection. A person could end up in Greenwich, but it was a silly place to begin.

Instead of being proud of Dodge, I began to wish he'd stumble. Nothing terrible like a cerebral hemorrhage or a car crash, but seeing him laid off might be nice. Or a sudden plunge in the stock market. At the time, these fantasies didn't strike me as mean but rather as divine justice.

Let things trickle up for a change. Let his Frisbee wobble.

Once I told my friend Rose that if Dodge disappeared tomorrow, I wasn't sure I would miss him. I said this and laughed, then turned it over in my mind trying to figure out if were true. I wasn't sure I felt anything for Dodge. There was just a windy space where I'd once felt affection. I blamed Greenwich for this; it was easier than acknowledging my own

121

hypocrisy. It never occurred to me that Dodge and I would never be close as long as I tried to pass myself off as the very thing I criticized: Greenwich perfect.

Then one night in Brooklyn, a man tried to rape me.

It was raining and the side streets had gone quiet for the night. Umbrella in hand, satchel over one shoulder, I made my way to the subway as rainwater rushed between the tires of parked cars. Up ahead, a man with a briefcase hurried up the hill. I watched him, grateful not to be walking alone.

It had been a good day's work.

Dem Party to Meet

Cops Step Up Patrol

The headlines I'd written, the stories twice proofed were pasted up, and, finally around ten, we'd put another week's paper to bed.

Stepping around a fat puddle, I saw my secret escort had disappeared, turned a corner or ducked inside. I walked faster, wishing someone else would come along, wondering, mindlessly, why no one ever makes umbrellas big enough and whether men in wingtips still wear galoshes.

Suddenly, a hand reached over my mouth. Out of nowhere, from behind, five leather fingers wrapped over my face. We fell onto the sidewalk, pulling at each other, making it hard to tell where he ended, where I began. Things slowed to a blur, like a memory already half forgotten.

Then he said, '*I want you.*'

I didn't see his face, maybe because he was behind me or because it was dark or maybe because I had my eyes closed or I'd just stopped seeing.

Then he said, '*Don't scream.*'

His saying don't scream reminded me that I could scream so I screamed. Loud, I think. I think it was loud. Maybe all the nightmares you have while safe in your bed, the ones where you scream for help but no sound comes out, maybe those nightmares are actually practice for being awake.

Somehow we unraveled. I was on my feet, stepping backward, heaving tears, eyeing the distance between us, wondering if he would come at me again. I pushed wet hair out of my mouth and sobbed: 'What do you want from me?'

He moved up the street, this man, a small man, not so very strong. Then he was gone or hidden or waiting in the shadows. My things lay scattered across the sidewalk – ballpoint pens, hair elastics, giant paper clips, a news story, a hairbrush, a half-eaten bran muffin wrapped in plastic.

Sobbing, I staggered toward the subway, wondering if he was lurking, waiting for a second try.

Two blocks later, at a bright intersection, I stopped to look for a cop car. At a kiosk, people huddled together, using their newspapers as hats. Traffic rushed through the rain. Finally, a blue sedan pulled over. I explained. The officers, a man and a woman, drove me back to the side street and waited in the car while I picked up my notebooks, my pens. These things seemed important.

Back in the warm squad car, scanner crackling out fresh news, the woman asked me questions and wrote my answers on her clipboard: Age: 25. Address: Stuyvesant Town. Could I identify my assailant?

'Maybe,' I said, not wanting to admit I hadn't been paying the right kind of attention.

The cops sounded bored. I hadn't been hurt, he hadn't had a weapon, he hadn't touched me down there.

'Some junkie,' said the woman, 'probably so doped up he didn't know what he was doing. Probably couldn't have done anything if he wanted.'

It was warm in the backseat, and I relaxed against the leather. It reminded me of being a very small child, how my parents used to take Chip and me along to dinner parties – this was before Dad's claustrophobia – and we'd fall asleep in the guest room and when it was time to go, they'd bundle us into the backseat and Dad would drive us home. As the dark houses slipped by, I wondered why some families left a light on all night and others didn't and hoped we were the kind of family who did. Then I'd drift off to sleep, smelling Mom's perfume, my fake fur hood soft on my chin, happy my parents were in front and in charge.

But who drives you home at night when you're twenty-five years old?

The cops, I hoped. But the woman said Manhattan was out of their jurisdiction and I said please and they said sorry and I got out of the blue car and stood on a busy avenue and waited for a cab in the rain.

Home in my apartment, my roommates asleep, I sat in the hallway and called Dodge.

'A man attacked me,' I said.

'*What?*'

I started to cry. 'He said he wanted me. Then he said, "Don't scream." So I screamed. Then he let me go.'

'Should I come over?'

'No, I'm all right.'

That's what we say in my family. We say we're all right.

'I'm glad you weren't hurt. Are you sure you don't want me to come over?'

'No, it's a long way.'

I said it's a long way so Dodge would say 'No, it's not, I'm coming over,' but he didn't say this.

'It's so weird,' I said. 'I can still feel his hand on my face. It's burning, like a brand.'

Dodge told me I was safe now and I should get some sleep and I hung up and walked to the bathroom, looked into the mirror at my face, expecting to see welts but there was nothing. Just the same old cheek. I washed and brushed and put on my nightshirt and climbed under the covers and looked into the apartment buildings where people were sleeping. I felt like the girl in 'T'was the Night Before Christmas,' the version my father used to read us on Christmas Eve, the girl who wakes up in the middle of the night and sees Saint Nicholas flying a sleigh pulled by reindeer, lively and quick. That's when she realizes the world is filled with magic. That's when she knows she's right to believe.

Cold air pressed through the windowpanes. Shivering, I pulled my socks back on, cinched the comforter around my waist. Then I held my hand to my cheek, covering the place where the stranger's glove had lain, warming my hand in his heat.

Dodge should be here. A lover is supposed to know when you're too proud to ask for what you need. I had no idea how to ask Dodge for all the things I needed. It was such a long list. It was easier to pretend to need nothing at all.

Getting herpes, the attempted rape, my anticlimactic sexual experiences all took their toll. I'd become two people: the inside me and the outside me. The outside me looked fine, but the inside me was tainted, vulnerable, a little scared. When I was away from Dodge, the outside me attracted entirely too much attention, from construction workers, from bosses, from suited men at bars. Young women wield an inordinate amount of sexual power, more than many of us know what to do with, more than we deserve. For some reason, I looked like the woman men thought they were looking for. While the attention was flattering, I couldn't help laughing to myself. *If they only knew. If they only knew who I really was and what was going down, they would run screaming in the other direction.* Meanwhile, the inside me went into hiding. I didn't share my secrets with friends, with Dodge, with anyone. The less said, the better. Why dwell on the ways I wasn't like other girls? Women have a lot of shit to deal with, and I was dealing with my portion as best as I could. I was passing. I was passing in Greenwich.

But day by day something was becoming ever more clear: While having a boyfriend was warm and reassuring, it was no guarantee that you wouldn't end up some day facing the hard stuff alone. Some men are happy to settle for the outside of a woman; some women – and I was one of them – aren't brave

125

enough to invite men inside. Being in a relationship can be like standing next to one of those grinning cardboard figures you pose with at the fair, Ronald Reagan or John Wayne or Elvis. In the Polaroid the photographer snaps, you both look real, but you're posing and your boyfriend is a cutout, just a look-alike of the real person, who's nowhere to be found.

So there was the rape that wasn't, and then there was this.

One afternoon, Dodge and I were trying to decide what to do that weekend, and I suggested we go to the Jersey shore.

'Nah, let's go to Greenwich,' Dodge said.

'We *always* go to Greenwich,' I said. 'Let's go to the beach.'

'Where?'

'I don't know.' I shrugged. Where was besides the point. The point was to get drunk and look at the waves. The point was to get lost. 'We could look at the map. Pick a place, have an adventure.'

I smiled that lame, hopeful smile my mother does when she's trying to convince my father to go somewhere he doesn't want to go.

Dodge looked away. The beach sounded like a hassle. Why bother when Greenwich waited at the end of the tracks?

'Let's not,' he said. 'Traffic will be bad, and we'll be driving around in our wet bathing suits all sandy with no place to change or shower. And besides, *where would we go to the bathroom?*'

Not long after that I met a boy named Andy. Andy had curly brown hair, blue eyes round as clocks, and long thick lashes. A dead tooth stained his lopsided smile. He walked with one shoulder leaning forward as if to fend off an imaginary tackle. His shorts drooped. His socks drooped. He looked like a shaggy dog that had just gotten out of the water and hadn't bothered to shake. From the moment I saw him, I wanted to sink my fingers into his fur.

We met at the dinner party of a friend of a friend in New Jersey; I'd moved to Trenton to work for a tabloid, the only daily newspaper that would hire me. Dodge was still in New York, and we saw each other on weekends. Though I'd never been unfaithful to Dodge – five years without so much as a fickle kiss – before dessert was served that night I felt doglike longings, ripplings of lust.

Andy sat next to me at dinner. I asked him what he did.

'I paint,' he said.

'Paintings?'

'Houses.'

'Where?'

'Right now this lady's house in Princeton. She's having everything marbled.'

'Cool,' I said, unsure how to talk paint. 'So you paint all day?'

Andy looked amused. 'If you want to get the job done.'

'Do you ever get . . . I don't know . . . bored?'

'No. Why? Would you?'

'No, I guess I wouldn't,' I said, hoping I hadn't offended him. 'You have all that time to yourself in a way. What do you think about, I mean, when you're painting?'

He looked at me coyly. 'Anything I want.'

Andy lived with his father and stepmother on a sixties-style compound called The Farm. It wasn't a moo-cow kind of a farm, more like a menagerie, a former hunting lodge, with a barn, a few cottages, a pond, a swimming pool that no one could bother to fill or clean, a donkey, a goat, two bitchy peacocks, chickens, cats, and a dog named Dave. His father, Alec, and stepmother, Joy, had ten children – five from his first marriage, four from her first marriage, one together. Alec, a former sex therapist who grew pot in the neighbors' corn-fields, was infamous for having patients do nude Gestalt on the front lawn, housewives working through their issues in the buff.

Andy was unlike any man I'd ever met. Forget Saab

127

convertibles. His Toyota Corolla had logged nearly 200,000 miles; he started it with a screwdriver. Before he left to go somewhere, Andy would grab a road beer, finish it driving down The Farm's quarter-mile stone driveway, stash the empty in the mailbox for the mailman to find. He was the only man who ever told me I needed to gain weight, a comment that made me feel simultaneously sexy and mothered. He was the only man I knew who would stop at a filling station and buy three dollars of gas. Maybe he only had three bucks in his pocket. Maybe three gallons was all he needed right now, and right now was generally as far ahead as Andy was looking.

Later on, after we were going out, I would press him about his long-term career plans, what he planned to *do* with his life. Andy would shake off my questions, flies on a tiger. One day, when I persisted, he told me he might take a job spraying down airplanes.

'Oh,' I said, trying to sound open-minded, like a career counselor whose client has announced he plans to join the circus. 'Is that really what you *want* to do?'

'Why do I have to *do* anything?' he asked. 'What's wrong with just *being*? Isn't that enough? Look at you. You're always *doing* something, *wanting* something, and then you get it, and then *oh geez.*' He slapped his forehead, pantomiming a fool with a fresh idea. 'You want something else.'

He had a point. Not that I was ready to concede it.

'That's so not true,' I said.

'Everybody I know is bragging about what they've done, their degrees from Harvard, but most of them are a bunch of phonies. So they have this degree, but they're not too bright. And are they happy? *Are they really happy?*'

Andy thought being happy was the most important thing.

Andy thought having children was the second most important thing.

Neither idea had ever occurred to me.

Andy was a lost soul; Andy was a prophet. I was convinced

of both even before I learned that when he was a kid, he had stopped speaking for two years.

'*You didn't speak for two years?*' I gasped, trying to recall whether I'd ever lasted a day and deciding, no, definitely not. '*Why?*'

Andy tucked a clump of hair behind my ear and looked at me as if it would take him until his dying days to give me a decent grasp of the obvious.

'Everybody else was talking,' he said. 'There wasn't much left to say.'

So I met Andy at a dinner party, a dinner Dodge knew nothing about. A week later, at a party, we kissed, a kiss Dodge knew nothing about. Then I spent an afternoon at The Farm and I knew there was no going back. Nothing much happened. Maybe that was the point.

It was a sunny summer day, and Andy took me for a spin on The Farm's all-terrain vehicle. I sat between his arms as he drove, leaning against his chest as we lurched over the bumpy terrain. Foot on the gas, he careened past the house, around his field of raspberries, a sideline of his, down a slope into the woods, down, down. We came to a pond basking in the sun, full and still with heat. Andy turned off the engine. We leaned against a big rock and watched dragonflies bounce off the listless water, each circular ripple radiating wider and wider until it finally disappeared. The pond was womblike in its stillness, in the comfort of all things grown used to each other, fused and whole. Hours passed.

Hours passed while we watched the stagnant water and listened to squirrels worry in the underbrush and lazed around together, touching and intertwined. While Dodge would have wanted to wind-surf, Andy was happy just to hold me. While Dodge and I would have rushed to meet friends, Andy and I sat alone. I couldn't remember the last time I had done so little. I couldn't believe that this, just this, was enough. But it was.

That Friday, after five years of dating and two trips to the Riviera and 5 million miles logged on the Metro North train to Greenwich, I walked into Dodge's apartment and broke up with him. He was stunned, asking when and why and couldn't we go to counseling. I didn't want to go to counseling; I wanted to see Andy.

'I can't say I won't see him,' I said. 'I can't say I won't go.'

Dodge lay stricken on the couch, bleeding to death from invisible leeches.

He hadn't seen this coming. Neither had I.

In the bathroom, I grabbed my earrings, then stood in front of his shower curtain with the world map and ran my finger over all the candy-colored countries I was never going to see. Istanbul, Hungary, the Red Sea. With Dodge I would have visited these places; without him, who knew? But I couldn't be with Dodge and not be with Dodge so I couldn't be with Dodge. For now, it was enough to know what I couldn't do. No was the accelerator. Yes was the brake.

'Will you call me?' Dodge asked.

'I'll call you,' I lied.

That night, I took the train back to Jersey, washed my puffy eyes, and met Andy for drinks. As we sat at the bar, I slid my thigh between his. Most of my breakups have been messy affairs that drag on for months, but not this one. This was the clean, cold work of an assassin.

So this is how love came and went.

Or at least, this is the version I told myself as I sat at a patio table at the Greenwich Field Club, surveying the empty tennis courts and the clouds pregnant with rain. Dodge and I had hung out here, playing tennis, ordering Cobb salads, signing the bill to his parents' account.

It was Monday, and the country club was deserted. I wasn't a member, but I looked like I was so no one bothered me. Drumming my dirty fingers, craving a cocktail, I tried to see myself, a younger me, making her way past Har-Tru courts

130

and the paddle tennis courts and grass courts and the squash court building.

I looked over my shoulder. A sign on the wall read:

All-white attire must be worn, including hats and all accessories. A minimum of trim (i.e., small logos, piping, etc.) is acceptable. Before May 15 and after Sept. 15, colored warm-ups and sweats may be worn.

I snickered. Oh, to live in the land of trim and piping. Had I been crazy to give this up? Dodge and I could have grown up together. He could have taught me to do a decent dive. I could have shown him the bathroom at the beach; I could have suggested he pee in the water. All these years, I'd told myself that I would have gone crazy here, but maybe this was pure confabulation, lies I'd fashioned to make sense of a time – a man – I needed to remember my way. I could have been a Greenwich girl. I could have been happy here, I think. Dodge had a good heart. Maybe I just hadn't been ready. Then again, maybe I never would have been.

As soon as I left Dodge, everything got harder. Herpes came back. Tears and struggle and worry came back. Then in Utah, where things really fell apart, I'd be up at night stalking the house, rocking on my love seat, listening to the gerbils in my head fritter and scratch.

I was alive. Miserable and utterly awake.

I reassured myself that it was worth it, that this was the proud route of artists and thinkers and women in love, but maybe that was pure bunk. Maybe self-knowledge was nothing more than a staircase to the basement, a dark and bumbling descent into the land of old boxes. And for what? If I'd had any sense, I'd have stayed in Greenwich, worked on my net game, met girlfriends for lunch, joined a circle of hungry young women waiting to order.

Block Island

My father and I both love seafood. We like clams smoked or fried or belly up on the half shell. We like oysters, raw or steamed. We like herring, pickled in sour cream or steeped in oil with onion. We like anchovies and sardines straight from the can. My mother thinks these delicacies are, well, too fishy. So does Chip, and so this passion for seafood is something my father and I share, a genetic connection he proudly traces back to his Norwegian ancestors, the ones we supposedly resemble.

Although we didn't eat out when I was a kid, from time to time Dad would take us to this fish joint in Wethersfield. You could sit at a counter or take out, and so we took out, cramming into Dad's Rambler with buckets of fried food. It was awkward, balancing drinks and catsup and passing around fries, and I never understood why if Dad had claustrophobia he didn't mind the four of us squeezing into his car, but he didn't. He liked it. There, among all the oohing and gulping, the high praise for small fish, we felt like a family, like a group of chummy passengers sailing out to sea in a small wooden boat.

* * *

The summer I was twenty-six, about six months before Dodge and I broke up, I invited my parents to spend the weekend on Block Island, an old fishing port off the coast of Rhode Island. It was the first time we had taken a trip together in as long as I could remember, the fulfillment of that fantasy I'd had eight years earlier on the dock of the bay with Rawl, a way of re-creating my childhood memories of eating seafood in the car.

The first night we ate at a family-style fish place with buoys and nets strung on the walls. It was the first time I'd eaten out with Dad in nearly twenty years, and we were all a little tense. Earlier that morning, he'd checked out the place to see if he could hack it, if there was enough light and air and space between tables. Now he sat in his captain's chair, like a man braced for a gun to go off.

'When are we going to order?' he asked.

'I'm sure the waitress is coming,' my mother said, looking over her shoulder. 'Do you know what you're having?'

Dad was confused by the menu. He wasn't used to deciphering what came with what. 'I guess I have some questions.'

The waitress showed up. Dad asked if the clams had bellies, if the entrees came with a salad, whether he could have French fries instead, what kind of beer she had, how much it cost, did the food come out all at once because that's how we wanted it, all at once, because we weren't in a hurry, but we didn't want to be here all night, if she knew what he meant. The waitress smiled and said she knew exactly what he meant and promised to put in the order right away. The three of us sat quietly, waiting.

'Are you okay?' my mother asked my father, touching his arm.

'Fine, fine,' said Dad, annoyed by what he took to be a patronizing question.

'Well, that was a beautiful day,' said Mom, her face flushed from sunshine. And it had been. We'd ridden bikes around the island, laughed as my mother struggled up the hills, stopped in a pottery shop where I'd bought a set of blue plates for Dodge. Things, I thought, were going rather well.

The restaurant was getting busy. We had purposefully arrived early, hoping to beat the crowds, but now the tables were filling and the room was getting loud and I wished everyone would shut up so that my father didn't wig out with all the noise. I'd never seen Dad break down, but it wasn't something I wanted to witness. Part of me wondered if the attacks were pure fiction, an excuse not to move, but it wasn't a theory I wanted to test.

Finally, the waitress returned with platters of fried clams for Dad and me, fish and chips for my mom. We shook catsup puddles onto our plates and dug in. And that's when Dad looked up and, apropos of nothing, asked me:

'So do you think you're ever going to settle down?'

My father generally waits for silence, a fixed silence where I can't run off somewhere, to corner me with questions on the way I am leading my life. He rarely gives advice, but the chosen path is illuminated by the direction and tenor of his questions.

'Do you think you might want to go to graduate school?'

'Don't you ever get tired of going to parties?'

This time, I played dumb, answering his question with a question. 'What do you mean by settle down?'

'Stop moving around so much. Get married. Have a family.'

I nodded, jamming a steamy fried clam into my mouth. Like my father, I am overly sensitive to criticism, direct or implied. This too we share. Oh, I know families are *supposed* to talk about personal things, but ours didn't – *hadn't* – and it felt entirely too late to start now. My parents seldom mentioned my boyfriends. They were extras, add-ons, non-essentials, not worthy of consideration when planning out the next step in life, unless, of course, you happened to marry one. Everything before marriage was practice, a temp job that didn't count for much.

'Of course,' I said, trying to keep my voice even. 'I'd like to get a good newspaper job and then stay in one place.'

'Where?' asked my father. 'Where do you think you'll go?'

'I don't know.' I shrugged, as if none of this mattered. 'Wherever I get a good job.'

Dad waited a moment, weighing his words. 'You know you can't just keep flitting around forever.'

Flitting around? Defensiveness rose in the back of my throat. I reminded myself that he loved me more than I would ever understand. He worried that I'd be left with nothing to hold in my hands. I worried about that too. But the more you stare at the hole in the road, the more likely you are to steer into it.

'Do you think you want to marry Dodge?' he asked.

'Maybe,' I said. 'I don't know. I want to get married some day, but I guess I'm just not ready.'

I looked at my mother for help. She was cutting her fish in tidy mouthfuls, rubbing on a dab of catsup with a knife. She smiled as if we were chatting about the weather, not letting on she knew how hard it was for me to talk about all this, not interceding to let me off the hook. Chip had gotten married when he was twenty-three, and I'd always thought his early marriage had bought me a little time. Apparently, my meter was up.

'But you *do* want a family?' my father asked.

'Sure,' I said, unable to keep irritation out of my voice. 'I would like to have kids some day.'

Dad sighed, balled up his white paper napkin, and tossed it onto his empty plate where fried clams used to be.

'Well,' he said. 'Whatever happens, you should know that your mother and I don't believe in divorce.'

I stared at the red-and-white checkered tablecloth, losing myself in the squares. My mother frowned into her French

135

fries as though she wished my father hadn't said that but it was too late now. She tried to patch things up.

'I thought maybe we'd scared you off from getting married,' she began, trying to take some blame for herself. 'That you took one look at your crazy parents and said "no thanks."'

It was true. I didn't want a marriage like theirs, as small and tightly wound as a Chinese woman's feet. But who wanted anyone else's marriage? Marriage was like underwear – you only wanted your own. The point was my parents were high school sweethearts who were still together, still loved each other. After thirty years, they still helped each other get by.

'No, Mom,' I said. 'It's nothing like that.'

My mother gave a bolstering mother's smile. 'We just want you to be happy.'

Dad finished his beer.

'Well, don't marry someone for *us*,' he said. 'Remember, you're the one who has to live with him.'

The waitress arrived with the check. My father pulled out his credit card. My mother showed him how to tuck it into the leather check holder with one corner exposed, a signal to the waitress that we were ready to pay. The waitress circled back, ran the card through the machine. My father looked at the carbon paper, puzzled, unsure where to put the tip. My mother showed him how.

'Well, wasn't that nice,' said Mom, folding her hands on the table. 'Wasn't it?' she prodded.

'Yes, yes.' Dad rallied a smile. 'Very nice. Thanks, Bugs.'

Bugs is my family nickname.

We pushed back our chairs and walked out into the dark. The sky was speckled with stars, millions of wishes, way out of reach. As we hiked up the hill to our rooms, my father's words spun around my head, like music from a merry-go-round in the foulest of moods.

Not until several years later, in Utah, when I was still not married, still not settled, still flitting around, did I see the three truisms that lay before me, a triangular trap from which there was no escape.

Hurry up and get married. No one is good enough. We don't believe in divorce.

Hurry up. Not good enough. No divorce.

Grampy walks out onto the deck in Maine and drags a director's chair into the sun. I am eating cherries, spitting out pits.

'Grampy, I bought some Hellmann's Mayonnaise to have with the crab tonight,' I say. 'I'm not wild about that Miracle Whip.'

'Yeah, right, okay,' he says, mulling this over. 'I have noticed an interesting gender difference. Males prefer Miracle Whip, and gals prefer Hellmann's.'

'Really?' I say. Somehow, in my two years as a gender issues reporter, I missed this.

'Say,' says Grampy. 'Did I ever tell you about this older neighbor of mine?'

I shake my head.

'This old gal had some kind of breast cancer, and they put her on testosterone. Well, a little male hormone and she kept her husband busy in bed three times a day. Finally, the guy calls his doctor and says "Doc, I can't take it anymore." So the doc took her off . . . That means, if you're a guy, you should look for a woman with one of those little mustaches over her lip. Boy, she'd send off some strong signals.'

He laughs at his joke and sighs happily. 'Ah, pheromones.'

The Greasy Pole

Gloucester, MA. By the time we found a place to park and made our way down a scrap of beach along Gloucester Harbor, the greasy pole contest was already under way. Hundreds of people hung off nearby porches, squeezed side by side on the sand, craning their necks, some drinking warm beer, others lost in binoculars, mouths agape. Rita nudged us to the front of the crowd.

'*Next up, Bobby Frontiero,*' a man with a circus barker voice boomed over a loud speaker. '*Brother of Jerry Frontiero.*'

When I'd called my college roommate Rita and told her about my trip, she said I should come to the Festival of Saint Peter.

'What's that?' I asked.

'It's this huge celebration to mark the blessing of the fleet,' Rita said. 'The Italian and the Portuguese fishermen go nuts. There are parades and rides and then on Saturday there's the greasy pole contest.'

'*The what?*'

'The greasy pole,' said Rita, laughing. 'You should come and see it for yourself.'

And I did, even though this meant backtracking, something I'd vowed not to do. In Connecticut, I turned the car around and headed north to Gloucester, the old commercial fishing port on the Cape Ann peninsula, famous for the fisherman statue pictured on fish sticks boxes, the one where the waterlogged captain clings valiantly to the spokes of his wheel.

We arrived late. The contenders, young men in swim trunks, were already clustered on a raised platform in the middle of the harbor, chatting, jeering, listening to the radio, waiting for their turn. About fifteen feet above the water, a telephone pole stuck out from the platform, parallel to the ocean, like a high diving board or giant tongue depressor. The pole was about forty-five feet long and covered in heavy black grease. At the very end of it, a red flag fluttered from a thin rod, sort of like a golf flag. The point of the contest was simple: Walk down the end of the slippery pole and capture the flag.

I squinted at Bobby Frontiero. His figure in silhouette advanced a tentative foot on the pole, arms extended like a tightrope walker. On his third baby step, he tilted to the right and then, to compensate, furiously spun his left arm, causing him, a split second later, to lose all equilibrium, and tumble into the bay, hitting the water with a loud belly flop. A collective groan ran through the crowd, followed by the humiliating sound of a gong.

'Ohhhh.' Rita grimaced. 'I'd forgotten that part.'

'That's gotta hurt,' I said. 'Seems like a guy could lose his sticky pole out there,' I said, pleased with my pun.

'Big time,' said Rita, reaching for a mint. 'It's a good thing they're drunk.'

Frontiero swam awkward crawl strokes past the fleet of motorboats and kayaks that had gathered in the bay to watch. He climbed the step ladder and rejoined the pack.

'*And now, Frankie California the Gentile walks. Guess they don't have this out in California. Do they, Frankie?*'

'What do you do if you get the flag?' I asked Rita.

'Give it back.' Rita laughed. 'But they carry you through town on their shoulders.'

'Do women ever get out there?'

'One did last year. She was terrible. A lot of guys dress in drag. Goofy stuff, you know, ball gowns and boas.'

Joe-Joe Favazza walked and fell. And Frankie 'the Godfather' Corolla fell. And Bogie the Castro fell. And so did B.J. 'My Mama's a Pajermo' Allen and someone named Sean Pulpo. Some twinkle-toed like Fred Flintstone bowling. Others charged, trying to power through the slime. One stud with pink hot pants pulled over his head ran and slid like a surfer. A couple guys turned their feet sideways and noodged along with careful fussy steps. When a contestant slammed his back or leg or groin into the pole, the spectators on shore howled in an empathetic chorus. They shook their heads sadly, threw cigarettes into the sand, snuffing the stubs with their flip-flops. And all the while the red flag blew in the sea breeze, the coveted prize beyond reach.

'Do you think Brando is all right?' I asked. We'd left him in Rita's apartment after a morning of stick and ball.

'The air conditioning is blasting,' Rita said.

'You're right,' I said. 'He's probably fixing himself a drink. Who are you rooting for?'

'Sean Pulpo. You?'

'Bogie the Castro. It looks like most of the grease is gone. Are they going to give everybody a second shot?'

'They keep going until someone gets the flag.'

'*Ohh, Andy the Guppie tries the straddle and slide and almost comes within range but nooooooo.*'

'Oh, shit,' shouted Rita, slapping her forehead. 'He almost had it.'

It was hard not to get caught up in it all. Somehow the struggle through the grease, the unsightly dives, the elusive red flag, looked eerily familiar. All at once, I realized why.

'Rita, this is my life,' I said. '*My life is a greasy pole contest.*'

'Really,' Rita said. 'That bad?'

'Messy, futile, flagless,' I said. 'In Utah, it was like that. For five years. And sometimes it still is. I mean it is now, really.

You can see the flag, but you can't figure out how to get there.'

'Run,' Rita said.

'Right, run,' I agreed. 'Or better yet drive.'

The guy who finally won was just another Joe, or Joe-Joe or Joey, a proud hometown boy, a little buzzed, a little cocky, who genuflected before venturing out from the platform's edge. Arms extended like a cross, he began with a deliberate walk that sped into a precarious half run that soared into a miraculous leap, grease flying, fingers grasping, and when he finally crashed into Gloucester Bay, the red flag went with him. The crowd let out a massive cheer and the gong gonged and the M.C. went wild.

As the winning Joe swam back to shore, I imagined how the brash son of a fisherman would be hoisted on warm shoulders and paraded through the streets of Gloucester like a saint. Flushed from sun and spirits, he'd feel the love of St Peter, the patron saint of fishermen, deep in his heart. He'd walked the pole for his father, and his father's father, and now floating above the crowd on his chariot, he was confident of his luck and talent. He knew now he was ready to begin.

That night at Rita's, I took Brando on a walk before bed. We strolled past the cottages toward the seawall at the end of the lane. Before we reached the third house, I felt hypocritical and unclipped Brando's leash. It was a pretty night, the sky freckled with stars, the houses warmed by yellow porch lights, the air alive with television laughter seeping through summer screens. It felt good to be walking a dog, my dog, my dog on loan. His tail flopped side-to-side, steady as a metronome. His girly toenails clicked the sidewalk. He sniffed tree trunks and flower beds and mysterious holes, jowls flapping, curious about the scents of earlier travelers. We were a team. A pair of outlaws, roving the seashore, trusting our bold hunches would lead us to water. I felt snug in the moment, a traveler who belonged nowhere to no one and while tomorrow this same set of facts would leave me feeling bereft – a leaf lost in the wind – tonight, chocolate lab at my side, I felt at home without one.

We reached the seawall, which wasn't a wall exactly, more a massive pile of boulders sloping down to the water. Looking through the darkness to the occasional boat light, rock-warning light, star, I thought back to the greasy pole contest and tried to imagine myself up there on that pole, struggling to maintain balance, fighting off gravity's pull. As we picked our way along the rocks, I let my mind wander back to Utah, the five years I spent slipping and sliding, my belly flops and nosedives and graceless missteps, and I tried to remember, to relive, the rhythm and velocity of each fall.

Zion

I was twenty-eight when I moved to Utah. This wasn't Manifest Destiny. This was Manifest Desperation. For two years I'd been wasting away at a tabloid in Trenton, New Jersey, writing dog-wedding stories, Stephen King-stole-my-manuscript stories, chasing down promiscuous girls to pose in bikinis for Page Six, our 'celebrity' page, and archiving my rejection letters from papers of record. When Mike, my old boss, called to offer me a reporting job in Salt Lake, I pulled out my atlas. (There was Utah! The square with the missing chunk.) I asked Andy if he'd go with me and he said he'd think about it, which I took to mean no, and I cried a lot and then reminded myself I was an independent woman, which made me feel better even though I didn't entirely believe it.

The editor asked for a two-year commitment; I grudgingly agreed. Two years: long enough to achieve CV respectability, not long enough to become another Jane Tarbox. Who was I going to date in Mormonland? A missionary? A prophet? Never mind. As long as I reached a *real* place before I turned thirty, I'd still have time to luxuriate in the wooing I'd so deserve after two years of desert starvation.

So like the valiant pioneer women before me, I packed my valise and headed west to seek my fortune. It didn't take long for things to start to go wrong. In fact, it took less than forty-eight hours.

My second night in Salt Lake, I went out to dinner with Alice, a sales executive who worked for my new employer, *The Salt Lake Tribune*. We were finishing a pleasant dinner of grilled fish.

'So you're starting in a week,' said Alice, well into her second Scotch. Alice was Catholic. 'They've gotten all your papers together. And you've had your drug test?'

The trout in my stomach did a violent flop. *Drug test?*

'No, not yet,' I said, strangling the neck of my wineglass. 'When do they generally do . . . *all that?*'

'Right when you get here,' Alice said. 'Mike will probably call you in to fill out papers and so on.'

I was suddenly aware of various illegal substances floating around in my veins. A puff or two of marijuana. A line or two of coke. Nothing terrible. I mean, I wasn't a drug user. I didn't have a drug problem.

Later that night, driving up I-80 nearly in tears, I pulled off at a shadowy truck stop to call Andy long distance.

'I'm going to be fired and I haven't even started my job,' I wailed into the receiver. 'They're giving me a drug test.'

'Really?' said Andy. He was cool. He was back on The Farm, that cozy anarchy of peacocks and pot smokers and Marvin Gaye. 'When?'

'I don't know. In the next couple days.'

'They're things you can do,' Andy said slowly. 'We'll figure it out.'

'*Like what?* Poppy seeds. I remember something about poppy seeds. Maybe I could just say I've been eating a lot of bagels?'

'Hold on. Let me ask Leonard.' Leonard, a friend of the family, was a drug user. Leonard had a drug problem. Thank God for Leonard.

Andy came back. 'Leonard says drink fresh-squeezed juice. Drink tons of it.'

'Orange juice?'

'Citrus. Orange, grapefruit . . . Drink it until you can't stand it anymore.'

'Oh my God, I can't believe this.' The world was swirling gray. 'What if I fail the test, and they send me home? What if I have to tell my parents that I didn't get the job because I failed the drug test?'

'Juice,' said Andy. 'Stall them with the test. Don't go into the office whatever you do. *Don't let them find you.*'

'But I'm *staying* with Mike,' I moaned. Though Mike was no Mormon, he was still my boss, and I didn't relish having to confess this little drug mishap before I'd even started work. 'He already said he wants me to come into the office and meet everyone, fill out forms.'

'*Don't go,*' Andy warned. 'Just say you can't go. Get up early and run.'

I set the alarm for 6:00 a.m. It was still dark when I tiptoed out of Mike's house. Just as I was making my escape, his wife, Jill, wandered out to the lawn in her motherly bathrobe, her long brown hair unbrushed, her eyes blinking away sleep.

'You're up early,' she called out. 'Where are you off to?'

I was standing in the driveway, hand on the car door, feeling like Jill's fourth and most depraved child.

'Apartment looking,' I called back. 'You've got to get an early start. It's a jungle out there.'

Jill nodded, perplexed. 'Don't you want some breakfast?'

'Thanks, but I've got to go.' I motioned toward my Rent-A-Wreck, a Coupe De Ville the color of eggplant. 'Wish me luck.'

The sun was breaking over the Wasatch Mountains as I drove into the city. Anxious to find an apartment, anxious that I'd lose my job and not *need* an apartment, I spent five or six hours circling Salt Lake and guzzling OJ until my stomach was a pool of citric acid. Every hour or so, I'd pull into a gas station to pee and buy mints or a soda so the pimply clerk didn't blow a gasket. Forget real estate ads. If I saw a moving van, I barged into the house to inquire who was moving out and when. I accosted contractors, called friends of friends of strangers I'd met in coffee shops.

That afternoon, I stopped a tall, stick-like guy who was riding his bike, golden retriever in tow. Underneath his brew pub cap, his smile was mischievous and willing.

'Excuse me,' I said politely. 'I'm new in town and I'm looking for an apartment to rent. Do you know of any, by chance?'

That's how I remember it. But Roger, the boy on the bike, tells a different story. He insists he was innocently riding down Sixth Avenue with his dog, Shane, when a blond woman pulled over in a large sedan and hollered out the window:

'Hey you. Do you know of any apartments to rent?'

In the coming years, so often would Roger and I disagree on the details of our common history that he took to saying, with a directorial wave, 'Okay, boys, let's rewind the videotape.'

As my version goes, Roger waved me over to the side of the road. I got out and he told me he too was thinking of moving and we should look for apartments together.

'Now?' I asked.

'Is there a better time?' Roger raised his eyebrow like a fishhook. 'Where are you staying?'

'In a condo in Midvale,' I said. Midvale is a suburb of Mormons, little boxes of sanctimony bursting with kids.

'Right now,' said Roger, stroking his jaw. 'You need me for this.'

I paused, looking him over, trying to see what I was getting into. Roger was not a handsome man, yet there was something winning about him. His red hair had made a bold retreat, and he made up for it with a goatee. His fair skin was scarred, I would later learn, from 'a youthful indiscretion' involving a friend's week-old Porsche. Doctors had spent hours bent over his face, extracting slivers of glass. When he

147

smiled at me – or was it a smirk? – his hazel eyes gave off a puckish glint, like he already had my number and was getting ready to dial. Apparently, I amused him. I could see he'd begun to rehearse this story in his head for a later performance, how he'd picked up the lost blonde in a purple Rent-A-Wreck. I have to admit I was falling for the story myself so I took off with Roger for the afternoon, peering in windows, knocking on doors. Later, we kicked back on the front porch of his apartment, watching cars wheel in and out of Albertson's parking lot, people dropping off videos, picking up eggs. I found myself flirting, flexing those old muscles, just to keep them in shape. Before I knew it, I'd confessed the horrors of my impending drug test.

'So you're running from the law,' Roger cackled, stretching out his long legs. 'A girl after my own heart. I've always prided myself on my swift exits. I imagine you've left a doting boy or two in your time?'

'One or two.' I pulled out a scrap of paper from my fanny pack. 'I have the name of one person in the state of Utah who I'm supposed to look up. Susanna Reed. She works in a sub shop.'

Roger whooped. 'Sub shop? I *hired* Susanna. Not subs, *please*. Wraps . . . Some friends and I started the business. Do you want a beer? Or are you sticking with the grapefruit diet?'

'What the hell. I'm going to be fired soon anyway.'

Roger returned with two green bottles. 'Susanna's a great girl. Now where did you go to college?'

'Brown.'

'Ohhh, the Ivy League. You'll fit in fine in Salt Lake. The women out west are generally smarter than the men.'

'Present company included?'

Roger made a check mark in the air.

'And you're from here?' I asked.

Roger looked pained. 'Please. Western Mass.'

'You like it out here?'

'What's not to like about Utah?' Roger opened his arms,

148

like a politician soliciting votes. 'The streets are wide, and the people are malleable.'

'And the Mormons?'

'K-Mart religion. Golden tablets found in upstate? I don't think so. So does Lili from Connecticut have a boyfriend?'

'Yeeees,' I said slowly. 'Back in New Jersey. He may move out here.' Already this didn't sound quite right.

'I see.' Roger nodded with mock earnestness. 'Boyfriend weighing his options.'

Two days later, I started work. To stave off my imminent dismissal, I tried to look busy, which wasn't easy with an empty desk and no assignments.

Roger called that afternoon. 'Lois Lane, I presume.'

'Speaking.'

'Still employed?'

'I'm keeping my head down.'

'How uncharacteristic.'

Roger invited me to dinner. I sat among futons and milk-carton end tables and skis and ice coolers and a slush of cassettes without boxes and boxes without cassettes and wrinkled snapshots of Roger, mugging on mountaintops, hoisting bottles of beer. Roger had been to the grocery store, an annual outing from the looks of his fridge. With great flourish, he prepared angel hair pasta with scallops. I was touched by the effort, although I would later learn this was his one and only dish, conjured solely for seduction purposes. While he cooked, I drank beer, hoping I was becoming light-headed and charming.

'It's delicious,' I said, spinning my fork through a jumble of pasta.

'Nothing at all,' said Roger with a wave of his hand. 'Just one of my many fine qualities.'

We went to the movies. Before leaving, Roger slid a Rolling Rock into his pocket; I stashed a second in my sock.

It was half-price ticket night, called 'Two-fifty Tuesday,' but Roger snuck us in without paying. A bunch of his friends showed up and piled in a few rows behind us, all big waves and grins, amused to have caught Roger on a date.

'Some of my worthless friends,' Roger explained. 'Bums. Slackers. You know you do the best you can.'

'That's what I always say,' I said, giving him the eye.

'Okay, missy. Eat your popcorn.'

'You didn't buy me any.'

'That's enough out of you.'

A half hour into the film, I turned to Roger and whispered, 'We should have brought more beer.'

Roger patted my hand. 'Oh, Lois, we're going to get along just fine you and me. I can see that already.'

It didn't take me long to realize that Utah had two worlds, and I didn't belong to either of them. The first group was the Mormons. The state's history, politics, its very geography was shaped by its dominant religion. The capital city is built on a grid; ground zero is the Mormon Temple, world headquarters of the Church of Jesus Christ of Latter-Day Saints. 'Third West' is three blocks west of the Temple, '3500 South' is thirty-five blocks south of the Temple. And so it goes, more than ten thousand blocks into the desert.

My first week at the paper, my editor assigned me to cover opening day of LDS Business College, a church-owned secretarial school. After the reception, I called back an administrator to double-check his title.

'I'm an apostle.'

I stopped typing. 'Excuse me?'

'I'm one of the twelve apostles.'

Yeah, and I'm Mary Magdalene.

I thanked the disciple and hung up the phone.

'Hey, Ryan,' I called over to my new boss. 'I'm a little confused. I just interviewed this guy from LDS Business College. He says he's one of the twelve apostles.'

'He is,' Ryan said. '"Apostle" is Mormonspeak for bureaucrat.'

So my religious education began. I learned how the angel Moroni had appeared to Joseph Smith in upstate New York and showed him tablets containing an entire religious history, and how the Mormons were chased to Nauvoo, Illinois, where they were persecuted and Smith was shot to death by an angry mob. I learned how his successor, Brigham Young, led Mormon pioneers west over the Rockies until they arrived at the Wasatch Front, and Young pronounced, *This is the place.*' I learned how early Mormons practiced polygamy until Utah territory wanted to enter the Union and then how church president Wilford Woodruff had a divine (and convenient) revelation that it was immoral for a man to keep more than one wife. I learned about garments, Jesus jammies, religious underwear that devout Mormons wear day and night (except while exercising or fooling around). I learned how every Mormon male in good standing holds the priesthood and communicates directly to God, and how not until 1978 did President Spencer Kimbell have the divine revelation that black men were real men too. (Women are still waiting for their revelation.) I learned that Mormon couples are encouraged to have big families because it's the only way the spirit babies can come to earth, and when good Mormons die, they rise to the celestial heavens where they have sex and procreate for all eternity, populating their own private planet. (While most religious doctrine strains credibility, it was particularly hard to imagine heaven as a place where women stagger around in perpetuity with morning sickness and hemorrhoids.)

Needless to say, the Mormons were not my lost tribe. While I liked many Mormons individually, the clan was oppressive. Week after week in the press, the good fathers railed against the three great threats to the faith:

Feminists. Intellectuals. Homosexuals.

Most of my friends were at least two out of three. My

151

greatest pleasures – coffee, alcohol, premarital sex – were deemed mortal sins, and their newfound illicitness only made them more desirable. Every cup of coffee became an act of defiance. Every cocktail, taboo. When covering the state legislature – 90 percent white male Mormon – I wore miniskirts, a tacit way of saying *I wasn't one of them.*

But no matter what you wore, it was impossible to forget who held the keys to the city. Just down the block from our offices soared the Mormon Temple, with its manicured gardens and Cinderella spires, with its fresh-faced tour guides eager to get your name and address, so they could come knocking with the Book of Mormon and a friendly handshake. All during the week, the sanctuary pumped out bride after bride, each freshly flushed from her top-secret service that sealed her for all eternity to her missionary man. Driving past the temple, you could get stuck at the crosswalk for a good ten minutes as streams of fair-skinned families in their Sunday best crossed South Temple: Grandpa Earl holding hands with sister LaRuth, sister LaRuth holding hands with Big Thor, Big Thor holding on to little Bucky and everyone smiling and overflowing with the goodness of God. They were so sure of themselves. I was so unsure of myself. It was all I could do not to mow them down.

As religious conversion held little appeal, I took refuge with Utah's other cult – the outdoors crowd. Back in New York, I'd always considered myself fairly athletic. I jogged, I swam, I looked good in black lycra. My idea of a good ski day was to make sloppy parallel turns for an hour or two, then head inside the lodge for a plate of warm fries. But people in Utah were another breed. These were ski bums, East Coast transplants who grew up cutting their edges on Vermont ice, huddling on windy chair lifts, nuzzling their chapped faces in damp wool scarves that froze and melted and froze as they breathed. They chose their college for its annual snowpack. They majored in Snow Science. Degree in hand, they moved out west to keep the dream alive. Bored by black diamonds, they ducked under warning cords to ski virgin drifts that threatened, at any moment, to crack into a deadly avalanche. It wasn't enough to ski down a mountain, they had to hike up it first. Skis hoisted high on their shoulders, they trudged to the tippy-tippy top of a ridge where they smoked a communal doobie and raced down a chute so sheer each turn was a leap. In the summer, they mountain-biked, pumping up rocky hills, tumbling over tree roots. At a post-race barbecue, the boys smoked dope in the garage while the girls showed off their war wounds, hiking their sundresses to reveal black stitches embroidered on soft stretches of thigh.

'What are you doing hanging around a cad like Roger?' asked the fleece guy/the ski lift operator guy/the bike shop trust funder guy – I could never keep them straight.

'That bad?' I asked.

'Worse,' said the fleece/bike shop/ski-lift operator with a smile. 'Much, much worse.'

Stories about Roger were constantly alluded to but never told. Escapades in lift shacks, mysterious smoke, petty scandals involving nurses and closets. Roger was infamous for one-upping *touristos*, East Coast hot doggers who thought they could ski. Playing local tour guide, he would lure them to the brink of a twenty-foot precipice lined with granite.

'You got it now,' Roger would prod. 'No problem.'

Roger leaned over the edge, grinning maliciously as the proud sucker jumped. Skis and poles scattered in the powder. (Such humiliations were called 'pulling a yard sale.') Then 'our hero' would leap after the chump, a blur of fearlessness, land feetfirst, scoop up the flayed poles, asking the ashen tourist, oh so kindly, if he needed a hand.

I was still in love with Andy but happy to cavort with Roger. Roger was not Mr Right and he knew it. We slept together anyway. It seemed like the next step, something that had to be tried. As usual, sex clarified nothing. I wasn't sure I was attracted to Roger. Or I was attracted but not in love. Or I was in love but not attracted. We were too

153

close. We were the same person. He was in my head. He could tweak my wiring, fix me like a phone. Of course, I felt guilty. (*Poor Andy. How could I? Why had I?*) Of course, I didn't stop.

Sexually active and verbally platonic, Roger and I communicated best with banter and insults until someone's feelings got hurt and there was a rapprochement when Roger would stroke the hair back from my forehead until I got woozy and limp.

'Scarlett, we could be really happy, can't you see that?' he'd say. 'We just have to make it work. You're the one I want. You want me too, you just can't admit it.'

I couldn't admit it. I couldn't even understand it.

Meanwhile, it looked like I was staying in Utah for a while because no one from the paper ever came to give me a drug test. It was a year before I had the nerve to ask our environmental reporter why I'd been spared.

'*Drug test?*' he scoffed. 'Do you know how many people around here would fail a drug test? We'd have to can half the staff.'

Francie Horsham perched outside the editor's office like a mother hen guarding one precious egg. Francie was the *Tribune's* office manager, the person who reporters sought out to get parking stickers, to sort out insurance snafus, to put in their order for chicken or steak at the annual summer barbecue. Francie, a Mormon mother of five, had faded pink skin and yellowish hair that floated above her head like a cottony halo. She wore flowered dresses belted at the waist, support panty hose, and chunky sandals. With her sick mother and her migraines, Francie personified middle age. Whenever I traveled to Mexico, she asked me to smuggle her back tubes of the antiwrinkle cream, Retin-A.

At office social functions, she played chaperone, worrying over single staffers who arrived unescorted, cornering our dates for a cordial interrogation.

'So now *where* are you from? . . . And *what* do you do? . . . How *long* have you known Lili?'

Francie considered it her duty to prod marital holdouts – Mormon or otherwise – down the aisle. Whenever I approached Francie's desk looking for an aspirin or an expense report, she'd whisper conspiratorially: 'So how's that cute fellow you're dating?'

Instead of asking which one, I'd mumble, 'Fine, just fine,' not wanting to explain Roger in Salt Lake, Andy in New Jersey to a Mormon mother of five.

If Francie was the quintessential busybody, her husband, Robert, was red meat, virile to the bone. He was too good-looking, cold as a carving. Bad things in handsome packages, it was disconcerting.

At the annual office Christmas party, affectionately known as 'the Prom,' while the electric organ band ompahed the seventies' disco anthem 'Celebrate Good Times,' Robert wouldn't budge from his foldout chair. Francie would elbow some poor reporter who, seeing no polite way to escape, asked her to dance.

Francie loved to dance. Once her white sandals hit the parquet, she floated from one partner to the next as if deep in a dream. She jitterbugged with the night city editor. She boogied with the bully cop reporter. As meddling as Francie could be, I forgave her everything when I saw her do the bunny hop, hands balanced on a copyboy's shoulders, grinning like a girl on her first date. Maybe she was imagining herself back in high school, when the boys were fresh-faced and eager and she'd had a string of summer nights to find just the right one.

The day I turned thirty, Francie pulled me aside to wish me happy birthday. She spoke with the concern of a seasoned woman sharing hard-earned wisdom with a prodigal daughter.

'Now don't you worry that you're all alone,' she said. 'My life didn't begin until I was thirty and I met Robert.'

Her words curdled my stomach. Clots of sour milk.

A moment later, I recovered, got defensive. I didn't need a man to jump-start my life. Not me, the *Trib's* 'gender issues' reporter, a woman on a personal and professional crusade to wipe out sexism at home, at work, overseas, in the ivory tower, in the army, the navy and the marines, and yes, even in the land of Zion. Yet I kept my feminist speech about empowerment to myself; I didn't have the heart.

'Thanks, Francie,' I said, turning away.

That afternoon, I repeated Francie's remark to a friend and we had a good laugh at her expense. Francie, Mormon wife and mother, it was all so funny. And yet, though I would have denied it to my deathbed, Francie's words filled me with hope. At thirty, Francie was an old Mormon maid, and yet she'd found a husband. They'd had a family. Her life *began*, whatever that meant. Maybe sex began, which might be confused with life, if you'd never had any. The point was: If Francie had waited until thirty to meet her partner, maybe I wasn't too late.

The harder I tried to find True Love, the more befuddled I became. Roger and I broke up, reconciled, broke up again, reconciled again. Andy and I did more of the same. Both men knew about each other; both were jealous; both vowed to fight on. My life took on the timing and theatrics of a French farce. Flowers from Andy arrived while Roger and I were smearing our bagels. When Andy flew out to Salt Lake unannounced, Roger stormed around my apartment in a rage, snatching his water bottle, his atlas, like a man whose ship is going down. When Andy went home, Roger suggested what Bonnie and Clyde needed was a little R&R in Cabo San Lucas. On the phone to Andy, I mumbled something about 'having to figure things out.' The real reason I went was it sounded like fun.

Roger would call at the office.

'Thelma?'

'Louise,' I'd answer. 'Can I put you on hold for a minute, someone is on the other line for me.'

That somebody would be Andy.

'Hey, Sweet Pea. Listen, I've thought about it. Why don't we just get married?'

I'd put Andy on hold, stare at the two blinking lights, look around the newsroom at all the dedicated reporters, the great Fourth Estate, fighting for truth, writing for justice.

Oh God, I hate myself.

Every day, I awaited a Mormonesque divine revelation telling me who was meant to be. Both relationships were so marvelous, so flawed. They went so well *together*. Though I knew good girls didn't behave this way, I couldn't help being the victim of my last conversation, allying myself with whoever sounded most convinced of our cosmic inevitability.

After putting up with a lot of this, Roger moved to Washington, D.C., to get into politics. After putting up with a lot of this, Andy returned to The Farm.

A widow, twice over, I donned black, went into mourning.

The next week, I started hanging out with Stuart, the vet, one of Roger's friends. Stuart and I didn't like each other much at first. He thought I was aloof. I thought he was a womanizer. I suppose we were both right. (Later, I would insist the reason I'd been aloof was because he was such a womanizer. Later, Stuart would insist he only came off like a womanizer to women who were aloof.)

With his eight pairs of skis, three bicycles, two kayaks, and one snowboard, Stuart was a poster boy for *Outside* magazine. One night, he took me to a kayak party where we nursed boutique beers and watched a videotape of the gang's latest excellent adventure down level-five rapids.

'There goes Skye!' a girl in braids shouted, pointing to a blob in a wet suit and helmet.

'There goes John!'

'There goes Laura!'

'That's not Laura, that's Jim!'

157

I stood in the corner, munching potato chips. On the way home, I pronounced: 'Nature is boring.'

'*How can you say that?*' said Stuart, shaking his head.

'Water,' I said. 'You realize it's everywhere.'

Spanish, of all things, brought us together. I was going on a month-long language program in Mexico that Stuart had already been on and we enrolled in the same Spanish night class and this seemed like Fate talking – in a foreign language, no less. For homework, we sat in his kitchen and conjugated. The imperfect. The conditional.

Pretty soon, it dawned on me that I was happy. Pretty soon, it seemed likely that Stuart might be The One. He was kind to my parents, calming my dad over the phone before a minor operation. He made me a jewelry box from an old cigar box. He wrote me a love poem. He painted me a picture. We went skiing, and I admired him from afar, the way he carved graceful telemark turns down the mountain, bending each knee like a prayer. What he saw in me, I am not sure. His greatest fear was that his life would be boring; perhaps I looked like a woman who could ward off such a fate.

When Roger heard the news, he fired off several death threats via FedEx. *We belonged together; we still had a chance.* As I read his letter, I couldn't help wondering if maybe he was right. I could have chosen Roger. And if I had, who would I be now? How would our lives have gone? I was always curious about the roads not taken (every dirt path, every sun-lit alley). Curious and sad. Why did I have to write off people who meant so much to me? Why was love an all-or-nothing game? Every so often it occurred to me that the Mormon polygamists were on to something. Maybe I wasn't built for monogamy. Committing to four husbands would be easy enough; it was winnowing the list down that troubled me. I wasn't prepared to make such a life-threatening choice. Somewhere along the line, the decisions had become adult but I hadn't. *How did anyone choose? How did anyone say yes? At what point were we all supposed to settle?*

All I wanted was a little certainty. A sign, a neon sign, a glaring Atlantic City arrow pointing over some man's head, ordering me to *Park Here*. That's what I loved about new love; it felt so destined, so inspired. Sometimes, it seemed the only way to get married was meet a man and hotfoot it to the altar before the initial spell wore off, before either of us knew too much about what we were getting.

And sex?

I had plenty of orgasms now. There was only one problem: I only had them alone. With a lover, I'd go right to the brink, and then my body would balk. I'd like to think this was some incisive feminist statement about not needing a man for pleasure, but no. I was a mermaid, stuck on the rocks with my mirror and comb and scaly green tail.

Like any good Yankee, I vowed to work harder. I tried to cultivate an exotic fantasy life. During sex, I summoned a cast of shady characters. Lesbians with baubles. Black men with sculpted chests. Rapists with heart. I dragged in scenery: chain link or spume. I turned off the volume. Faded to black and white. I dreamed up Italian men, all passion and meatballs, not a subtitle in sight. I tried not to think. I tried not to think about not thinking. I saw myself headless, mindless, just a body, all chicken reflexes and fresh appetite. Animals doing what animals do. I rose to the ceiling, a movie camera on a riser, peered down at our bodies, the sheets, the ways we connected, communicated, his hand, his skin, his ass. *It's not the penis, it's the man attached.*

None of it worked. None of it ever worked.

Not that my lovers didn't give it the old college try. Each man attacked my problem with great bravado, confident *he* had the Midas touch. It reminded me of those Test Your Brawn games at the county fair, where men slam a giant mallet on a disc and try to ring the bell. Roger once told me not to worry, one of his exes, another girl from Connecticut, had a similar problem. (Was there something in the water? Had anyone done studies?) Apparently, when Miss Connecticut finally climaxed she was so enraptured she wanted to get married. Roger told her not to be ridiculous. 'People don't get married for orgasms,' he'd scoffed. While this seemed like fine advice, did people get married without them?

And Darwin? What would the old bugger have had to say about the evolution of female gratification? If men didn't climax, the species died on the vine. If women didn't climax, the human race merrily rolled along. And if we women weren't satisfied, well, we could always go shopping.

I had no idea why I couldn't do what everyone else did without thinking, without any effort at all. Maybe herpes held me back. I worried about it all the time, convinced I'd spread disease like a street rat or a tsetse fly. Forty-five million Americans have herpes, but not one of them has ever talked to me about it. We're all just supposed to keep our mouths shut; we're supposed to be ashamed.

In my experience, most people treat sexually transmitted diseases like a big, fat joke. At parties, I'd ask some guy for a sip of his beer, and he'd smirk.

'Sure you don't have any diseases I should know about?'

Ha ha ha ha ha ha.

'Clean as a whistle,' I'd say, wrapping my lips around his green bottle.

One night, my neighbor told me how his buddy was pissed at him for fixing him up with a woman he knew. 'So he calls me after his date and says "thanks a lot." And I say, "What?" And he says, "At least you could set me up with someone with a clean bill of health." Oops. I had some serious making up to do after that one.'

I smiled sympathetically. 'Imagine that.'

Of course, compared to AIDS, herpes is small potatoes. It's not going to kill you. It's not going to ruin your life. But it's no fun either, especially when you're single and you know that in every new relationship there will come the moment when you have to cough up the goods. Even though, after the college boy, none of my partners contracted the virus, the threat was always lurking. In the middle of lovemaking, I pictured the virus swirling around in bodily fluid, evil amoebas eager to land. Rawl was wrong about one thing: Men still wanted me. Men couldn't imagine any such thing would happen to them. I'm not sure they really believed I *had* the virus. Bad things in handsome packages, it was disconcerting.

Looking back, I should have talked things over with my girlfriends. And once I tried. One rainy night after work, I got up my courage and confided in a friend, hoping she would offer advice or at least reassure me I wasn't the only sexual flop. Outside my apartment, we sat in her car, the rain beading and tumbling against the windows.

We were talking about sex. 'Sometimes I just can't get there,' I began. 'I'm almost there, and everything feels great, but then it doesn't happen. I fall short.'

'*You're kidding*,' my friend gasped. 'Orgasms, that's one thing I've never had problems with. I've always enjoyed sex and things just . . . well . . . Gosh, I'm so sorry for you. I just never would have known. I mean, *you're so pretty*.'

One day, riding back from a vacation in Seattle, Stuart let me drive.

Usually Stuart drove us wherever we went because he liked driving and I didn't and he was good at it and I wasn't, but the traffic was heavy and Stuart needed a breather so he pulled into the breakdown lane and we switched places. I bounced along the highway's edge and then, with a rush of adrenaline, merged into the afternoon traffic, shiny with sun.

Move over, you fat Ford, make way.

As I shifted into the center lane, my favorite (in the middle, there are more ways to change your mind), Stuart assumed the crash position, right arm braced against the door handle, legs braced against the floor mat, jaw braced against the air.

'It's not that bad,' I said.

'Just relax,' Stuart said.

161

'I *am* relaxed.'

'*No, you're not.* Look at you. All hunched up. Leaning forward.'

I dropped my shoulders. Sat back against the seat.

'I'm relaxed.'

'*No, you're not.*'

A bread truck steamed up on my left. A moving van squeezed in on my right. I throttled the wheel, felt the car shudder as the sixteen wheelers rumbled past. Somehow I had become the kind of woman my father swore at on the highway, the kind of overly cautious bumbler who sent him careening into the passing lane muttering his ultimate put-down: '*Woman driver.*'

'I remember back in driver's ed in high school,' I began, talking not because I had something to say but to prove I could manage two difficult tasks at the same time. 'The guy used to say you're not supposed to look at the horizon or down at your wheels, but instead keep your eyes on some middle ground.'

I waved my hand at this vague, pregnant space.

'He's right,' Stuart said.

'No,' I said. 'You have to look at what's right in front of you, right where you are. What if some little kid runs into the street after his ball and you're staring way down the road into no-man's-land? Whammo.'

'You'll see the kid,' Stuart said. 'Your eyes adjust. You brake.'

'How do you know?'

'It's just the way it works,' he said impatiently.

'The way it's *supposed* to work.'

'Right.'

We didn't say anything for a minute or two. Stuart watched me drive, and I pretended not to notice.

'Stuart?'

'Yes.'

'When you're driving, do you ever space out?'

Stuart didn't say anything so I continued.

'Forget you're driving altogether, sort of disappear, have some kind of out-of-body experience? And then, suddenly, you wake up and you've got no idea how much time has passed or where you've been, but the whole time you've been driving, not even *thinking* about what you're doing. As if someone else were driving the car, as if it were driving itself.'

Stuart gave me an exasperated stare.

'Don't you get it?' he said.

'Get what?'

'*When you forget you're driving, it means you're driving well.*'

'No.'

'Yes, yes, yes, yes.'

'But I only do that when I'm driving alone,' I said, waving my hand again, trying to explain. 'I can't forget I'm driving when you're here.'

My eyes smarted. Driving, sex, it was the same sort of battle.

'What do you want me to do?' Stuart asked.

'I don't know,' I said. 'If I knew, I'd tell you but I don't. I have no idea.'

'Do you want me to drive?' Stuart asked.

'No, I'm driving.' I pressed the accelerator to prove it.

Stuart sat back in his seat, stiff as a security guard, and I gazed purposefully into the middle distance and awaited transformation, but I couldn't forget the four wheels spinning underneath us and the three exits to go before we changed highways and the two trucks roaring up from behind and the one of us who was still here, who was always still here, doing her best to drive.

Another day, Stuart announced his pet theory about me: The reason I didn't understand love was that my heart had never been broken. I had no idea what it felt like to be on the receiving end.

'That's so not true,' I protested. 'My heart has been broken.

163

Many times. Ending relationships is terrible no matter who does it.'

'Maybe,' Stuart said. 'But it's easier to leave than be left. Has anyone *ever* broken up with you?'

'*Yes*,' I said. '*Once*.'

'When?'

'*In high school*.'

Stuart rolled his eyes.

'*It counts*.'

His named was Jack. What I remembered most clearly was he drove like a maniac. He knew exactly how big his car was, down to the centimeter, and he wove through Boston traffic steering the wheel with his knee. He was a clownish guy, a prankster, but the day he broke up with me was no joke. He sat me down on the carpeted stairs of my dorm and told me that our relationship wasn't working. He never knew what I was thinking; I kept my feelings to myself.

As he told me this, I started to cry because he was leaving me and because I didn't understand what he meant. *What was I supposed to be telling him?* I kept any bad thoughts about him to myself, so I wouldn't hurt his feelings. Maybe he was mad because I couldn't say I love you. I had tried, but for some reason, the words wouldn't come out. It was too large a feeling, too raw an exposure. Like slicing yourself open with a knife, then inviting friends to come watch you bleed. No, that wasn't it. It was like a bubble coming out of a fish. Only the air bubble was life itself and if it ever escaped, the fish would collapse, be empty, be nothing at all.

Then I wondered if maybe this was one of those things I was supposed to be telling Jack, but I felt stupid telling him about the knife and the fish.

'The whole point is to share things,' Jack said.

'We share things,' I mumbled.

Jack wiped a tear from my cheek, stroked my chin with his thumb.

'Some things,' he said, 'but not enough to feel close.'

164

I felt close, but he didn't. I had failed him somehow. Apparently, other people were giving things I didn't even realize were missing.

That afternoon in Utah, I told Stuart a short version of this story – how this high school boy had broken up with me and how sad I had been – but he still wasn't convinced I knew much about love and I wasn't either, though I wasn't going to admit that to him.

The rest of the day, I kept thinking about this breakup, growing ever more unsettled and amazed. What unnerved me was not that this adolescent high school kid had left me for the reason he did, but that in all the years that followed no one else had.

To my complete astonishment, I won a journalism fellowship to go to Mexico for nine months to study Spanish and write about NAFTA. I had applied on a whim; my Spanish professor graciously exaggerated my fluency on his recommendation, and somehow I'd been chosen. I read the acceptance letter over and over again, tears in my eyes, amazed that a bunch of strangers had an iota of faith in me.

Now that I was leaving, Stuart looked better than ever. We decided to date long distance. We would write and call; he would visit. We'd grow together, two thousand miles apart.

The last thing I expected when I moved to Mexico was to fall in love again – this time with a country. Originally I lived in Guadalajara, but after a month of dragging around in the city heat and pollution, riding buses past *la catedral* while men stared at my breasts and genuflected, I relocated to an artist colony with more modern sensibilities. Though I hardly spoke Spanish, I felt more at home in this Mexican village than I ever did in Utah. After three years in the sagebrush with the Mormons, Mexico felt like a sensual paradise: the bougainvillea blossoms, the coconut masks, the smells of ripe fruit and brush fire, the brash mariachis, the hand-patted tortillas warm in brown paper, the donkeys wobbling down cobblestones. I didn't even mind when the rancheros hissed '*Güerita*' (little blondie) as they passed on the street; it made me feel, well, blonde.

I adored studying Spanish. It was a way to begin again, to pare down my life to simple objects and verbs. How could you worry about major life decisions when you couldn't even tell your professor what you had eaten for supper? I moved into an apartment next to three Mexican painters: a druggie surrealist and two women, Leila and Sara, who became close friends. My grant required me to do a research project, so I reported on a clinic that sent teenagers out to remote ranchos to teach sex education. Under thatched roofs, as the chickens pecked in circles, the girls explained that trusting God's will was not the most secure form of contraception.

All the while, I sustained grand illusions of getting my romantic life in order. Instead, I discovered my *telenovela* had merely moved south of the border. All the boys had my number. All the boys had my fax. Stuart planned to visit for a two-month sabbatical. Roger phoned in for updates. Every blue moon, Andy called to see if I was single again. For days, I drifted the cobblestones thinking about the verb *esperar*. It means to wait, to hope, to expect, all three things at once. It was the perfect verb for me; my whole life could be encapsulated in a single word – *espero*. Frustrated by my lack of progress, I crept off to the neighborhood witch for a *limpia*, a spiritual cleansing. In a shack lined with dripping candles and offerings to the *Virgen de Guadalupe*, a diminutive crone in a shawl muttered a murky incantation and wiped me down with raw eggs and green aftershave. When I left, I didn't feel cleansed; I felt minty.

One afternoon, Roger called from Washington to suggest I visit his old Salt Lake buddy, Louis, a botanist in Costa Rica. Louis and I started a fax correspondence, trading witty rejoinders about expatriate life. He was charming. I was restless. I booked a flight.

Louis was boyish. Louis liked ferns. Louis was thirty-seven and had never voted in a single election. He told me this over our first dinner together, after we'd worked our way through a bottle of Merlot.

'*What?*' I gasped. '*Never?*'

Louis didn't see what the big deal was; he was usually out of the country and absentee ballots were a pain in the ass and I gave a drunken lecture about civic responsibility, conveniently forgetting all the elections I'd missed.

We went to the beach. We went to the rain forest, Louis marching through the wet plants with his umbrella and rubber boots. He looked like Christopher Robin.

Our fourth night traveling together, in a tent on the beach, doing shots of tequila, Louis professed his undying love. Camping . . . you'd think I'd have known.

'I have never met a girl like you,' Louis said, hand around an empty bottle of mezcal. 'I can't help it. I'm falling in love.'

'Do you realize how utterly *impossible* that is?'

I had enough problems. The wire service, as Roger and I called our Salt Lake social circle, well, there had been an unflattering story or two. About the string of men in my life. The infamous Overlap.

'First off, you don't even *know* me,' I said. 'Secondly, I am already dating one of Roger's friends. *I can't start dating another.*'

'*Oh, Roger.* Oh, no,' Louis wailed. 'He'll *kill* me. But I can't help it. *I love you.*'

He was so convinced.

After a week of watching monkeys and eating hearts of palm, I was convinced too. Louis was The One. I'd been listening to the wrong voices, heeding the wrong muse. A few weeks later, Louis flew to Mexico City, and we traveled to Tecotihuacán. At the top of the Pyramid of the Sun, he gave me a gold ring as a present. He wanted to show me how

167

strong his feelings were. I was ecstatic, petrified. Things were happening so quickly they had to be real. As I slipped the ring on my finger, I tried not to think about how the Aztecs had performed human sacrifices on these very rocks, killing handsome young warriors, offering their beating hearts to the Gods.

Meanwhile, back in Utah, Stuart was preparing to drive a couple thousand miles through the Mexican desert in an unair-conditioned car to come see me. Collapsed in an over-heated telephone *cabina*, I tearfully called him long distance to confess my transgressions, as a warty *abuela* glared at me for hogging the line.

'I know all about it,' Stuart said dryly.

'*You what?*' I asked, wiping back tears.

'I know all about it. *Everybody knows all about it*. The night you flew back to Mexico, Louis called his sister in Salt Lake. His sister told Russell, and Russell told the entire state of Utah.'

Stuart came anyway. We reconciled. The faxes from Costa Rica kept coming. Then came the preposterous day when I woke up next to Stuart, received a starry love fax from Louis, and flew my broomstick to Mexico City to see Roger, who had arrived 'on business.' Roger congratulated me on the fine pickle I'd gotten myself into this time.

'It's all working according to plan,' said Roger, lifting his Dos Equis in a celebratory toast.

'Whose plan?'

'Mine, of course. Why do you think I sent you to Costa Rica? I know you. I know Louis. Camping at the beach? What did you think would happen? I just wanted to make Stuart suffer. The bastard. Oh Calamity, you do such good work.'

'*You didn't.*'

Roger smiled. 'You're right; I didn't.'

'*You did.*'

Roger held up both hands, feigning surrender. 'Don't be ridiculous. How could I? Not even I could be that devious. It was just an innocent suggestion. How did I know what would happen?'

'*You knew.*'

Roger winked. 'Pretty good, huh?'

At that moment, it occurred to me for the first time, that all this hoopla was not about me and not about love; it was about winning. This was Darwin in action; let the fittest survive.

Later that night, Roger pinned me on his hotel bed. 'Okay, Mata Hari, tell me I'm the one you really love. Say it.'

'No,' I said, laughing, wrestling back.

'Say it.'

'No.'

'Say it.'

'*I love you.*'

The sad part was it was true.

Stuart left Mexico. A week later, Louis showed up at my door unannounced. We started where we'd left off, lounging in cafés, daydreaming about the travel company we would open. We'd give tours, teach Spanish, never go home.

Three months later, I was back in Utah.

One month later, so was Louis.

I had told him not to come – I wasn't sure our affair was more than just that, and I didn't want the responsibility of having an unemployed botanist on my hands, but Louis insisted.

Much as I feared, our relationship didn't import well. We needed a jungle; we needed a fax. There seemed to be no end to Louis's naïveté. He'd never heard of Gloria Steinem. He'd never heard of flappers. Contemplating a career change, he interviewed for a job selling megavitamins door to door; he could, he assured me, make millions. And yet here was a guy who sprayed my perfume on a card to keep in his wallet.

He pressed flowers; he bound our faxes into a softcover book. He was entirely too sweet to fall for a girl like me. Loath to hurt Louis, loath to chalk up yet another failure, I dragged to work and back each day, wondering how I'd let things get so out of hand.

Meanwhile, Stuart had moved on to no. 43, a leggy blonde who was exceptionally aloof. Now that Stuart was gone, I missed him terribly. Now that he was gone, I wanted him back.

Despite what it sounds like, I did not spend my every waking moment trying to ferret out true love. Most of the time, I was eating, sleeping, driving to Albertson's for low-fat milk; I worked long hours at the paper, fussing over language, poring over quotes. I wrote articles about pay equity and child care and the glass ceiling and the sticky floor. I sat through tedious legislative subcommittee meetings where Utah's cowboy caucus discussed higher education enrollments, headcount versus FTE. I wrote stories about Evergreen, the Mormon therapy group that claimed it could cure homosexuality by having gay men play softball. I fought to get my stories on the front page, to have them placed above the fold. Work was a haven where most things made sense.

Every so often, I'd give myself a rousing pep talk about independence and autonomy, freedom and feminism, and I'd imagine how thrilling my life would be if I never married, if I remained single, flexible, a foreign correspondent forever on assignment. The only problem was I didn't really buy it. I wanted work *and* love. Of course, marriage wasn't the be-all end-all, the Hoover Dam against loneliness, but I wanted to share my life with someone. It comforted me to think there was someone on the planet who cared that my plane didn't crash, that I hadn't drowned at sea. I couldn't very well return from a business trip and call my friend Bonnie and say, 'I just wanted to let you know, I got home safely.' Don't get me wrong, I'm all for women sustaining themselves, being

170

firefighters or governors or president of the Mormon church. But I have to agree with old D. H. Lawrence on this one. 'That people should all be stuck apart, like so many telegraph poles, is nonsense.'

At age thirty-two, I decided to seek professional help.

I noticed a sign on the *Tribune's* bulletin board advertising a counseling service. The ad showed a picture of a young woman sobbing at her desk. The copy read: 'Are you feeling Depressed? Do you have Mood Swings? Are you having problems with Personal Relationships?'

Yes, yes, yes.

I went and saw Angie.

Angie was a social worker with a voice like Little Bo Peep. When she sat in her plastic chair, she curled her legs under her bottom, like she was too small to reach her desk and needed a booster seat. With her freckles and kinked hair, Angie looked ten years old, max. I confided in her anyway.

'I am having problems making decisions,' I told her, starting to cry. 'I don't know what I want. I don't know what I'm feeling anymore.'

Angie made a sad little girl face and passed me the Kleenex.

'Close your eyes,' she said. 'Listen to what your gut is telling you.'

I closed my eyes. I listened. Faint gurgling, nothing more.

Angie made me stand up and try to knock her over like a TV gladiator to prove I had inner resolve. She told me to write my own obituary. (*Lili Wright, a newspaper reporter infamous for her 15-year legacy of failed relationships, died yesterday outside the Mormon Temple when three suitors faced off in a pistol duel and shot her instead. She was 32 years old.*) After one session, Angie told me to draw a line down the middle of a blank piece of paper. On one side, I should write the qualities I required in a man – 'the nonnegotiables.' On

the other side, list the qualities I'd like but weren't required –
'the negotiables.'

'That will help,' Angie said, twirling her hair. 'I promise.'

I took my assignment seriously. On the left, I started my
list:

NONNEGOTIABLES:

1. Honest
2. Intelligent
3. Kind
4. Funny
5. Hardworking
6. Attractive (to me)
7. Faithful – in love (with me)

I admired my work, then reconsidered. Maybe seven requirements was too many. Maybe *this* was my problem. But I
was all seven, wasn't I? Okay, maybe I needed work in the
Faithful department. And Kind? Well, I tried. And Honest,
well, lies of omission shouldn't count against me.

I nervously shifted over to the right-hand column.

NEGOTIABLES:

1. Likes to travel
2. Gets along with my family
3. Great in bed

The next week I sheepishly presented my list. Angie
nodded.

'Looks good,' she said. 'Aren't you glad you sorted this out?
Now put this someplace safe so you can refer to it when you
get confused.'

I tucked the paper into my pocket. The list wasn't even
remotely honest. I'd jotted down all these noble qualities
for fear of revealing my true callow nature. Here was the real
list:

172

NONNEGOTIABLES:

1. The man of my dreams must have bigger thighs than mine.
2. He must never light up a joint before we play tennis.
3. He must sing in the car, pitch being secondary to gusto.
4. When giving piggyback rides, he must never groan and complain about his sciatic nerve.
5. He must have a paying job. Spraying down airplanes does not count. Pyramid schemes do not count. Being a Washington spin doctor counts.
6. He must know who Gloria Steinem is.
7. He must like or pretend to like (all) my friends.
8. He must be able to hold my face, look into my eyes, and tell me he loves me – all three things at once, not one out of three or two out of three, but *all three*, convincingly, without yawning.
9. After sex, he must wait at least twenty minutes before falling asleep, unless I too am dozing, in which case we are dozing together, which is just the kind of tender moment that keeps two people together.
10. He may, under no circumstances, juggle tennis racquets for a living.
11. He must never pick out chunks of mushrooms, zucchini, and eggplant from my stir-fry and stack them on his dinner plate like a compost pile and then insist he *likes* vegetables, just not *these* vegetables, and then, to prove his point, recite his list of *acceptable* vegetables, which includes three items: carrots, celery, and lettuce.
12. He must never tell anyone that I am the smart one in the relationship.
13. He must never send flowers in lieu of an apology. No you're-still-mine flowers. No fuck-you flowers. Or who-are-you-sleeping-with-now flowers. Flowers are

not a weapon. Out-of-the-blue-coming-home-from-work-I-saw-them-and-remembered-how-much-I-love-you flowers are a good thing. They should arrive once a month. In summer, wildflowers are preferable. These should be picked by hand and delivered immediately.

14. When both of you are in the bathroom getting ready for bed and he takes a pee, he must never spit into his urine and then justify this decades-old habit by explaining that the fun part is trying to aim the spit bomb so it pops the bubbles floating around the toilet bowl.

15. He must never use smiley faces as a form of punctuation. (This is bad enough from a girlfriend.) Ditto hearts. Ditto arrows shooting through hearts. Exclamation points should be avoided at all cost!

16. He must never give updates on the state of his solar plexis.

17. Finally, he must never, ever, even *think* of asking me to squeeze the zits on his back.

Angie never saw this list.

One weekend, Roger flew back to Salt Lake for a visit. He had met a woman he liked and wanted to see me before things progressed. I told Louis that Roger and I needed time alone to talk. And we did talk, among other things.

In the thin mountain air at Snowbird, we got drunk on margaritas and swam in an open-air pool on the lodge roof, snowflakes melting on our faces. Roger held my waist and spun me through the warm water, our bodies enveloped in mist. I flashed my tits. We made out. An erotic game of uncle. I wanted him to know what he was missing now that he was seeing someone else. He wanted me to admit that I should have chosen him, should have packed up and followed him to Washington.

I felt bad for Louis, but just a little. The way I see it, once you've dated someone, you always have the right to go back to him. That's not cheating, really. Because whatever you two share came first, was part of who you were, always would be, and so that relationship had its rights. It's like old boyfriends are grandfathered into your psyche. Or maybe that's just what I told myself to justify doing what I wanted to do.

Moving from the pool to the sauna to the weight room to who knows where, we had fun being bad. Sex for sex's sake. Sex for power neither one of us felt. A few hours later, we staggered out into the snow, wide-eyed and hung over, then drove down the winding canyon, following the precarious curves, careful not to ride the brakes.

At the foot of the mountain, we stopped at a 7-Eleven. It was past midnight. My tequila buzz had worn off, and I wanted it back. We sat in my car in the parking lot, gazing into the flat convenience store light. I bit into a candy bar, waiting for the chocolate to warm in my mouth. Roger was talking in circles, his eyes alive with this dream of his, this dream that I was part of, had always been a part of, only now all we had left was 7-Eleven, high talk, and chocolate bars.

It was time, Roger said, for Bonnie and Clyde to make their final exit.

'So you thought you could get away from me that easily?' he taunted. 'Ahhhh, Cinderella. You underestimate me. Big mistake. The fat lady's not singing yet. I always knew I'd have to beat you over the head and drag you back to my cave. I'll tell our kids, "You wouldn't believe the fight I had getting your mother in line." You're the one I want.'

'But you're not with me,' I said stubbornly. 'You're with her.'

I clung to these facts, proof of his betrayal, proof in the intransigent order of what would be. There was somebody else now. Someone who mattered.

'We've been on a couple dates, for God's sake,' he said. 'No one is getting married yet. I have no idea what's going to happen. Besides what about you? What are your options?

175

Marry Louis? I don't think so. The guy lives in a rain forest. Marry Stuart? Be the good vet's wife?'

'I could,' I insisted. 'I could marry Stuart.'

'Listen, Thelma. You've waited this long. Don't go settle now.'

Neither one of us said anything for a moment or two. I watched the clerk make change, scrub the dirty counter. Then Roger started up again. We had to decide to be together; we had to decide tonight. Screw the wire service. Screw everyone.

I tried to imagine us running away. I'd pack my clothes and books and Mexican fish, and load them into Roger's broken-down Jetta. In the dark, we'd drive up I-80 through Parley's Canyon, past the enormous highway sign for Cheyenne. I'd open the sunroof and stare up at the moon. Roger would say I didn't need all that shit back there, and I'd start chucking stuff out the sunroof. A T-shirt, a work dress, a shiny black shoe, old photographs, old coat, old pants, old belt. Then Roger would pass me a beer and we'd listen to Ry Cooder's guitar on the tape deck and I'd smoke a cigarette to cinch the pact we'd made.

This was his proposal. Marriage as flight.

But I couldn't do it; I couldn't trust what I couldn't name.

When Roger left, he gave up on me for good. From time to time, he'd call with friendly updates about how his relationships were progressing and I tried to play coach from the sidelines, half hoping his affairs would fizzle so he'd be around to give me one more chance. But before I knew it, in a sunny New England garden, a woman slid a gold ring over Roger's fourth finger while I paced around my apartment in Salt Lake, looking up at the lonely snow-capped mountains, convinced I'd lost the one person who knew who the hell I was.

After nine years of reporting, I was sick of newspapers, sick of the stingy columns, the two-inch news briefs, the

176

overviews and wrap-ups and explainers, the dull-tool columnists amusing themselves, the cop reporters with their crackly scanners, the editors slicing six inches off the bottom. I was beginning to see that life didn't always have a nut graph, a tidy summary paragraph outlining the main point of the story. Life was a murkier pond than that. Life was what happened at 7-Eleven after midnight, and afterward it was all a blur and no one would ever agree exactly what had transpired. Forget objectivity. There was no videotape. The stories I wanted to tell, newspapers didn't print. Like the story of my Spanish professor who climbed up to the seventh story of his apartment building and jumped.

My editor said that wasn't a story.

I said it was.

Then she said: 'What makes it a story, that it happened to you?'

I applied to a creative writing program in New York and got in.

Louis and I broke up; he loped back to the jungle.

Roger reported that he loved marriage, loved his wife.

Stuart dumped number 43 and came back to number 42. I vowed to make everything up to him, vowed to make everything right.

A few months before I left for New York, Stuart and I drove down to southern Utah to hike in Zion National Park. We climbed two and a half miles up to the top of Angel's Landing, a granite peak in the heart of the park. At the top, 1,500 feet above the canyon floor, the air was thin and cool and smelled like iron. We looked down at a series of red rock faces streaked with black, which must have been mineral deposits but looked like a paint job cut short. Along the plateau, hikers lay belly up to the sun, munching bits of grub from zip-lock bags. As we sat and admired the view, I wondered whether the angels were headed up or down, deciding this must be a stopover for both, an uncomfortable congregation of the chosen and the lost.

After a long hike down, we took Brando for a walk in a grassy field by a brook. We drank a warm beer, and Brando swam in a cold brook as the aspen leaves quivered in the breeze. Then Stuart pulled a black box out of his pocket.

'I was going to ask on the top of Angel's Landing, but there were too many people.' His face broke into a gentle smile. '*Will you marry me?*'

Everything got quiet. Dead quiet. The brook, the bugs, my breathing. Stuart was proposing. He was proposing with an antique emerald ring. In all my silly daydreams about this moment, it never occurred to me that when it actually happened, I wouldn't know what to say.

'It's a beautiful ring,' I said, trying to buy some time.

'Just a stand-in. A fun ring. I thought we could pick out the real one together. Try it on.'

I slipped it on my fourth finger. It was too big. I moved it to my middle finger. The ring looked odd, like an heirloom I hadn't earned. Stuart's face was killing me. He looked so proud of having found a place whose beauty matched his intentions. It was time for me to answer, and I frantically searched for my feelings like a woman who has lost her keys.

'If you have to think about it,' Stuart said, 'that's not a good sign.'

'Are you serious?' I asked. 'You want to get married?'

'Yes, *of course* I'm serious. *It's been two years.* You're moving to New York for school. We should make a commitment. It only makes sense. But you're terrified. I can see it. You're absolutely terrified.'

'I'm not.'

'*You are.*'

It was true. One word and the deed was done. One word and my life would have a big fat dividing line through it, like a timeline showing B.C. and A.D. This would be how my story

178

ended. This would be the story we'd tell our children. Stuart would tease that I'd kept him hanging for a few minutes. I would deny the truth.

Suddenly, I remembered how Stuart had once confessed I wasn't the woman he'd imagined himself marrying. The real Ms Right had appeared to him in dreams. She had long, wavy hair and wore a flowered sundress, and she was walking through a field of tall grass, looking for him. She was sweeter than I was, more earthy and patient and kind. From his description, she sounded so nice I wanted to marry her myself.

'Can I think about it a bit?' I said. 'Sort of get used to the idea?' *Oh, God, I hate myself.* 'I had no idea you'd ask . . . I just . . .'

'It's not a limited-time offer,' Stuart said quickly.

Suddenly, we both got terribly busy, packing up empties and gathering fleece and whistling for Brando. Back in the car, Stuart drove and I propped my feet on the glove compartment and Brando wriggled his snout between our seats. I could barely look at Stuart for fear he'd ask me questions I didn't know how to answer. We shared a beer and pretended that nothing had happened, that everything was the way it had always been, except, of course, it wasn't. This was either the beginning of a beginning or the beginning of an end; the trick was figuring out which. The green ring sat on my middle finger. And I worried it round and round.

Not long after, I learned Dodge had married.

A mutual friend gave me the poop. Apparently, his bride was a Harvard Business School grad, a dry cereal executive who wore silk scarves and carried a patent leather briefcase. Dodge had proposed in the shower. Showering together, my friend confided, was one of their favorite rituals.

The wedding was a grand affair. The couple rented out a Caribbean island and the good people of Greenwich flew down for a week of mixed doubles and local crafts with the natives. Every guest got a gift bag of trinkets: sunglasses, sun block, and Dodge-and-Susie T-shirts. The bride floated to shore on a boat at sunset, strolling under a trellis of thatched palm fronds while dark-skinned boys played love songs under the stars. Or something like that. On their honeymoon, the newlyweds sailed the South Pacific, gliding through cerulean waters as a hired captain trimmed the sails and fixed seafood hors d'oeuvres.

Was I jealous?

Not in the slightest.

I was happy to be hunched over my terminal, writing a ten-inch daily about a groundbreaking ceremony for the new Mormon Temple. Let Dodge and Susie Corn Flakes have sex in the shower and squid on the grill. I didn't need to be a princess bride.

I'd gotten over that princess stuff a long time ago.

I left for New York. Stuart and I agreed to date long distance; we'd had plenty of practice. A few months after the move, I called Francie Horsham to track down a check. She answered the phone with a familiar sugary lilt. '*Editor's office.*'

'Francie. It's Lili. How are you?'

'*Well*, I never thought my life would come to this.'

'Francie.' I gasped. 'Are you okay? What happened?'

'Oh, you didn't hear? Robert is divorcing me,' she said. 'He doesn't love me anymore. Can you imagine living with someone for twenty-four years, and one day he tells you he doesn't want to live with you? *I am just devastated.*'

Poor Francie. What could I say?

'I'm so sorry,' I said.

'The papers go through Friday morning,' she said. 'Afterward, Lloyd (the editor) is taking me to that swanky joint, the New Yorker.'

'That's nice,' I said. 'I mean, the lunch.'

Some masochistic impulse overcame me. I had to ask.

'So, Francie,' I said. 'After going through all that, I mean marriage, children, divorce, do you have any advice for those of us on the other side? How do you know when you've found the right guy?'

Francie didn't miss a beat.

'Well, I'd say go with a fellow who will court you right,' she counseled. 'And marry a man who loves you more than you love him. That way you know he'll never leave you.'

Grampy walks out onto the deck in Maine and drags a director's chair into the sun. He's spent all morning studying his alternative medicine journals and now hands me something to read.

'Did I show you this?' he asks.

It's an ad for a homeopathic creme that supposedly increases women's sexual desire. One in four women don't experience orgasm from intercourse, it claims; 46 percent of women are sexually dissatisfied.

'Do you believe these statistics?' Grampy asks.

'It seems high,' I say, 'but then again, maybe not.'

Grampy nods. 'The French always said the problem was there aren't enough good lovers.'

'That's right,' I agree. 'All the good lovers are over in France.'

Grampy stretches his arms over this head, an exercise designed to keep him from slouching.

'You know testosterone helps women get things going,' he says. 'And pheromones. I used to spray myself with pheromones before I went out with my lady friends to the movies or the theater, but it never worked. Then one day, I brought my spray to the dentist. I have a female dentist – a young woman – and she gave me two of the most passionate kisses.'

Grampy holds his arms out wide as if preparing to succumb to his dentist and her drill.

'Imagine what would have happened if the assistant hadn't been there.'

Progress Report

New York City. After three weeks on the road with Brando, I decided I couldn't travel with him anymore. It was impossible to care for him properly and go all the places I wanted to go. Most beaches didn't allow dogs, so I had to keep him shut up in the car when I went exploring. It was July now and terribly hot. While Brando is generally an enthusiastic companion, his spirits wilt in the heat. Who could blame him? Being overweight as he is and covered in fur.

Still it was hard to let him go. I'd grown accustomed to his affection, his doggy smell, his perpetual wag. Whenever I felt at a loss, I'd stare into his milky eyes, dime-size pupils rimmed in brown, and ask his sage advice:

'Where to brown dog?'

My companion wasn't big on particulars, just thumped his tail and panted, which I took as a sign of unqualified support and optimism for whatever lay ahead. So long as there were sticks involved, so long as there was water.

When I reached New York City, I stopped by my apartment. Brando jumped for joy at the sight of Stuart. Stuart jumped for joy at the sight of Brando. With me, Stuart was cordial, no jumps, no joy. He was looking for his own apartment now, preparing to move out of mine.

I felt horrible about this, and it was all I could do not to try to convince him to stay. But this would have been purely selfish, and so I told myself no. At the same time, I missed Peter, my writer. I was hallucinating about Peter. I drove lame circles past his apartment on Riverside Drive, staring at his door, willing him to come out and greet me.

Being back in New York made me realize just how little I'd changed. All this traveling and things were just as screwed up as when I'd left. This trip wasn't working the miracles I'd expected. I didn't want to stay in New York, and I didn't want to go. Driving to Key West alone was a stupid idea, lonely and pointless, a dare I was too proud to take back.

'Well, Brando will miss being with you,' said Stuart, which seemed to be his way of saying that he would miss me.

'I'll miss him,' I said, swallowing hard, watching Brando scratch his ear with a foot, tags jingling, eyes rolled back in his head.

'No more "Travels with Lili,"' said Stuart, with a sigh. 'It could have been quite a story.'

'I feel bad enough,' I said. 'Don't rub it in.'

'You're the one who's turning him in.'

'That doesn't mean it's easy.'

I tried to get Brando's attention to say a proper good-bye, but he was chewing the short hairs by his crotch and couldn't be bothered. It had always hurt my feelings how he was so nonchalant when I came to visit Stuart in Salt Lake, sometimes barely lifting his head when I walked in the door. Once, in the airport parking lot, he walked right past me to waggle at Stuart, as if I were invisible, as if I didn't matter at all.

Now, standing here in my apartment, watching the lab remove his snout from his groin and cross his paws, like a lady at high tea, I realized it was time to face facts. Brando had one and only one true love. And so it should be between a dog and his master; so it should be between a woman and her mate. But it wasn't that way between Stuart and me. I wished it were but it wasn't. And no amount of waiting or hoping or expecting was going to change that.

Stuart and I had broken up. I could see that now. It was over.

No matter what I said or did, he wasn't taking me back. I couldn't tell if I was relieved or terribly sad.

The best I could figure, I was both.

Sandy Bottom Beach

Nana marched toward the ocean like a dodo defying extinction. Her short, spindly legs suspended a broad belly and bosom. On her delicate feet, she wore swimming sneakers, white canvas shoes that came to a point. Her straw hat was rimmed with madras ribbon, and her plastic sunglasses were studded with rhinestones that caught tiny sparkles of light.

Behind Nana trailed Grampy and then, a few steps back, Chip and I. We were children, spending the afternoon in Maine with our grandparents while our parents took much-needed naps. The tide was nearly low and dead calm. Brown clumps of seaweed stretched over the rocks like soggy mops refusing to work. Against the horizon, the gentle roll of the Camden hills stretched out before us.

Nana stopped at the water's edge, peered into the sea, and frowned.

'Herbert, this needs a lot of work,' she said.

'Yes, Virginia.' Grampy looked at me and winked.

Our beach on North Haven is rocky, a chunky mixture of gray stone scattered with broken crab shells, sea urchins, driftwood, periwinkles, and sea glass. The higher up the beach you go, the smaller the rocks become, until at the high-tide mark, it's mostly pebbles, soft underfoot, almost like sand. But down at low tide, the rocks are large and covered with seaweed and barnacles, making swimming treacherous. And yet for some reason – no one knows why – just above the low-tide mark, thirty yards down the shore, there's a swatch of beach that's unusually sandy. Nana, who loved to bestow grandiose names on unassuming places and things, dubbed this patch of shore Sandy Bottom Beach.

Once the beach was christened, it was up to Chip and me and especially Grampy to see that it lived up to its name. Throughout the summer, we'd make pilgrimages down to the shore to remove rocks that had rudely wandered where they didn't belong. It was all part of Nana's great dream. One day, there would be an unbroken path from high tide to low tide, and swimmers could stroll down to the sea barefoot. No cuts, no sloshing about, just luscious sand underfoot. It could be that good.

Mother Nature, apparently, was unaware of these grand plans. No matter how many rocks we cleared, the winter tides ferried them back. Come summer, Sandy Bottom Beach was hardly recognizable. But Nana was not one to give up. As she supervised from shore, Grampy waded into the water, flinching with each step. I followed, then Chip.

'Where did it go?' Chip asked, rubbing the goosebumps on his thin shoulders.

'Herbert, I think it's to the left a little,' Nana said.

'Here it is,' said Grampy, shirtless, red chest hairs glinting in the sun. 'Or what's left of it.'

And so the three of us started to work, reaching down into the clear water, pulling up rocks, throwing them to the left or right, listening to the syncopated plunks as they sank back into the sea.

As a child, I found this project silly, if not a bit cruel. Like most children, I believed even the most lifeless objects were sentient beings who should be treated with care and so I worried about how the rocks felt, being uprooted this way. It probably took them months to secure a sandy spot, and then

187

here we came, careless giants, tossing them about willy-nilly, not even looking to see who they were.

But Nana was confident she could improve what nature had wrought. Just as she was sure she could transform her quirky husband into a scholar from Yale or turn Chip into an engineer or me into someone better than whoever it was I was starting to become. Things and people could always be better. It was simply a matter of not settling for less. Of not looking too carefully at any one rock before you picked it up and threw.

The Tipping Point

Atlantic City, NJ. Dogless, ex-boyfriendless, for all practical purposes homeless, I drove south down the Garden State Parkway in a daze. I didn't know where I was going and, wherever it was, I didn't want to go. It was becoming patently clear to me just how big a jerk I'd been, dragging Stuart from Zion to Gotham just to say *Surprise, you've been recalled.* By now our friends in Utah were surely wagging their heads in amazement at the audacity of my latest stunt. And Stuart's parents – such kind, *sensible* people from the Jersey suburbs, people with oak cabinets and storm windows, people I'd tried to impress in a relaxed, casual sort of way, in case they turned out to be my in-laws for the next thirty years – they would conclude my good manners were the clever front of a duplicitous woman, a B-I-T-C-H with a cold, cold heart. Dumping their boy. Before he'd so much as unpacked his Tevas, his Scope.

And here was the real irony: You'd think if I were going to pull such a schmucko move and become, as my friend Dan calls commiters of such low crimes, 'a life ruiner,' you'd think I'd at least have the good sense to be uproariously happy. Sipping Tanqueray and tonics, rubbing noses, blissing out with my new Don Juan.

But where was I?

Alone in my Mazda, wilting in the humidity, chugging along in the slow lane, debating which rest stop had the cheapest gas.

In a word: miserable.

I wanted to pulled a U-ey, go back to New York, but there was no going back now. Stuart would be in my apartment for at least another month. Peter was queasy about seeing me before Stuart was gone. 'It's not the right way to begin,' he'd said, on more than one occasion. He was right, of course, if we were actually *going* to begin, which wasn't entirely clear, as the last time I'd seen Peter I'd still been so mixed up about Stuart. And who was Peter seeing in the meantime? He was probably back at the wine bar, running his finger down some other girl's arm, some other girl who wasn't *really* on a date.

The Quakers on Nantucket have a saying for such ludicrous mishaps: *going ashore to windward*. Returning home with the wind in your face is theoretically a foolproof approach, and yet even in such auspicious conditions, buffoons still manage to run their boats aground. A person who *goes ashore to windward* would go wrong with no excuse. As far as I could tell, I was just such a sailor.

It didn't help any that the backseat was so quiet now. As with most men in my life, now that the wild one was gone, I wanted him back. It was the little things I'd miss: filling his bowl with water, wandering with him behind gas stations looking for trees, rubbing my finger over the short hairs on his snout, friction like velvet. I thought about Brando so I wouldn't have to think about Stuart. And so I wouldn't have to think about Brando, I listened to Howard Stern.

On his morning radio show, Howard Stern was measuring the tits of some porn star named Marlene, fantasizing about what he'd do if he got her alone. An exotic dancer named Roxanne, who knew Marlene in a former life, phoned in to say Marlene's breasts were fakes. Marlene denied it, then later admitted she'd helped God's hand along. Howard Stern didn't care: *'Who could blame a girl for wanting to better herself?'*

Better herself. Weren't we all trying?

Peering through the windshield at the traffic, I tried to rally some adrenaline. The weather wasn't helping much. The sky was that shade of gray that looks like pollution. The air, heavy and slow. I'd planned to stop somewhere on the Jersey shore, my old stomping ground when I worked in Trenton, and I'd even bought a history book of the area, but somehow I couldn't muster the energy to exit. One beach town after another slipped by until, with a long sigh, I turned down the Atlantic City Expressway.

Oh, God, I loathe this place.

Casinos always leave me feeling depleted, emotionally more than financially, although sometimes a bit of both. And yet I've been to quite a few. Reno, Nevada – for a wedding. What I remember best was the cat fight over the bouquet. Vegas – with Andy. Cruising down the main drag at night, it looked as if the whole city had been plugged into an electric socket. Pulsating signs urged us to drink for FREE. At the tables, Andy quickly lost $100 and traipsed off to the cash machine to refuel. At midnight, we ate fried eggs and the waitress used a paintbrush to slather my wheat toast with butter.

Wendover, Nevada – popular with Mormons because it's just over the border. At the *Tribune*, I'd written a story about a nursing home that took residents out gambling each month; most were frail or senile or both. On the bus, I sat next to a great-great-grandfather who hid a wad of cash under his Bugs Bunny cap, then asked me to remind him where he'd put it, in case he forgot. For six long hours, the seniors dumped coins into lucky slot machines; their fingers turned gray. Partially paralyzed from a stroke, one elderly woman smoked and gambled with her left hand, unaware ashes from her Capri cigarette were landing on her blouse.

I asked her how old she was.

'Too old to start over,' she said. 'Too young to settle for this.'

Up ahead the casinos of Atlantic City paraded across the horizon – Trump Plaza, the Clarion, the Sands, Bally's, the Claridge, Caesars, thc Tropicana – as the expressway funneled us into their greedy grasp. On either side of the highway lay raw empty fields, a wasteland no one had bothered to claim. Every few hundred yards, another billboard advertising lounge singers I could have sworn were dead. WAYNE NEWTON. BURT BACHARACH. BARBARA MANDRELL.

When the expressway ended, I circled up the parking garage and swung into a spot. The garage elevator opened directly into the casino as if management was afraid we all might escape. This was the Sands, but it could have been any casino with its crimson carpets, hyperoxygenated air, sunken people anchored at slot machines. No clocks. No windows. Mirrors repeated the room so many times you couldn't tell what was real and what was reflection and it seemed possible that if you came back tonight or tomorrow or twenty years from now, the same sunburned guy would be losing his paycheck and the laid-off nurse would be winning the Perfecta and the lounge singer from Red Hook would still be singing '*I want money. That's what I want.*'

The only redeeming thing about Atlantic City is the beach, although the casinos never make it easy to find. But eventually I spotted an exit and walked outside, squinting hard at the sun. On the boardwalk, listless tourists drifted about, eating junk food, killing time, breathing a few gulps of salt air before heading inside to change their luck. I leaned against the railing and looked out to sea. A cloudy tide dutifully chugged up and back, but it seemed, like the boardwalk, exhausted. Far in the distance, at the end of a pier loomed an amusement park; a Ferris wheel, a roller coaster, and a giant roulette wheel with people attached spun furiously but silently, screams lost in the wind.

On a bench, I pulled out my history book and started reading. In its heyday, Atlantic City was the country's premier seaside resort. The first Ferris wheel was built in Atlantic City. So was the first boardwalk. In the old black-and-white photographs, dapper men in top hats and ladies in sunbonnets strolled the jammed boardwalk, literally elbow to elbow. A railroad conductor proposed the walkway because he was tired of guests traipsing sand in his rail cars and hotel. Atlantic City quickly became famous for its wacky attractions, many of them human – from Alvin 'Shipwreck' Leon, who sat atop a flagpole for forty-nine days, to the High-Diving Horse, who earned his keep by plunging sixty feet into a swimming pool. The promenade grew so popular, the local paper reported: 'Nearly everyday somebody falls off the Boardwalk. In nearly every instance, the parties have been flirting.'

It was hard to imagine those glory days now. The board-walk was dry and splintered, covered in bird crap. The shops along it peddled acres of plastic schlock. Passing over the Everything for 99 Cents store, I ducked in a shop specializing in soft-porn posters and T-shirts with such clever sayings as:

It's a Blonde Thing, I Wouldn't Understand
Zero to Horny in 2.5 Beers
Mean People Suck. Nice People Swallow
Money Can't Buy Happiness. That's What Shopping Is For
If You Won't Smoke, I Won't Fart
I May Be Shy, But I've Got a Big Dick

Who buys this stuff?

A line had formed at the cash register.

Outside, I was disoriented and asked two cops on mountain bikes what cross street we were on.

'This is Illinois,' said an officer, 'but we allow them to call it Martin Luther King.'

What the hell was I doing here?

193

Disgusted, I ventured off the boardwalk, down a short flight of steps leading onto a side street. I was curious about the *real* Atlantic City. People had told me the casinos were a façade, showy scenery that fronted for a community beset with drugs and poverty and crime. Sure enough, not a block off the boardwalk, things started to deteriorate: empty sidewalks, boarded-up stores, vacant lots and scrub grass. I sidestepped a used condom and watched a mealy pigeon peck a puddle of oil. The quiet was eerie.

Then something crashed.

It startled me. I looked up but couldn't figure out what happened. Then a chair flew out the window of an old brick hotel and crashed onto a giant pile of debris. The building was being gutted. Every few seconds, a pair of arms appeared out a fifth-story window and hurled boards or chunks of old furniture, refrigerators, bureaus, bedposts, and end tables.

I stood there, fixated. The sun burned my neck, and I was starting to sweat, but I couldn't stop watching the furniture tumble and crash. At first, it seemed sad, a piece of history was being ripped down to its core, but then again, maybe someone was fixing up the place, giving the sagging hotel a second chance at life, buying new mattresses, rolling on fresh paint. Thinking of it that way made me wish I were up there with the construction guys – giving the ratty armchairs the old heave-ho.

That's when it occurred to me that this is exactly what I needed to do.

Throw out my old furniture.

No wonder I was getting nowhere, hashing over the past like some masticating cow. It was time to throw out Rawl and his *razzamatazz*, throw out Greenwich and Dodge and his shower proposal, pitch all those bad feelings about herpes – it was a rash, for God's sake, a goddamn rash – lose the Negiotables, the Nonnegiotables, forget Jane Tarbox, who was probably hugely successful by now, with or without the Frenchman and his shoes, blow off the old threats, '*the moving*

194

finger,' 'Your mother and I don't believe in divorce,' 'love can burn or love can last' – Ha, I say, Ha – pitch 'I love you, Pumpkin,' pitch the little zucchini squash too, shut up the chorus, the voices, the egg beaters and their frothy batter, forget going back to New York and instead press on, press on until I figured out . . . well . . . until I figured out what to do next. Buddha was right; I needed to rid myself of all thoughts of past and future; I needed to focus on nothing but liberation. I was too old to start over, too young to settle for this.

I went swimming.

The water was warm and murky with red tide. Paddling about, fishing seaweed from my top, I saw, for the first time, how this road trip could add up to something. Like a Cubist painting, it would begin as blocks of color, promising abstractions, but if you looked closely, you'd make out a table, a treble clef, a vase. My trip could be like that, if I climbed out of my head, if I stopped looking back. Word by word, object by object, I'd fathom and name, slowly uncovering the shapes hidden in the rush and go of the road. The key was to find what I wasn't looking for. The key was to see not what I expected but what was there.

As I walked over the sand to the boardwalk, a deep pressure lifted. It felt as if I'd thrown a two-hundred-pound desk out the window, as if all my hanging files and telephone bills and tax returns were fluttering in the breeze, lilting like paper airplanes with no particular place to go.

Waiting for the Blue Crabs to Shed

Grampy walks out onto the deck in Maine and drags a director's chair into the sun. I am stretching out, getting ready to run.

'That was your dad on the phone. He was going on . . .' Grampy shakes his head. 'I just don't know how your parents got so straitlaced.'

'You noticed?'

'Good God,' Grampy says. 'How did they get so proper?'

'I hold you responsible for Dad,' I say.

'Well, we tried to teach him how to behave properly, but Nana always had quite a lot of leeway in things, being an anthropologist.'

Nana did graduate work in anthropology at Cornell.

'I grew up quite strict,' Grampy continues, 'but then I realized that's not the way things should be. I had to rediscover The Way. You know, Taoism. That's where I am at today.'

'And where is that?' I ask.

Grampy leans back in his chair, pausing a moment to consider.

'Well,' he says, looking up. 'Wherever I am.'

Back at the Bar

Fenwick Island, DE. On good days, I felt alive and invincible, driving through summer without worry or care, knocking about, taking things as they came, cruising down the coast on a saltwater breeze. I like this image of myself. It was the woman I wanted to be.

But la-dee-dah meandering doesn't come easy to a worrier. Oh, I could bumble along for a couple hundred miles, proud of my new Buddha-like faith in the interdependence of all things – gas to car, car to road, road to getting lost, getting lost to acceptance, acceptance to inner peace, inner peace to life's great journey, life's great journey needs gas – but eventually the rootlessness, the utter haphazardness of my trip grew exhausting, and I vowed to, as my father would say, get organized.

Getting organized began with scrounging up a legal pad from backseat clutter. Then, while the other campers kicked back with a cup of instant joe, I'd perch in the driver's seat, road map spread over my lap like a giant napkin. Across the top of my legal pad, I'd print the future. It seemed like a good place to start. In a neat column, I'd list the states remaining:

DE
MD
VA
NC
SC
GA
FL

Then I'd scour the map for red tent symbols, measure my finger against the mileage scale, page through guidebooks for wisdom. Around and around I went, debating the pros and cons of various tourist attractions. Now that I wasn't looking for the ghosts of my exes, I wasn't sure what I was looking for, which made it tricky to know where to begin. Getting organized was dull work, and before long, a throbbing headache would nestle in around my temples, the by-product of road fatigue, coffee withdrawal, and anxiety. I'd stare stupidly through my dirty windshield at the license plates of parked cars, watch a beach towel dry in the wind, smell someone else's bacon. No one else was worried about THE FUTURE. Or if they were, they were keeping their fears under wraps. Zippered up in their pup tents. On ice in an igloo.

Then, for the millionth time, I'd vow to forget planning altogether. Traveling was a crap shoot. You can't reserve an adventure, book the weather, anticipate a mood. No matter how meticulously you plan, you can't see everything. Choosing one route means not taking fifteen others, like marrying one man means not sleeping with all the rest. Then it would occur to me: This journey was a royal waste of time. No matter how light I traveled I still had to bring myself along, like a rolling black suitcase you drag through the airport. No matter where I went, *I was still me*. There was no such thing as genuine change. No true transformation. If I'd had any sense, I'd have stayed in New York and spent my money the old-fashioned way: in therapy. With that dead-end conclusion, I'd slam the car door, turn the silver key, and merge onto any road heading south.

I took the ferry from Cape May to Lewes, Delaware, then drove along the coast, hunting for a place to spend the night. I got lost following signs for something called Camp Henlopen, which sounded like a campground but was actually a day camp. Inside a cafeteria smelling of sandwiches and sun block, I asked a table of adults for directions back to the beach. One middle-aged guy with thick forearms and a low cap said he was driving back that way and he'd escort me, and before I knew it the folks at the table were waving him off with a chorus of 'See ya, Stan.' As we walked outside, I asked what Camp Henlopen was and Stan explained it was a camp for inner-city kids run by the police department and I asked if he was a cop, and he said he was. Then he asked where I was staying, and I said I was looking for a campground, and he said I should stay in his RV, which was sitting empty at a park called Treasure Beach.

'Stay with you?' I asked.

'Not *with* me,' said Stan, sounding annoyed. 'I've got to stay here with the kids. I'm saying you can stay in my place.'

At his place? At his place without him? I looked under his cap trying to decide if he was some kind of weirdo or the man he said he was, a good cop trying to show poor kids a bit of summer. Meanwhile, he was peering skeptically into my crapped-out Mazda, sizing me up.

'I can trust you, right?' he asked.

'I'm a student,' I said, as if that were some guarantee of good intentions.

He paused. I paused. Each of us trying to make up our mind.

'All right then, let's go,' he said.

We drove to Treasure Beach, a neighborhood of mobile homes that weren't going anywhere. Each house had a minia- ture lawn appointed with wooden geese and garish geraniums.

Stan's RV was neat as an airplane, each thing in its place. He reached into the fridge and pulled out some fried chicken in a plastic take-out container and said I could have it for dinner and I said thanks, not mentioning that I don't eat chicken because Stan seemed like the kind of no-nonsense guy who thinks vegetarians are loons. Then Stan pulled down a map and asked me what I liked to do and I mumbled something about seeing the sights and Stan said he wasn't exactly sure what I was looking for and I thought to myself that makes two of us. He asked if I liked oysters and I said yes and he said I should try Smitty McGee's down the way and he pointed and I looked. Then he showed me the rock where the extra key was hiding and, with a quick wave over his shoulder, took off up the drive.

Unsure what to do next, I wandered around his RV, checking out his stuff, the lemon air freshener, his soap. I always get this unsettled feeling when I'm in someone else's home without them. There's the urge to snoop, yet I'm half afraid what I'll find. *Who was this guy?*

I dialed up the phone numbers he'd given me to see if they checked out.

First, his work number.

'Camp Henlopen?' a woman's voice answered. I hung up. I called his beeper; it beeped. I called Stuart. I had no business calling him but I did anyway.

'Where *are* you?' he asked. His voice sounded warm and familiar, like a favorite shirt you can't wait to put on.

'In some guy's RV in Delaware. Or Maryland. I'm not sure.'

'*What?*'

I explained. Getting lost. Camp Henlopen. Stan.

'Do you think I'm crazy to stay here?' I needed a reality check. 'He's a cop. He gave me his numbers, and they're right. His friends know he brought me here.'

'Well, you've got to decide that for yourself,' Stuart said in his best you've-made-your-bed-now-lie-in-it voice. I wanted him to say I should hotfoot it to a hotel and charge it to his credit card but he refused to be ruffled. If he'd sounded worried, then I would be brave and say 'Oh no, everything's fine.' That's what we say in my family. Everything's fine. But since he was being blasé, I had to match his bluff or lose face.

Stuart continued, 'Now, in the back of his mind, he's probably hoping something will happen . . .'

'The old would-I, wouldn't-I?'

'Right, I mean, here's this pretty woman on the road willing to stay in his trailer. Maybe she's up for fooling around? But if you give the right signals, I doubt he's going to try anything rash.'

I'd never been good at giving signals.

'Well, let me give you my number here,' I said.

Stuart jotted it down.

'Okay,' he said, like that settled that.

'Okay,' I said, searching for an excuse to stay on the phone. 'Well, okay then . . . I love you.'

I hadn't meant to say this but it slipped out. This is what we always said when we hung up the phone, only now we weren't supposed to say it anymore. Or feel it either.

'Be safe,' Stuart said.

And I said: 'I'll try.'

I don't know, you're a woman. Why don't you tell me? Where does love go?

It was a damn good question, and Carl knew it. He looked pleased with himself as he stared into the Happy Hour crowd at Smitty McGee's, the drinkers and smokers, the couples and singles, all doing their damnest to make love go *somewhere*.

Carl's question was clearly rhetorical, yet I felt compelled to weigh in anyway. 'I don't know where love goes,' I began. 'I mean, maybe it never really *goes* anywhere . . .'

I looked to him for help, but he was lost in his memories, tapping his cigarette on the ashtray. Then he remembered something and nudged in close to share it.

'It got to the point the only sex my wife and I had was

hallway sex,' he said conspiratorially. 'Ever heard of hallway sex?'

I shook my head. My thumb cuticle was bleeding. I wiped a thin smear of red on my shorts, then drank more wine.

'You haven't heard of hallway sex?' Carl asked with mock surprise. He lowered his voice as if letting me in on a secret. 'Hallway sex is when you pass your wife in the hallway and you both say "*fuck you*."'

Clearly, it was time to go. I asked the waitress for my check. Carl looked surprised. 'You're not leaving?'

'I'm pretty wiped out.'

'Here I've gone told you everything about my life and I don't know a thing about you.' Carl sounded indignant. Maybe he felt bad for telling these stories, or angry with me for leading him to them. 'I want you to come out with me tonight. I'll take you to this place by the water. You'll like it there.'

'That's nice of you,' I said. 'But I've got to get some sleep.'

Carl mashed his cigarette, exhaled the final puff through pursed lips, then spoke, pronouncing each word slowly, as if taking aim.

'*I . . . am . . . asking . . . you . . . out.*'

I smiled idiotically as if I didn't notice his tone. This was my fault. I could have stuck with Buddha, drunk mindfully in silence, but no. I should have known by now that everything with men and women ends in the same place. It wasn't about sex, it was about loneliness. It was about sex and loneliness. We all want someone to wrap ourselves around, someone to stroke our heads until sleep came. Well, I couldn't be that person for Carl; now he felt rejected. Everybody wants someone until they don't want them anymore.

I knotted my cotton sweater around my waist and tried to look, well, aloof.

'Nice to meet you, sir,' I called over to Carl's father. The old man looked around, nodded, held up two fingers good-bye.

I offered Carl my hand.

He seemed calmer now, maybe a tad embarrassed. He shook my hand but kept holding it, bobbing it up and down like a water pump.

'You can't be scared about marriage,' he said softly.

I was still thinking about hallway sex, how you pass each other in the hallway and both say *fuck you.*

'Being scared is not going to get you anywhere,' he said. 'You've got to try.'

My throat winced. This stranger had gotten under my skin; somehow he'd seen the fears bundled at the end of my hobo's stick. All of a sudden I couldn't remember what I was doing in Delaware – the five Ws of this silly trip of mine. The who, the when, the what, the where, the why.

Carl let go of my hand.

'Good night,' I said. 'Thanks for the wine.'

I pushed open the heavy glass door and stepped into the night. Unlocking my bike, I mounted the thin seat and headed onto the road, still busy with cars. The headlights of oncoming traffic made it nearly impossible to see. I felt fragile, hovering an inch or two from the pavement's edge, trying to balance my tires on the brink. Round and round the pedals spun, slowly at first, then faster, until summer blew past my face, this summer and last summer and the summers before me, as if I were riding through time, as if I might lift into the sky and fly up to the stars. Up, in some frozen galaxy, where there would be no want. No need or emptiness. No having and holding, holding and losing. No shaky compromise between together and alone.

Back at Treasure Beach, I stretched my sleeping bag on Stan's bed so I wouldn't dirty his sheets, then lay down, knees tucked close to my chin. Noises drifted in, television and telephones and traffic. As cars drove by, diamonds of light slid across the ceiling and down the window frame. The trailer walls felt thin as a T-shirt, as if anyone could punch through them with a well-aimed fist. I wondered if Stan would show up unexpectedly in the middle of the night. I wondered if he was a violent man, if there was even the remotest possibility I would die in this trailer tonight, just another six o'clock news story about a man and a gun.

I rolled over. This was paranoia talking. I wasn't going to die tonight. I wasn't going to die until I was grandmother-old, with my family encircling my bed, nodding that I could go now, it had all been enough. I tried to sleep but couldn't and instead thought about love, where it went and why and whether I would ever find a way to catch it, tame it, teach it to come back to me when I shouted its name.

Dancing

When I was around ten years old, my dad fell in love with a Billy Joel song called 'I Love You Just the Way You Are.' It was a jazzy love song that bubbled along about how this girl shouldn't go changing to try to please him. My father called it 'schmaltzy,' which sounds like a putdown but was actually high praise. Schmaltzy meant romantic in a good way, straight from the heart. Dad discovered the song on a.m. radio and bought the single and from time to time played it on our record player in the kitchen. After blowing dust off the needle stub, gently releasing the arm on the spinning 45, he'd walk over to my mother and ask her to dance.

'C'mon, Chubby,' he said, pulling her hand.

No one who didn't love my mother would ever call her Chubby. My mother weighed a scant one hundred and nine pounds on her wedding day and, fifteen years later, weighed only fifteen more than that. But Dad has a knack for turning insults into pet names. As a boy, Chip was nicknamed 'I gotta I wanna' because reportedly that's all he ever said. I was Bugs and, in later years, Moose. I forget the origins of Moose; I only know it felt funny and flattering coming from Dad.

When my father offered his hand, my mother would smile and stand. Just home from work, she was swaddled in a pink flannel nightgown and robe. My father would wrap his hand around her waist, what little there was of it with all that thick cotton, and pump her right hand with his to the beat.

And so my parents began to dance, carving lazy arcs between the stove, our 1938 hulky refrigerator, the black-and-white television propped on a stool. Overhead, the electric light beamed a caustic glow, warming the dead flies trapped in the shade. On the Formica counter lay an uncooked meatloaf, a box of brown rice, a colander of frozen broccoli trying to thaw.

Though a smooth dancer, my father did not cut a debonair figure, mainly because he wore too many clothes: thick khakis, hung low on his hips, an undershirt, a flannel shirt, two wool sweaters, two pairs of socks. He'd lost much of his hair. The lenses of his glasses were covered with particles of dust, a galaxy of stars he was too close to see. When the horn section stepped up, he'd close his eyes, appreciating the harmonies, and drift off to some party a long time ago.

Mom looked drained from a long day at the office. You could see it in her face. Her cheeks without blush, the way her silver earrings screwed tight around each lobe. My mother is a pretty combination of hard and soft. Her nose, which my father calls 'the Beak,' is long and narrow. Her mouth is small, eyes a gentle brown. Back then, she wore her thick curly hair up in a bun like a teacher on TV. A shy, analytical woman, she chooses her words with crossword-puzzle precision, while my father is the master of the malaprop. Mom likes happy endings. Dad likes film noir. Mom is pure brains. Dad is all heart. They'd been bickering for as long as I could remember.

And now Dad hummed along the words as Mom's slippers went *thwis-thwis* along the broken red tile. For a few beats, they pulled apart, then back together, circling round. My mother always knew where my father was going, as if following him were the most natural thing in the world. As I sat on the staircase, admiring them through the spindles, I could see that they loved each other, that something real and palpable held them together.

> *I could not love you any better*
> *I love you just the way you are.*

I wondered if these lyrics had special meaning for my dad. He was a hard man to love the way he was: a house husband who hated to keep house. And yet, in my eyes, he was a romantic, and this, of all qualities, I judged supreme. My father lit kerosene lamps at dinner so we could eat in their glow. On Christmas, he gave each girl in his life – my mother, my sister-in-law, and me – a small piece of jewelry. Dad was the one who told me the story of how he and Mom had won so much money gambling during their honeymoon in Italy, they had stayed another week. My mother had forgotten the incident entirely.

'I don't need a memory,' she once said. 'I married one.'

And tonight, Dad had put a love song on the stereo. Tonight, he had asked my mother to dance.

Billy Joel wound down with one final *I love you just the way you are.* He held the final *aaaarrrrrrre* forever, carrying it up and down a bunch of different notes until he completely ran out of breath. I wished the song wouldn't end, that it would go on all night and the meatloaf would never be cooked and the TV would keep quiet and there would be no arguments, not one, but my father never played the Billy Joel song twice.

When the song ended – was it three minutes, maybe four? – everything went back to normal. Someone had to wash the lettuce. The rice needed to boil. As I watched my parents separate, my mother fixing a hairpin, my father hoisting his trousers, I understood, as I always did when my parents danced in the kitchen, that three minutes might just be long enough to hold two people together.

Grampy walks out onto the deck in Maine and drags a director's chair into the sun. I am sitting in my bikini, trying to even out my tan.

'Now, Lili, when you get to my age, you see, most of the females aren't interested in sex anymore. They just want to get married.'

I laugh. 'Really?'

'That's right,' Grampy says. 'Now I've given up sex and gambling and smoking and religion. Pretty boring. Did I tell you I took dance lessons with a girlfriend of mine?'

'No,' I say. 'What kind?'

'We took swing and a bit of tango. Then I'd had enough. But after my friend learned how, she asked other men to go dancing with her. One day I asked her, "Did they ask you to go to bed afterward?" And she said that several did and then one didn't and she was disappointed.'

Grampy slaps his thigh and chuckles.

'That's the female species for you. She's disappointed because she didn't get a chance to reject him.'

We Believe

Tangier Island, VA. As the small wooden ferry left Onancock, a quiet town on the Delmarva Peninsula (so named because Delaware, Maryland, and Virginia each claims a piece of it), I felt a surge of joy and adrenaline, the one I often get when I'm going somewhere new.

My stay in the RV had passed without incident – no bloodied axes, no midnight tap-tapping on the door. Before leaving, I'd scribbled a thank-you note to Stan the cop, tucked it under a quilted placemat by the toaster. As I locked his door behind me, I felt a rush of traveling bravado. As my friend Dan likes to say after the successful completion of a risky caper: 'We got in. We got out. No one got hurt.'

Here I was, alive and alert in this bright, sunny morning, heading to Tangier Island, one of the biggest producers of soft-shell crabs in the world. That was all I knew about this spit of land tucked in the Chesapeake Bay; that and a man I'd met in Assateague said people on Tangier were crazy.

'What kind of crazy?' I asked. There are so many kinds.

'Well, it's pretty isolated out there,' he said. 'Natives pretty set in their ways. No cars or anything. Not much communication with the real world.'

Leaving the real world sounded just fine to me so I drove to

Onancock, parked my car in the small lot, packed a few clothes in a backpack, and rolled my bike on the ferry. As the small boat left shore, I leaned over the railing and took in the view. The Chesapeake Bay looks like the ocean, only greener, its waves more condensed and confused, as if they were not so much going somewhere as undecided. Brown sea grass floated like linguine in a cooling pot. Inside the cabin, a dozen passengers, older folks in sweatshirts, huddled together, fussing with bags. The captain's door was open. A solid, middle-aged man, white cap and uniform, sat behind the wheel. I decided to ask a question or two, hoping to drum up a little conversation.

'Excuse me,' I said. 'Does this boat run all year?'

The captain turned his head, turtle slow, stopping when one brown eye met my gaze. He was a handsome man, with a wide tanned face, brown hair hidden under a cap. An ironic twitch at the mouth. Eyebrows thick as paint. He looked bemused or annoyed, it was impossible to say which. Without a word, he turned back, as if he'd seen all he needed to make up his mind.

'She runs till October. Why? You acoming back?'

His accent was heavy, each vowel stretched long as a wet sweater.

'Am I coming back? Well, I don't know. I haven't even arrived. What's Tangier like?'

He took his time before answering. 'Well, you'll find out won't you?'

There was no denying this. I leaned against the cabin wall, turning my face to the sun. The cabin smelled like warm wood, and through the bay window, the water shattered in the sunlight, like a mirror that had fallen off the wall and looked better that way.

'Are you from the island?' I asked, in my most polite tone.

'Born there,' he said. 'My family's there from the beginning.'

'Do you know a place where I could spend the night?'

'You should stay with my brother, Norman. He has a place. Betty's Bed and Breakfast. Betty puts out quite a spread. There's a brochure in the cabin.'

It reminded me of Mexico, how strangers invariably guide you to the hotel run by their cousins.

'How'd you come about here?' he asked.

'Well, it's kind of a funny story. In Assateague, someone standing in line for a fried oyster sandwich told me to come,' I said, proud of my impulsiveness. 'I'm driving from Maine to Key West.'

The captain raised an eyebrow. 'Why?'

This guy reminded me of my father, who could deflate even the most magical plan with a simple one-word question like 'How?'

'I guess I just like to travel,' I said.

'You traveling alone?'

'Alone,' I said in my most upbeat voice, trying to convey alone was good, that I'd had offers of company, not that I had, but I *could have*. Maybe. Anyway, the point was I was choosing to be alone, that alone *meant* something, *proved* something about independence, self-reliance, pup tents, and—

'Got yourself a boyfriend?' asked the captain.

'Yes,' I said, trying not to sound defensive.

'Why didn't he come with you?'

'He had to work,' I said. I wasn't sure whether I was referring to Stuart or Peter, but hell, both had to work.

'You got a lot of nerve,' he said, shaking his head. 'I wouldn't be taking a trip like that if you paid me a million dollar. Not a million, I wouldn't be going.'

I had never taken a trip that made so few people envious.

'Why wouldn't you?' I asked.

'I hate being alone,' the captain replied. 'What are you . . . a loner?'

I couldn't tell if he was being playful or condescending.

'A loner? I don't think so,' I said. 'I'm a writer. Well, more of a reporter. Well, I'm a reporter trying to write, only I'm not writing now. I'm traveling and then I'll write about it. Maybe. If there's anything worth writing about.'

'It's going to be a book?'

'I don't know.'

'What you going to call this book?'

'I haven't thought of a title,' I said. 'I haven't even begun.'

The captain said nothing. I felt as though I'd failed him. His sturdy fingers turned the wheel a hair this way, a hair that, as if years of experience went into these fine tunings, which they probably did.

'Call it *South on the Chesapeake*,' he said.

'But it would be about the *whole* coast, from Maine to Key West,' I said, feeling the need to defend this unwritten, unstarted book from a hypothetical, erroneous title. 'Not just the Chesapeake.'

The captain didn't answer for some time.

'Call it *South of Maine*.'

This time I didn't object. Through the window, I could make out a strip of land in the distance.

'What was it like growing up on Tangier?' I asked.

'Child's paradise,' said the captain, his voice softening a bit. 'No crime. No drugs. Simple living. Didn't have no storm windows, no television, no electricity, no electrical heat. The men worked the water, and the women tended the house.'

'Everything had to come over by boat?'

'How else was it going to get there?' he asked. 'When the bay froze, nothing to eat but what came from the water. Imagine running a house without electricity? Nowadays women couldn't do it. How would you run a household full of children in the dead of winter on an island without electricity?'

He bestowed one of his signature stares, waiting for my reply. I couldn't imagine having a house, let alone a household.

'I don't know,' I said respectfully. 'It sounds very hard.'

215

He nodded and turned back, satisfied that I had conceded his point.

'Did you ever want to leave?' I asked.

'I did leave,' he said. 'I live on Onancock.'

'I mean leave the area.'

'What, move to the city?' He swiveled to face me. 'Where do you live?'

'New York City.'

'Now what would I do in New York City? Where am I going to go fishing in New York City? Do you think some banker is going to move to Tangier? What's he going to do there? There's nothing there for him.'

He paused, then added: 'No reason to go where you don't belong.'

He made it sound so simple. You are who you are. You live accordingly.

'I guess you're right,' I said. 'Can't see you in Manhattan.'

He nodded. 'Now, if you're interested in island history, you should go see my aunt. She's ninety-one. Dorothy Walker is her name. She'll tell you how it was.'

The island skyline came into view, a pointed steeple, an enormous water tower, bunches of houses. A thick summer haze muted the colors, softened the details, rounded the corners.

'They can say what they want about Tangier, but it's a beautiful place,' said the captain, lifting a reverent hand. 'This would be a beautiful picture to paint. Looks like the town is just sitting on the water. Have you ever seen anything prettier than that?'

I knew better than to answer the question. 'It *is* pretty,' I said.

A young girl walked into the cabin, picked up a clipboard, and started reading a canned speech over the intercom: '*On either side of the boat, you'll see crab shanties. This is where the watermen store the soft-shell crabs. Tangier Island is the soft-shell crabbing capital of the world.*'

216

I thanked the captain and told him I was going to get my things.

He nodded. 'You'll like Tangier,' he said. 'No place like it.'

We rode into harbor between nautical markers, telephone poles topped with green squares and red triangles, leaving green to port, red to starboard. The old sailing rule rose from foggy memory, '*Red Right Returning*.' An osprey that had thatched a nest on top of a marker watched us float by, like an old woman admiring a passing parade. We motored past the crab shanties, small work sheds suspended on pilings, each equipped with a stack of crab pots and a tethered dory. The names of the boats reminded me of country singers: *Loretta Star, Kathy Lee, Miss Nancy, Bette Bee, Ginna-Jack.* One shanty had large sign saying '*Jesus Never Fails*.' Another had one of those religious fish encasing the words '*We Believe*.'

The ferry nudged the dock and we unloaded ourselves, all curiosity and confusion. The downtown was nothing much, a grocery, a couple restaurants advertising crab cake specials on hand-scrawled signs. A half-dozen stocky women sat in golf carts waiting to give tours. Cutting through the crowd on my bike, I pedaled down a narrow street of white houses. Almost every house had a fence; some white picket, some chain link, rusty and bent, like dog kennels without the dogs. I was surprised to see that many homes had private graveyards, gray stone markers tipped like dominoes frozen midfall. The corner church had a huge cemetery with aboveground vaults, slabs of white concrete slightly bigger than a coffin, like a field of bed sheets drying in the sun. *Parks. Pruitt. Crockett. Dise*. The same names appeared over and over again.

I crossed a wooden bridge and surveyed the island as a whole. Basically, Tangier was one big marsh with a strip of houses on either side. Looming above everything was an aqua green water tower, which looked like an alien spaceship that had forgotten how to return home. Through the island's core, turgid water wended through acres of marsh grass, buttery green like the insides of avocados. Here and there, mud pockets or a rowboat. It was beautiful, in a quiet, empty way. The heat was building into a swelter. Sweat rolled down my chest as I pedaled on.

Eventually, I came to the house I'd seen in the brochure. A cheery three-story gingerbread Victorian with a long porch, flower beds bordered with ship's rope, and a satellite dish yawning into the sky. Betty's Bed and Breakfast.

The woman who answered the door was around fifty, solid with a bowl of brown hair. Her shoulders tipped to one side, as if work had gotten the best of her.

'I was wondering if you had a room tonight?' I asked. 'I just took the ferry from Onancock, and the captain recommended I come here.'

'Yeeeeah. That's Norman's brother,' the woman said loudly with a nod. 'But I'm sorry, don't have no rooms. Had a girl going to rent the couch. She's coming after work today from Washington, awanting to get out of the city. Then I had a cancellation, so she got that room. Don't know what to tell you.'

Her accent was a thing of wonder. Some kind of twangy mixture of long vowels and words chopped short.

'So the couch is free?' I asked.

The woman looked amused, as if I'd asked to buy her underwear. 'Well, yes, you can look at it. It weren't nothing special.'

She held open the door. A man appeared, handsome with strong forearms, hazel eyes, and heavy dark eyebrows. Unmistakably the captain's brother.

'Norman, this girl's awanting to rent the couch.'

Norman smiled. 'Two in one weekend. We ain't never had nothing like that before.'

I felt like a stray dog, ready to curl up on any carpet scrap.

'What's your name?' he asked.

'Lili.'

'Norman. Nice to meet you, Lily,' he said, shaking my hand.

We went to look at the couch. The living room was decorated with crocheted doilies, china tchochkes of angels and sheep. The couch in question was, well, a couch. Beige. Square cushions. Long enough to lie flat. The three of us stared at it, as if expecting it to speak.

'It looks great,' I said. 'I've been sleeping in a tent, so a couch would be a luxury. That is, if you don't mind.'

'Nah,' Betty said. 'You can have it. Maybe that other girl who's coming would let you share her room. Her room goes for sixty-five dollars a night. You could ask her when she comes. Then you'd get a bed.'

'Either way,' I said. 'Just glad to be here. So how much would you charge for the couch?'

'Twenty-five dollars,' she said, 'full breakfast included.'

The porch thermometer read 90 degrees, but the humidity made it seem hotter. Norman smoked while I swatted mosquitoes and skimmed magazine articles about Tangier. Seven hundred people, 80 percent of them belonging to one of four families, live on the two-and-half-mile-long island. Many still speak with an old English brogue. The highest point on island is four feet above sea level, thus the above-ground crypts. 'We do bury the dead on the island,' one brochure explained. 'They are buried three feet under, and in some of the older gravesites, the top of the vault is showing, often compared to those in New Orleans.' There are seven gift shops, two groceries, two churches, a post office, a school, but no doctor, bank, movie house, liquor store, or jail. 'We are staunch Methodists. We have our own high school. We also have a modern airstrip. Some might say that we are isolated. That is a matter of opinion.'

I looked up. One of those golf cart tours drove past us. *'This is one of the oldest houses on the island, built in 1918. It was featured in the November 1973 edition of* National Geographic. *It is also a bed and breakfast.'* The cart rounded the bend and disappeared from earshot.

'They do that all day?' I asked.

'When the boats get in,' Norman said. 'The women take them round the island. Give them their history.'

I loved listening to Norman. He had a gentle way about him. While Betty seemed frazzled, Norman was lemonade calm.

'Smoking keep the bugs away?' I asked, rubbing a welt.

'Reckon so they don't like me so much.'

'So it says here people on Tangier have Elizabethan accents. Is that what you have?'

Norman looked faintly annoyed. 'That's what they *say* we have. Don't right know what to tell you about that, Lily. People used to have accents, but not much anymore. Used to be you wouldn't no more know what they were saying for nothing in the world. But not anymore. It's TV that's done that.'

I had to say something. 'Norman, my name is pronounced Lee-lee.'

He nodded. 'That's a hard one.'

Another golf cart approached. *'On the right is Betty's Bed and Breakfast. Rates are seventy dollars per night for couples, and children under twelve are free.'*

I heard Betty talking to other guests out back. While the visitors' voices were indecipherable, Betty's orange twang zagged round the house like comic strip lightning. She managed to sustain a conversation by saying virtually nothing at all.

'Yeeeah.'

'They surely do.'

'Ease that right?'

'Well, that's niiiice.'

'They get some reeest.'

'Wouldn't you know?'

'That she can.'

'Well, that's good.'

'Yeeeah.'

Norman lit another cigarette. The guy could smoke. And yet the easy way the clouds drifted past his cotton shirt, it was hard to believe such a peaceful habit was lethal.

'So, Norman, it says here there's no doctor on the island, but there's a cop. What's he do?'

'Well, Leela, that's a good question. We'd *all* like to know,' he said. 'He slows the scooters down to fifteen miles an hour, that's about it. Gets some people drinking beer for public intoxication. Makes good money, too. Not a bad check.'

'But you can't buy liquor on the island.'

'No, island's dry,' Norman agreed. 'Some tourists get right disappointed when they come to find out they can't get a drink. One lady chartered a private boat – eighty dollars – to take her back to Crisfield.'

'To get liquor and come back?'

'No, she left for good.'

Yet another golf cart whizzed by. '*It costs sixty dollars a night per couple, and that includes a full breakfast. They have a patio in back where you can . . .*'

'Didja hear there was supposed to be a movie shot here?' Norman asked. 'Kevin Costner and Paul Newman.'

'You're kidding.' I sat up. 'Which movie?'

'What was it called . . . oh, I'll think of it, but it was set right here on the island. Going to build a restaurant on my sister's property. Had all my cottages rented up for weeks. Plus' – he leaned forward for emphasis – 'they were going to hire a hundred and ten head. *Message in a Bottle*, that's it. But the city council voted them down. You know why?'

I shook my head.

'Paul Newman was going to drink a beer.'

I laughed.

'Paul Newman was going to drink a beer. Not even a real one. One beer at the restaurant and there was some un-dressing scene. Robin Wright, only just from the back. The undressing wasn't even happening here. She was undressing somewhere else, only people would have *thought* it was here.

221

Two hundred people signed a petition saying they wanted the movie. The city council voted it down. A couple church people and the mayor killed the whole thing. Made me sick.'

'Isn't the mayor also the minister?'

'He's the mayor, the preacher, the assistant principal, *and* the undertaker. He's making $150,000 with all those jobs. What's it matter to him whether we got the movie? He's got his.'

'What was the movie about?' I asked.

'It was a love story. Nice story. Paul Newman thought the island was perfect. Ooooh, we got some bad press. Jay Leno said something. Surprised you didn't hear about it. What's that radio fellow, Howard Stern, he knew about it. One woman who came here said, "Norman, I'm not even going to tell you what he said." I said, "Go ahead, I'd probably agree with him." She said, "I'm too embarrassed," so you can imagine. Think what that movie would of done for the island. I just wanted to watch 'em do it. I'm interested in those things. Never seen a movie being made.'

'Were people worried it would bring too many tourists?'

'No. It was the beer.'

'I guess people here are pretty religious.'

Norman ground his cigarette into his ashtray. 'They like to think they are.'

'Norman, do you know anybody who'd take me out and show me how to soft-shell crab? I'd love to see how it's done.'

If I had any agenda for my stay it was this: to meet a real waterman. I'd always harbored romantic feelings about men who worked the sea, none of which were based on experience or fact. After spending so many summers in Maine, you'd think I'd have gone lobstering, but no. We were 'summer people,' a label that always made me feel hopelessly effete, like a person better suited to croquet than fishing, which, of course, I was. But Tangier seemed like an ideal opportunity to observe the legendary Maryland watermen up close.

Norman thought for a minute. 'I could ask my neighbor

Malcolm. He lives right over there,' he said, pointing to the bushes of the neighboring house. 'He once said if there were girls visiting, he'd take them out.'

'Just girls?' I asked, half smiling.

'Well, visitors, you know.'

'*Up here on the left is Betty's Bed and Breakfast. It was established in 1904, and now you can spend the night . . .*'

The tour guides were getting on my nerves. The way they circled the island, parroting facts as if nothing had changed, as if nothing had changed, as if nothing had changed since the last go-round. It took me a minute to realize why they bugged me.

They reminded me of the cat show.

My first year in Utah, on a slow news day, I was dispatched to the state fairgrounds to cover the cat show. Determined to make the most of this lame assignment, I earnestly interviewed fanatics from the Cat Fanciers' Association. I wrote:

Bandito looked like a winner with his long legs, playful spots and prestigious pedigree. But then the final competitor turned on the sex appeal. 'It was even-steven until the Scottish fold reached over and gave the judge a kiss,' said Cheryl de Young, as she cuddled her second-place kitten. 'It is really hard to beat the cute factor.'

It was a decent fifteen-inch story. Over and done. But before I knew it, a year had passed. As luck would have it, I was working cat show weekend and was dispatched again. I drove to the fairgrounds, seething: This is who I am now – the reporter who covers the cat show. I started to see how life ran away from you, how the years blended together like some cheap cake mix.

As I watched the golf cart circle back into town, I realized something I hadn't before. My restlessness, Dad's claustrophobia – it was the same sort of fear. He was scared of being boxed in by airplanes and movie theaters and loud people. I was terrified of routine, rote emotion, a gradual numbing of flesh to the bone. Dad eased his worries by staying home. I eased mine by taking off, reaching for whatever was new, causing a romantic ruckus so no one got bored. Partnership led to routine led to stagnation led to the cat show.

'Now we come to one of the oldest houses on the islands. The rates here are seventy-five dollars a night . . .'

I had to move. 'Norman, I'm going for a bike ride.'

'Okay,' he said, lighting another cigarette. 'Got plenty things to do round here.'

It took me three whole minutes to get back into town. I stopped outside a house where dozens of plastic cups hung from a chain-link fence. A sign read: *All Recipes are 5 for $1.00.* I unfurled a couple; They were heavy on mayo and canned goods. I suppose island women had to be inventive with what came over on the boat. The Peach Pie recipe read as follows:

1 *baked pie shell*
1 *box peach Jell-O*
1 *c. sugar*
1 *quart peaches*
1 *rounded tsp. cornstarch*
1 *small Cool Whip*

At Jim's Gift Shop, I bought a book of local sayings, which I paged through as I ate an ice cream cone on a shady bench. Native Tangiermen are called *been heres*. Newcomers are *come heres* or *foreigners*. Something temporary *won't last a good high water*. Drinking is *having a smother*. To eat a big meal is to *run ashore*. Dating is *sparking*. When you have to pee, you're *taken short*. To age is to *break*, like she *broke* since the last time I saw her. *Huck* is grime, usually on your neck or back. *Kaflugie* is an indefinite distance a long way away, as in, 'I could throw that to *kaflugie*.' The thick scum that forms on old paint is *mother*. Something dangerous is a *tickly bender*. And my favorite, a person who's living the good life, especially a child, is *eating his white bread*.

I wandered over to the island museum, a single room in the back of another gift shop; it was filled with kerosene lamps and maps and arrowheads and a table full of news clippings about Tangier, many concerning the movie. Norman hadn't exaggerated.

'We don't want any loud, alcoholic parties or bad language from the filmers,' Miss Annie Parks, 97, was quoted as saying. Parks had never seen a movie and wasn't about to start now. 'Like Pop used to say, I'm against it tooth and toenails.'

Councilwoman Nina C. Pruitt, a school librarian, voted against the film. 'Even Howard Stern is talking about us. If he calls us idiots, we've got to be doing something right.' Town council member Betty Dail Parks had no trouble sleeping after she voted no. 'I've got to answer to my God, not Kevin Costner.'

What a crew.

Tangier was one big extended family and, like most families, a little nuts. For years, I thought my family held the patent on craziness. There was a great-aunt called Tanta, who sat in a wheelchair one day and never got up. And my second cousin Louise, who wafted through Greenwich in a see-through black witch's robe, wooden staff in her hand. And Aunt Mary, whose first husband made a fortune selling corsets and whose second marriage to Mr Wright (no relation) ended abruptly one morning with a series of loud bangs. Aunt Mary asked the maid what the commotion was about. 'It's Mr Wright,' the maid explained. 'He's moving out and taking the furniture with him.' Thereafter, Aunt Mary lived an Eloise-like existence at the Sherry Netherland Hotel in Manhattan, eating warm milk toast, seldom changing out of her silk bathrobe. She collected snuff boxes, cameo glass, and went through a lace period. She had a passion for late-night TV, particularly women's wrestling.

As a child, I dreamed of being orphaned. In my fantasies, the Rodericks, the parents of my Barbie friend Page, would open their doors to me, outfitting me in Alligator shirts, whisking me to the Bahamas for a much-needed vacation. The fact that Mrs Roderick disappeared briefly into an 'institution' did little to dissuade me. This too felt exotic.

It took years for me to see that every family is its own Tangier, an island where you can propagate your own brand of weirdness, design a world in your own flawed image. Or as my brother Chip likes to say, 'The nice thing about having kids is you get to fuck them up in your own special way.' Every family has its customs and rules, down to the most trivial detail. As a girl, grocery shopping with my mom, I always knew when a stranger had mistakenly dropped food in our cart. Cabbage, half-and-half, shredded coconut would leap out, bright as a checker. Those weren't ours.

In most families, newcomers remain *come heres* no matter how many years pass, like my sister-in-law Sue, who struggled to join our tightly wound family. Sue cut cheese in cubes, not slices. She ripped open her Christmas presents, instead of saving the paper for next year. Up in Maine, Sue repainted Nana's gray room yellow, the blue room cream . . . having no idea she disturbed a natural order. At dinner with my parents, glass of wine for courage, she asked questions we had spent a lifetime avoiding.

'Mr Wright, *do you think you'll ever go back to work?*'

'Mrs Wright, *don't you get lonely living up here on this road?*'

As I waited for my parents to explain themselves, a delicious chill channeled up my spine. When they tactfully finessed her probes, I was disappointed they hadn't been exposed, as if public acknowledgment of their foibles would prod them to change. But who was I to talk? I wasn't exactly meeting my parents' expectations. And yet I expected them to understand me no matter what I did; I expected them to understand me without asking too many questions. In my family, the stranger we become, the less we have to say about it. It may not be healthy, but it's just the way we are.

It was Grampy, of all people, who helped clear the air. Grampy once told Dad that he didn't think I'd *ever* get married, that I'd travel and write. Mom and Dad must have chewed that one around for a while because Dad later repeated it back to me, his way of giving his blessing, I suppose. Things with my parents improved after that. They stopped hinting about marriage and starting imagining how their daughter might live a different sort of life. This helped *me* imagine how I might live a different sort of life.

And now I was becoming rather proud of my family's Tangier-like eccentricities. Being daft is its own sort of club, exclusive, with a hefty set of annual dues. Better peculiar than bland. The stories are better. And it's comforting to know that no matter how odd an apple you become, Great-Aunt So-and-So has already done you one better. Or as my father once put it: 'Just think, if you were born a Roderick, you wouldn't be kooky like us.'

Watermen wake up at 4:00 a.m. so people on Tangier eat supper before six. That night I ate dinner at a restaurant in town. The meal came in various shades of yellow and brown: pan-fried crab cakes, macaroni and cheese, hushpuppies, iced tea. By the time I finished, my boat had definitely *run ashore*.

Riding my bike through town after supper, I saw how the island had changed since morning. The day-trippers had departed. Except for the handful of tourists spending the night, the people of Tangier had their island to themselves. Women chatted over fences. Young men did their best to look cool in golf carts. Legs akimbo, left hand sly on the wheel, right hand dangling between their legs, eyes squinty and smug. A peach-fuzzed boy steered his girl to a corner Pepsi machine. She leaned over his lap, her breasts falling before him, slid her quarters into the slot, pushed root beer, sat back down with her pop. The boy slipped his arm round her bare shoulder, then motored on.

When I got back to Betty's, Norman had two pieces of good news. Malcolm, the neighbor, had agreed to take me out on the water tomorrow evening, and the woman from Washington would share her room so I wouldn't have to sleep on the couch. I thanked Norman, then walked to the back porch to watch the sun set behind the sewage treatment plant. The whole sky turned a misty pink. Tangier reminded me of the Little Prince's planet, how the sun rose on one side of the island and set on the other, an entire world no wider than a boy's outstretched arms.

Suddenly an engine roared. A black sedan shot down the landing strip that spread before me in the distance. Kids drag racing. What else is there to do on a two-mile island? Driving for driving's sake. Driving to feel speed. I imagined myself in the passenger seat, tingling as my boyfriend pressed the accelerator to the floor, wondering, as the houses and marsh and bay blurred past my open window, whether I would ever move fast enough to be someone who mattered.

The next day I swam and read and, in the early afternoon, went to visit Dorothy Walker, the captain's ninety-one-year-old aunt. Dorothy lived in a trailer home on a small plot of land with gravestones in back and a chain-link fence all around. When she opened the door, I explained I was staying with Norman and that I wanted to learn about the island. She seemed accustomed to greeting uninvited quests and graciously said, 'Yes, come in.'

Dorothy was a delicate woman, brittle but not broken. Pale red hair. Face soft with wrinkles. Her large glasses were tinted pink. I sat down on the couch, and she sat in her rocking chair, which afforded her a view out the window of her neighbors milling on the street. As we talked, Dorothy threw a ball to her cat Pitty Pat.

Dorothy was born on Tangier. Her father, a merchant,

owned a general store and a movie theater, which she pronounced thee-*ate*-her. And oh, Tangier was such a wonderful place to be a child. They ice skated and had dances and went to taffy-pulling parties where everyone sat on the oriental rug and played the Victrola and listened to songs. In those days women didn't work, they kept house, had children. Dr Gladstone born all the babies and never lost a one.

Dorothy had gone to college; she and her sister were the very first ones on the island to do so. After college, she'd taught school. Between divorce and death, Dorothy hadn't much luck keeping husbands. Three of them in all. But before then, Dorothy and her daughter, Lynn, and her son-in-law, Paul, had taken lots of trips together, to the Bahamas and Egypt and Greece. Paul's friends thought he was nuts to vacation with his mother-in-law, but they'd had such fun. She'd even tried one of those parachutes that lift you up and drag you behind a boat. Parasailing? I asked. Yes, parasailing. She'd gone parasailing and her daughter thought she was nuts but she went up and came down and had the bruises to prove it. Not long after that her daughter, Lynn, died of cancer. She was only forty-one.

Dorothy got teary thinking about Lynn. I got teary watching Dorothy, a mother who had outlived her daughter. We stared at the framed photograph of Lynn that stood on top of the TV set. It's hard to look at a picture of someone you don't know and see what their mother sees, but I tried. Dorothy started a scholarship fund at the island school in her daughter's name.

'I'm thinking about selling my wedding ring.' She held out a diamond, big as a dime. 'It's four carats.'

I was more interested in Dorothy's fingers, the heavy wrinkles, the arthritic bent.

'It's so important to travel when you're young,' Dorothy said, 'because you just never know.'

I asked about the winters on the island. Dorothy said she spends winters in her condo in Maryland, but she comes back to Tangier each summer because this is where her family is.

Literally.

Her parents were buried out back. Her father had died in his late forties from a stroke, but her mother made it to ninety-one and she lived her whole life on the island. Her father was heavy, that's what killed him. That's why Dorothy didn't eat greasy food, though she did like her sweets.

Dorothy told me how she loves her golf cart and how she meets Betty's guests at the ferry and over the years she'd made so many lovely friends. She couldn't remember all the friends she'd made, but they remembered her and they came back to see her and would say, 'Dorothy, do you remember me?'

I wanted Dorothy to remember me if I ever came back, but how would she? I was just another *foreigner* sailing in one afternoon. Dorothy asked when I was leaving Tangier. I said Tuesday morning, three days from now on the morning boat to Onancock. Dorothy said she'd go down to the ferry to say good-bye. I said she didn't have to do that and Dorothy said she wanted to.

Before I left, Dorothy gave me a yellow crocheted butterfly with yellow pipe cleaner antennae and a small magnet on the back. She said I could put it on the refrigerator. Put it on the refrigerator and think of me, she said. I crocheted it before my hands went bad.

'Maybe I can come back some day,' I said.

Dorothy nodded. 'We get a lot of repeats.'

'I'll stop in and see you,' I said.

And Dorothy said: 'We'll be here. Someone will be here.'

At quarter past five that evening, a man strolled up to Betty's front porch. He wore jeans, a muscle shirt over slouched, freckled shoulders. His head was perfectly round, the bottom half dipped in reddish whiskers, like a Sesame Street muppet. My waterman had arrived.

'Yooou Leela?'

230

'Lili,' I said.

He nodded, sat down on the porch swing.

'I'm Malcolm. I'm sorry but I can't take you out,' he said. Each word lilted, singsonging to the next. 'My boat's getting repaired. Maybe tomorrow though. Might be ready.'

'Tomorrow would be great,' I said, trying to hide my disappointment.

'Yee-ah, well, tomorrow might work. Why you want to go?'

'I wanted to understand more about soft-shell crabbing,' I said. 'I was just curious how it's done.'

He nodded, digested this reason, seemed to find it satisfactory.

'How long you been crabbing?' I asked.

'Since school,' he said. 'Dropped out in tenth grade. My friends were workin' on the water, saw them makin' money and wanted to make me some. I love it. Never wanted to do nothin' else. Never knew how to do nothin' else really, but this, just this, you know.'

He gave a quick smile.

'So have you done well this year?' I asked.

'Hard to make a livin' now,' he said. 'There's so many regulations. They say they're tryin' to save the bay, but they don't know what they're talkin' about. There are plenty of crabs out there. From here to the road, throw out your net, you get hundreds. These regulation people, they sit in an office, you know. Never been out on the water a day in their lives.'

I started daydreaming about our adventure tomorrow. I'd wake up at 3:00 a.m. and feel like hell but sort of noble, like a better brand of tourist. Out on the bay, in the black of old night, we'd loft giant nets over the stern or grind a rusty crank. (I had no idea how to crab.) When the time came, we'd haul in the catch and, *oh my God*, look at all those crabs, stretching and clicking and tangled in wet line. With one final gasp, the crabs would lunge for freedom, but we'd grab the old grouches with black rubber gloves, men's gloves, thumbs four times the size of my own, and chuck them in a storage basket or a tank or a box. Then we'd start again. Throwing and hauling until my back ached. It would be like . . . like . . . like a Winslow Homer painting. When the work was done, we'd sit back and sip black coffee from a dirty cup. Malcolm would chew out a story or two. He'd teach me to read the ripples on the bay, to forecast the weather from whispers of early morning wind and—

'You married?'

This took me a minute. I was still in the crab boat, sipping black coffee from a dirty cup.

'No,' I said, quickly adding the obligatory, 'but I have a boyfriend.'

'How old are you?'

'Thirty-three.'

'Me, too.' Malcolm smiled. This one lingered a second longer before it too disappeared. We both shook our heads at this coincidence.

'I'm not married,' Malcolm said. 'My brothers are married. You think you'll get married?'

'I hope to some day,' I said, trying to think of a way to move the conversation along.

Malcolm nodded. 'Now, last time I took a girl out crabbing, my girlfriend got right jealous,' he said. 'Don't know if I could do that again.'

His girlfriend got jealous?

Malcolm continued. 'The woman, Lydia Brown, she keeps coming back, trying to change things here on the island. Got these ideas. She's from Minnesota. Says she was sent by God *to save the island*,' he said facetiously. 'Some people say the Devil sent her. She's got death threats and all. She's trying to break up the watermen, divide the Christians and the sinners.'

I didn't have to wonder which membership he claimed.

'Doesn't seem like it's any of her business what happens

here,' I said, hoping to make it clear I wasn't another Lydia Brown interloper, armed with God and an agenda.

'No, it's not,' said Malcolm, hands between his knees, eyes focused on the marsh. 'But she's here now, trying to divide everyone. We sinners ain't so bad. Anyway, last year, I took her out and my girlfriend, well, she got right jealous. No, she waren't too happy about it. I could ask her about you, but I don't know what she'd think. Nothing against you and all.'

I had no idea what to say. Did this woman really think I would crabjack her man?

'Well, I was only interested in learning about crabbing.' I crossed my legs chastely. A little body language never hurt. 'I don't want to put you in an awkward spot with your girlfriend. That wouldn't be fair to you—'

'Thank you for saying that. Well, I'll ask her, but she gets mighty jealous. I'll see how she takes it.'

'She wouldn't want to come along? So she'd be comfortable that—'

'No, she's got to work.'

Malcolm stood. I sensed I was losing ground. 'If it doesn't work out, do you know anyone else who would take me?' I asked, trying not to plead.

'You shouldn't have a problem finding someone. You're a pretty girl.'

I was utterly confused; somehow he had turned everything around.

'So how will I know one way or the other?' I wasn't going wait around forever on the porch.

'I'll stop by tomorrow,' he said unconvincingly as he ambled across the lawn.

It was all I could do not to ask what time.

That evening, I saw Betty and Norman sitting in the garden.

'Lylee,' Norman called out. 'Didja go out crabbing?'

'No,' I said, walking over. 'Malcolm's not sure he can take

233

me out. Says the last time he took a girl out, his girlfriend got jealous.'

Norman looked confused. 'I ain't never met a girl,' he said. 'Unless she's new.'

'He ain't got no girlfriend,' Betty said.

It hadn't occurred to me Malcolm was lying.

'He said he's been dating her since last year,' I said.

'He lives right there,' said Betty, pointing to the fence. 'I would know if he got a girlfriend and he don't . . . Nawh.'

'Maybe he didn't want to take me out,' I ventured.

'Well, then, why did he tell me if there were any girls interested in going out to let him know?' Norman looked genuinely puzzled.

'He said the last woman he took was Lydia Brown,' I said, 'and his girlfriend got jealous.'

'*He ain't got no girlfriend,*' Betty insisted.

'Maybe he thinks you're with Save the Bay,' Norman said.

'Maybe he just didn't like me,' I said. 'He said he just came back from Williamsburg with his girlfriend. They went to Busch Gardens.'

'He ain't left the island,' Norman said. 'He's had to crab.'

It seemed pretty clear my waterman fantasy was going to stay just that. Betty chimed in one last time with her signature triple negatives.

'I ain't never seen no girlfriend.'

Needless to say, Malcolm never dropped by. The next day, we passed each other on bicycles. He grinned and said 'heyyah' and didn't stop. Maybe Malcolm really did have a girlfriend or maybe he didn't want to take me out once he heard I had a boyfriend or maybe he wanted all the lady *come heres* to request crabbing expeditions so he could reject them. Maybe he just liked to be asked so he could say no.

I guess I knew a little about that.

That Sunday, I went to church. Not that I am religious, not at all. The only times my family went to church were to marry people or bury them, and then once for my tardy Baptism as an Episcopalian at age three. We never talked about God or faith or read the Bible, and I had always been fine without that, grateful we hadn't cluttered up our weekends with dull religious obligation. I'd always found the idea of God vague and overwhelming. When pressed, I say 'I am spiritual,' the divine escape clause. The way I see it, we live, we die, we return to the earth like old dogs and swatted flies, and there's something poetic about this, something decent and fair. Bad things happen for no good reason. Good is its own reward. No afterlife for the martyrs, no judgment day or second chance, just the here and now, which is scary enough to be inspiring. If anything, I believe in Mother Nature, the biology of flowers, the healing power of the sea. Grampy was lobbying for me to become a Wiccan or a Druid. He liked the idea of worshipping trees and wanted to build a ceremonial stone circle up in Maine. Grampy was tempted to become a Druid himself, but with the mail-order catalogs stacking up and so many sweepstakes to enter, well, he just hadn't found the time.

So for thirty-three years, I'd gotten along fine without God, but lately I'd been wondering, as I did about most things, whether I was missing out on something. Before I left home, I decided to go to a bunch of different services, shop around, see if I could find a faith to suit my style. Nothing with too much Jesus on the cross. Not too Lord Above, Holy Father. Just a preacher who inspires you to do better next time. So far, I'd played hooky, but Sunday morning on a two-mile Methodist island, there was literally nothing else to do.

I spotted Dorothy in the back pew and sat down next to her. She smiled and patted my knee. The church was pretty in a chaste sort of way, with pink stained-glass windows and a funereal bouquet on the organ. Several hundred people lined the pews, more women than men. Before I knew it, we were going through the motions, sitting and standing and listening to some warmup reverend talk about how he'd once been oh so lost – 'What chance did I have, being a Parks *and* a Pruitt?'

Everyone laughed because most people there were a Parks or a Pruitt.

But, sure enough, Mr Parks-Pruitt had been found again. When the found man sat down, a minister, substitute for the $150,000 reverend/headmaster/undertaker/mayor who was off-island, took to the podium saying he was going to preach as long as it took to get out the message, never mind if the soft-shell crabs got hard.

This can take half a day.

The morning's sermon was the story of the prodigal son. Being a prodigal daughter, this got my attention. The minister told how a young man ventured out into the world, squandered his inheritance, and returned home a beggar, pleading forgiveness. The father bore no resentment but welcomed him with open arms, even killed a cow in his honor.

'Too many young men are like the prodigal son. Their priorities are out of whack. All they care about is the dollar bill. So long as the boys has the *monies*, the boys has the *honeys*.'

He got himself all worked up thinking about avarice and sin. His jowly face turned red and sweaty. He implored east and he implored west, trying to wring evil out of us as if we were sponges. The greatest honor, he thundered, is not monies or honeys, but to be a Christian, a man or woman of God. 'You have a responsibility to walk in fear of the Lord.'

The last thing I wanted was to walk in fear of the Lord. I had enough fears already. Church was always such a letdown. So much bluster. So little heart. I looked over at Dorothy. She sat patiently, hands grasping a hanky, and I wondered if she was taking this all in or thinking her own thoughts. I studied her ring, the one she might hawk for her scholarship, four carats, third husband. I thought about her travels. *It's so important to see the world when you're young because you just never know.* Old women were people you could travel into, people who understood only the story survives. I'd sensed that as a girl, wanted that for myself; I still did. Old hands. Old rings. You could worship the church of a person. The stained glass of their being. Broken chunks of color fused with the stickiest glue. Something stirred inside me. Something like grief and something like love. All that living bundled into one small woman. A woman who didn't travel much anymore but remembered clearly the places she'd been.

After church, back at Betty's, I stopped to talk to Norman, who was sitting on the steps having a smoke. He asked me if I'd found a waterman to show me the crabs.

'No,' I said. 'Maybe you know a married one so there wouldn't be any confusion.'

'No-uh.' Norman wagged his head. 'Don't think their wives would think much of that.'

I kicked the grass. I only had one day left.

'Well, Lila, Marie might show you round,' Norman said. 'She works with her father. She's a good girl. Her husband died in a boating accident some years back. Got two children. See that house over there with the shutters, opposite the church?' He pointed to the main ridge with his cigarette hand. 'That's her house. Go over and ask her. She could show you round the crab houses. When Lydia Brown comes, she stays with Marie.'

I biked over and knocked on the door.

'Come on ieeen.'

A woman my age with a mop of brown curls was balancing on one leg, trying to jam her foot into a sneaker. With a quick sweep, I took in the kitchen: the white bread, the child's art, the furniture that looked not so much bought as come by, the Christian proverbs stuck to the fridge.

'Hi. My name's Lili. I am staying with Norman and Betty and I wanted to learn about crabbing. They said you might take me out.'

Somehow Marie looked familiar, though I was quite sure we'd never met.

'We-ell,' she said, sizing me up. 'Can you be here nine tomorrow?'

'Sure. Great. Thank you.'

'You going to church tonight?'

'I went this morning,' I said, glad I could report this true fact.

'You could still go tonight,' Marie said with a grin. 'I go morning, night, whenever I can.'

'I think once is enough for me,' I said. 'But we can talk about all that.'

'Ohhh. Ye-ah.' Marie shook her finger playfully. 'We'll talk about that.'

At five of nine, I knocked on the door. A small blond boy let me in. Marie was in the kitchen. She wore baggy shorts and a T-shirt with an iron-on picture of Oliver North.

'Right on time,' she said. 'My girl Vicky is staying home today, but Tommy's coming.' She turned to the boy. 'Hurry up, Tommy.'

Marie darted about the kitchen, grabbing dirty clothes, shouting to Tommy to get a move-on. Her lean shins were a bit bowed, her shoulders square. I liked watching her move. She was the kind of girl I envied as a child. A tomboy. A sexy tomboy, born with her eye on the ball. At times, my admiration for such girls spilled into full-blown crushes. Marie was the kind of woman I would date if I were a man, the kind of woman who made me wonder if I could ever love a woman that way, if such a thing were in me. I liked the *idea* of loving a woman, of there being some new brand of ecstasy or communion, something still untried, but it seemed doubtful I'd ever consummate the impulse.

Only once had a lesbian tried to pick me up. It happened one Sunday in a bar in Park City, Utah. I was there with my friend Tad, who found the whole thing hysterical and did his best to egg her on.

'Isn't she beautiful?' said this red-haired slip of a woman gazing up at me as if I were the Statue of Liberty.

'Oh, she's beautiful all right,' said Tad, giggling into his Guinness.

'I have things I want to do to you,' the woman cooed. 'I know what you *need*.'

For a moment, I wondered if she did know what I needed. As she spoke, I could see she was imagining us together, moist and entwined, and it bothered me that she had put me in her mind's eye without my permission. She was a little drunk and wouldn't let up, until finally I pulled the old bathroom-disappearing trick, hiding in the dank stall until finally she left.

Marie walked back into the kitchen, stopping at the sink long enough for me to read the lettering on her pink shoe-laces: *'Jesus Loves Me.'*

My eyes widened; I was going straight to hell.

The three of us rode our bikes down to the docks. We climbed into a weathered motorboat, and Marie fastened a life preserver around Tommy's thin chest.

'I hate these,' he whimpered.

'You got to,' she said. 'Ain't got no choice.'

Marie pulled the motor's cord, and we headed across the water. The harbor was bustling with small boats.

'Hanny!' Marie slowed down near a chubby woman in a whaler. 'How you doing?'

Hanny nodded, then looked hard at me. 'That Lydia Brown?'

Marie shook her head. Good God, she thinks I am Lydia Brown, the disciple, the fanatic.

'No, another one,' said Marie. 'A writer.'

The woman nodded as if she made no distinction. I smiled, trying to appear simultaneously harmless and sincere – no easy feat. We pulled alongside the crab shanty, and Marie

239

fixed the boat with a practiced knot. We walked along the dock to the floats, a row of waist-high wooden vats that resembled a crude assembly line. Each bin was filled with circulating water and a couple dozen blue crabs.

Compared to the crabs up in Maine, these were enormous, most larger than my hand. On elegant tiptoes, they darted sideways underwater, claws raised like a boxer ready to jab. A few lay stacked on top of each other, mating or fighting, I couldn't tell which. Their faces ran horizontally. Mean teeth in the middle. A cold black eye on either side. Each leg had a patch of slate blue. With their intricate joints and tarnished carapaces, they looked like ancient warriors, crustaceans who demanded respect.

With a short net, Marie began fishing out crabs, feeling the seam under the legs where the shell cracks. Then she either dropped them back in the floater or threw them in a short cardboard box. I'd always thought that soft-shell crabs were a special *kind* of crab, but it turns out all crabs shed their shells as they grow. Every few months, they squirm out of their old shell and grow a larger one. Before the new shell hardens, which takes half a day, the 'soft-shell crab' is utterly defenseless against predators, aquatic or human. Naked to the world, they hide in the grass and hope for the best.

Watermen capitalize on this skinny window of opportunity. Using a dredge, they drag along the bottom of the bay and then pick out the crabs with a special red mark, which indicates they are ready to molt. These 'peelers' are stored in floats until they shed. Every six hours, someone like Marie weeds out the dead crabs, dumps the discarded shells, and collects the crabs that've shed. Keepers are put on ice; the cold stops a new shell from forming. Marie's family sells crabs frozen, but most watermen ship them live on the morning boat. The whole process is incredibly labor-intensive, thus the high prices. The largest 'whale' soft-shells sell for $22 a dozen. If a crab hardens before it's harvested, it's sold as a hard shell, at a fraction the price.

'The hard ones are called jimmies,' Marie explained.

'Can you tell which are male and female?' I asked, ever the gender reporter.

'Yee-aah.' Marie netted a pair and turned them on their bellies. 'You see that?' She pointed to a cupola-shaped pattern. 'Those are females, the sooks. And these,' she pointed to a pencil-shaped tab. 'These are males.'

Marie laughed. I laughed. Even in the crab world, women were orbs, men had erections. Still laughing, Marie added, 'We call them, what's it called in Washington? . . . the Capitol and the Monument.'

Marie scooped and sorted, and I studied the bucket of empty shells. It was amazing how crabs made all that shell just to chuck it, how they were constantly growing, shedding their old selves to become something larger.

'That's all for now,' Marie announced.

We walked into the crab shanty, which wasn't much to speak of – an ice machine, some chairs and buckets. On the counter sat a stick that measures the size of crabs: whales, jumbo, prime, medium, cull. Marie started lining up the crabs in a box and sprinkled them with crushed ice. I hoisted myself onto the counter where, through the two sets of windows and two open doors, I had four different views of the bay. Outside on the docks, Tommy was playing boy games, amusing himself.

'You a big Oliver North fan?' I asked, noticing her shirt again.

'He came here.' Marie turned around and held up the back of her shirt. 'Signed my shirt. You can't really see it, it washed out mostly.'

'He was running for Senate from Virginia?'

'Don't right know. He must a been if he'd come. I'm not smart about politics. You could ask my sister. She knows all that stuff. Anyway, he flew into the airport. Gave out shirts and all. Stayed long enough to get votes, I guess.'

Marie turned on a transistor radio and sat in a plastic chair, tipping back on two wobbly legs.

'You married?' she asked.

I shook my head. 'You?'

I knew the story but wanted to hear her tell it.

'My husband died eleven, twelve years back. Feels so long ago. Like it happened to someone else.'

'What happened?'

'Sort of a mystery, really. He was fishing. Fell overboard, didn't find his body for four days. But he knew how to swim. They say it was a heart attack. He was only twenty-four. I was pregnant with Vicky at the time. He was her daddy. Tommy, his father, I don't know where he's at. I was in a *baaaad* way. You wouldn't have wanted to know me back then. I did everything. If there was beer or drugs, whatever, I was the first one there. Tommy's father wasn't from here. He didn't stick around.' She waved her right hand as if washing a dirty window clean. 'But two years ago I found the Lord, so that's all over now.'

'How did you find him?' I asked.

'Well, there was a revival. Went on for six weeks. That's when I was saved.'

'Saved?'

'Two hundred and seven souls were saved in six weeks. The two churches got together. They had service every night. Every night folks got saved. Everyone on island was talking about it. The air round town was real thick, like you'd have to cut it with a knife to get through. The lady who cuts my hair she told me, "Marie, you got to go." I said "I ain't going." I waren't churchgoing at the time. I said, "No thank you. Get that 'way from me."'

Marie shooed the air again with her hand. 'But I started thinking about it. I guess it was right then, I knew I would be saved that night.'

'What happened, I mean, how did they actually do it?'

'It waren't nothing really,' she said. 'They say: "Do you admit you're a sinner?" I say yes. "Do you blah blah?" Yes. "Do you blah blah?" Ten to fifteen souls was saved that night.'

It seemed entirely too easy. A bunch of handwaving and presto – redemption. Or maybe change could happen overnight. Maybe I just hadn't had the right night. Hell, you could get pregnant in a night. Or married. *Or both*, if you were making up for lost time. (On more than one occasion, I'd used this line of thinking to reassure myself there was no great rush to do either.)

'What did it *feel* like?' I prodded.

'It was the greatest feeling.' Marie hiked her leg over her knee like a boy. 'I've had a child and I've been married, but no joy compared to that. This weight was lifted off me, and I felt joy and peace. In one night I was delivered from all that sinning. I know people that have been good all their lives, but they're still going to hell. I done everything in the world. I was into so much sin, and then I was clean.'

'But what made you go in the first place?' I asked.

'I just knew the Lord had more in store for me than what I was doing.' Marie shook her curls. 'And I knew it was one of my last chances. He'd done tried and tried and was 'bout to give up on me.'

'You think you'll get married again?'

'Well.' Marie grinned. 'If the Lord see fit and sends me a good Christian man, well, okay. Frankly, it would be nice to have a man to provide for me. But I'm doing all right. In the summer I work here. In the winter I go on welfare. I just don't see me getting married because I am real contented like this.'

'I noticed yesterday in church, there were a lot more women than men.'

'That's the truth,' Marie agreed. 'I was like, "What's wrong with this picture? Where are all the Promise Keepers?"'

She paused for a second.

'Now I don't want you to think I'm saying I'm perfect. *No, no, no*. And I'm not saying it's easy. *But by His grace*. It's an hourly thing. It's not what *Marie* wants. It's what *He* wants.' She tapped her bracelet, a black nylon band with the Day-Glo letters WWJD. 'What Would Jesus Do?'

What *would* Jesus Do? I had no idea. Hell, all I was doing was what Lili wanted to do, and it wasn't working out so well. Marie genuinely believed she'd walked in a sinner and come out a saint. It seemed so simplistic, but maybe that was the point. She believed she had changed, so she had.

An electric guitar riff came on the radio.

'Oh, Led Zeppelin reminds me of my sinning days,' said Marie, sounding nostalgic. 'I went to one of their concerts, so you can imagine what I was into.'

She changed the channel to some bland Christian chorus humming with hope.

'So what did you think about that movie?' I asked, smiling in anticipation.

'You know where I stood.' Marie sat back down and shook her head. 'We didn't need none of that round here, no sir. The Lord will provide in other ways.'

'But it wasn't even a real beer.'

'Yeah, when I go telling my son I'm against drinking and cussing and then he says, "But what about that movie? I mean, I don't know where you stand." No sir. We don't need none of that.'

Now that we'd talked about crabs and Ollie North and marriage and Jesus and the movie, there really wasn't much else to say. Not in a bad way, more as if we'd walked the property and could now sit back and ride time. I gazed through the doors and windows at the pilings and traps and boats. It was peaceful, watching the bay lap along, swinging my legs under the counter. Here we were, two women in a wood shack surrounded by water, biding our time till lunch, waiting for the blue crabs to shed.

Later that morning, I met Marie's mother, sister, and two aunts, all of whom work on the docks preparing crabs for market. We ducked inside a wooden boathouse on the water and Marie introduced me around to the women and I sat and watched and listened. It reminded me of a sewing circle only fishier. Each armed with a pair of orange-handle scissors, the two aunts snipped off the crabs' aprons, faces, and gills and stacked them on a pile of ice, where the faceless creatures twitched in the cold.

'Sort of like a chicken with its head cut off,' I said.

Everyone said *yee-ah*, like that.

Marie's mother and sister folded each crab in plastic wrap, tucking legs under body in a neat bundle. When a cardboard box was full, off it went to the freezer. Every so often, one of the women held a dripping crab to her nose, smelled, made a face, and chucked the offender in the garbage.

'You'd get real sick if you ate one of those,' said Marie's mother. Then she asked if I had been to the beach.

I said, 'Oh yes, it's wonderful.'

She agreed, saying, 'Oh yes, isn't it?'

Then the women took up the movie controversy and explained how the whole island was dead set against it. I thought it better not to mention Norman and the petition with two hundred names. The younger aunt said, Paul Newman is too old anyway, but I'd take Kevin Costner. Someone asked me if I had ever traveled out of the country. I said to Europe and Mexico and then didn't know whether to ask her where she'd been and decided against it, and then later wished I had. They asked where I worked and I told them about how I go to school and moonlight at *Good Morning America* and they said, *Good Morning America* had come to Tangier, five years, no ten, no twelve years ago now, or maybe it was that other morning show, and no one was quite sure but someone had taped it and then erased it by mistake. Then the aunt mentioned how Bell Atlantic shot a TV commercial on Tangier last year and the TV people went to the rec center and handed people sixty dollars just for talking, just to see if they wanted to use them or not. Imagine, sixty dollars just to talk. And the people who got on the ad – why, it was a most beautiful ad – they were still getting checks in the mail and always would. I said I thought this was called residuals, not wanting to be a know-it-all, but trying to add something. The women all nodded. Residuals.

Then the younger aunt showed me where Governor George Allen signed the fridge when he came three or four or was it five years back. All this talk about numbers got me thinking, and I asked how long a crab lives. The older aunt said until they're caught and go to market. I asked how often crabs shed. Someone said three times, and then a red-eyed waterman who'd slipped in a few minutes back and slumped in an armchair announced that a crab sheds twenty-two times before it matures. That was news to everyone. Twenty-two times. Imagine.

Then it occurred to me that I acted an awful lot like these blue crabs, only instead of growing my own shell, I let men do it for me. I wore each man like a new set of armor, checking my reflection in the mirror – *Who was I with this person? Was this who I wanted to be?* – and when it was time to grow again, I'd squirm out of my old shell, leaving it to drift to the bottom of the bay. There I'd be, naked, for all of twelve hours, until I found a new shell and began parading it about. It was one way to grow up, but it wasn't very kind. It was time to stop using people to discover myself; I needed to grow my own goddamn shell and do it soon because I was not going to shed twenty-two shells before I found one that fit.

So I decided I would change. Then I tried to believe it.

I'd walked onto Tangier one person; I'd walk off someone else. Maybe not saved, but moving down the road in that general direction. The thought of this made me happy, as if I had accomplished something and could take the rest of the day off, like a fat person deciding to start her diet tomorrow.

Having settled the matter, I sat back and relaxed and focused on being right where I was. And as the women worked through the pile of soft-shell crabs, snipping faces and gills and aprons with their orange-handled scissors, as I listened to the crabs click click about the mountains of ice,

I realized it didn't matter that I'd missed going out with a real waterman. I was eating my white bread right here.

The next day, I left on the morning boat.

As the ferry was about to leave, I spotted Dorothy Walker parked at the landing in her golf cart. I'd forgotten that she'd promised to come see me off. I waved but she didn't see me. She looked small behind the wheel, her face lost behind oversized pink sunglasses. Her head turned side to side, surveying the crowd. I kept waving, wondering if her eyesight was poor.

Good-byes always leave me feeling sad and depleted, and I see why most people avoid them. My old roommate Chris used to joke that you knew the relationship was over when your girlfriend stopped driving you to the airport. That seems about right. The reverse was true too: Only someone truly gonzo in love sticks around to watch your plane leave. Louis did this for me the first time I left Mexico. He drove to a grassy field alongside the airport and sat on the roof of his truck and watched my plane take off, actually waited until it disappeared into the clouds. It was one of the nicest things anyone had ever done for me.

Suddenly, it seemed doubly important that Dorothy see me. I leaned over the railing and waved hard and then, sure enough, she saw me.

She saw me and smiled and waved.

Then I gave one of those goofy two-armed waves, like a castaway pleading for rescue. Dorothy laughed, then touched her hand to her lips and blew me a kiss that sailed out over the green water of the Chesapeake Bay to deliver its promise.

Mom

Virginia Beach, VA. I called Mom from a pay phone to see how she was doing. For the past year or so, law work hadn't been going well. Her partners at the firm – there are six or seven of them, all male, all younger by a decade or two – wanted to can her because she didn't bring in enough business; she wasn't, they told her, a 'rainmaker.' Periodically, I gave her pep talks, which never seemed to do much good. I told her to fight back or find a job somewhere she was appreciated, but she didn't do either.

'But you do good work,' I protested, walking out of the sizzling phone booth as far as the cord would allow. 'Doesn't that count for anything with these guys?'

'It counts, but it's not business,' said Mom. 'Hartford is in the dumps now, and there used to be plenty of work for everybody, but now the work's dried up, and there's not enough to do. The boys are all protecting their little fiefdoms, and I'm just a drain on resources. Good-bye billable hours.'

I pictured a rowboat stacked with legal briefs drifting out to sea.

'Well, Mom, call some of those lady lawyers and get your own work. *Go, Mom, go. Network, Mom, network.*'

'Network . . . yeah, well, I try. I'm having lunch with a friend next week.'

'That's great.'

'I'm just no good at this,' Mom said with a wistful sigh. She sounded exhausted. 'I never was. I don't want to pick up a phone and ask people for something, for money, for lunch. Your father was always the social one, so easy with people. I relied on him.'

It was one of the confusing things about Dad: He's a misanthrope who gets on well with people.

'Dad says you're *weeping* all the time.'

'He exaggerates.'

'He says you get up in the middle of the night and listen to talk radio and eat cookies and milk.'

'Not cookies, graham crackers.'

I used to love dunking graham crackers in milk. The way the crackers get so soggy they fall to the bottom of the glass, drift around so you have to rescue them with a spoon. But the idea of my mother's doing this in the middle of the night seemed unbearably bleak, like some kind of regression, a kid thing you were supposed to outgrow.

'Mom, you've got to cheer up. Don't let those jerks get to you.'

'Now, don't *you* worry,' said Mom, putting on her perky voice. 'It's not that bad. I'm all right.'

'That's what you always say. If you're up all night crying, everything is not all right. Mom, don't let those men define you. You still get to be you. And you still have a husband and two kids and three granddaughters who love you and a house in Maine and no one can take *that* away from you. This is just a job.'

I stopped to breathe. Why was I lecturing when I should be listening?

'Can you pinpoint exactly what you're sad about?'

My mom groaned. 'I don't know. I can't explain it. I guess, for the first time in my life, I'm experiencing emotion that can't be explained by reason.'

I thought for a minute, then reached for a pen to jot this down. It seemed important and sadly beautiful, a yellow butterfly tacked in a wax tray. *Emotion that couldn't be explained by reason* – wasn't that what love was? Love often had no good reason, no matter how hard you looked. With love, the irrational made sense.

'I was always good at everything,' Mom continued. She sounded far away now, like a graham cracker drowning in milk. 'I got good grades; I had a nice figure. Now they're telling me I'm no good.'

'They're not telling you you're no good,' I objected.

'No, in a way, they *are*,' Mom insisted, defending her injuries. 'Ellen says I'm not used to taking risks.'

Ellen was the psychologist she'd started to see.

'Risks?' I said. 'What does she mean by that?'

Even as I said this, I knew what Ellen meant. Dad had complained about this for years. 'She can't make a decision,' he'd groan. '*She can't pull the trigger.*'

I agreed with him, though I had to admit I was sticky fingered myself.

'I was always behaving, obedient, waiting for a pat on the head, waiting for approval,' Mom said. 'A good girl.'

Mom was a good girl. She *liked* being a good girl. It worked for her; it worked for her until now. She raised me to be a good girl. Not to hurt anyone's feelings. Not to trust luck or magic, not to extend blind faith. We are Yankees, Swamp Yankees, Connecticut Yankees. We work hard and expect the grade.

'Yeah, I guess I've got some of that good girl stuff, too,' I said. 'I try to please everybody and then I get frustrated and say forget it and start pleasing myself and then I feel *guilty*—'

Mom didn't seem to be listening.

Finally, she sighed and said: 'I told Ellen the other day that all my life I was raised to believe that if I colored between the lines everything would come out all right.'

'Color between the lines?' I sputtered. I pictured a fifty-cent coloring book. Stupid duck cartoons. Cheap grainy paper. The kind Mom refused to buy us when we were kids. She insisted we draw on blank paper so we'd have to dream something up. Turn nothing into something. Turn nothing into art.

'Mom, you hate that.'

'Coloring between the lines,' Mom repeated, her voice foggy, as if she were conjuring up some distant, orderly utopia, some blissy no-fallout zone where we'd never be held responsible for the mangled choices we made, the ways we'd fallen short and let people down, where every ending was happy, every heroine heroic, where any dabbler with a blue crayon could bring the sea to life.

'*Mom*—' I was losing her.

'Oh, I know,' Mom said, snapping out of her daydream, grumpy at having been woken up so soon. 'Of course, I hate that, but I am so good at it.'

'But you're good at other things, too.'

'Yes, but they are so much harder.'

I felt better. We agreed: enough of this passive good-girl stuff. We wouldn't settle for coloring someone else's lines; we wanted to draw our own. We'd fumble along, take our licks. We would make rain, or we wouldn't. Let the weathermen stand around with their pointer sticks and wonder.

'I don't know where this whole good-girl business came from,' I said, 'but it's got to go.'

Mom laughed a hard laugh, practically a cackle. 'You know what I like to say?'

'What?'

'Good guys come in last,' Mom said. 'But good girls come in even laster.'

Grampy walks out onto the deck in Maine and drags a director's chair into the sun. I am admiring the sea glass I found at the beach.

'There goes Watson,' says Grampy, pointing to an airplane crossing the sky and leaving cottony contrails in its wake. The Watsons, the IBM Watsons, live just down the road; they have their own airstrip, their own fleet.

'It's pretty,' I say, 'but I'm glad I'm not up there.'

Grampy nods.

'Nana preferred to travel by ship,' he says. 'She didn't like big airplanes. They scared her. The seats were so crowded, and she always ended up sitting next to some guy who tried to pick her up. Actually, she didn't mind that part so much. She liked knowing she still had it.'

I laugh. 'So the guy would try to woo her in the plane?'

'Right, he'd say all these flattering things. One time I asked a lady friend of mine "Why do you women believe all the crazy things men tell you?" You know what she said?'

I shake my head.

'She said, "Oh, we don't actually believe all those things, we just like to hear them."'

The Sound

Currituck Sound, NC. To avoid the major roads around Norfolk, I took the free ferry across Currituck Sound. It was a hazy day, the sky sleepy with heat. The crossing took about forty-five minutes and I struck up a conversation with one of the guys who worked the ferry. He was a beefy man, broad-chested with a dark crew cut, and he started telling me that he'd met his wife on this ferry and I said *really* and he said not his first wife, his second. His first wife had been difficult, always telling him what he ought to be doing, *pick pick pick*, and one morning it struck him. 'This is my life. *This is my life.* I can do what I want.'

He left her. He lived alone; it waren't easy but he done it.

One day working the ferry, he met this pretty woman and it turned out she was blind but that didn't seem to matter much and he asked her to dinner and gave her the telephone numbers of good people who would vouch for his character. It took some convincing, but by God she went. They had a fine meal and took a long walk together. After that, they saw a lot of each other until one day he proposed and she accepted and now they were happily married, quite happy indeed.

That's such a nice story, I said, and he agreed that it was.

Then he excused himself to take care of business and I tried to find the horizon in all that haze. You could sort of sense where it was, though there was no way to know for sure. Then I closed my eyes, grabbed hold of the railing, leaned back on my heels, and pretended I was that blind woman, falling in love.

Learning to Float

Grampy walks out onto the deck in Maine and drags a director's chair into the sun. I am sitting in a wet bathing suit, dripping.

'Did you go swimming?' he asks.

'I dunked,' I say. 'The water was freezing.'

'Cold water is good for you,' Grampy says. 'Did you know Jean Harlow's mother made her put cold water on her breasts every day to keep them from sagging.'

'What?'

'Right, well, it was supposed to restrict the blood vessels.' Grampy makes swimming strokes with his arms and grins. 'But she died young so I guess that didn't work out so well. You know Nanny and I used to go in once a day, twice when it was hot. Nana loved to wallow about in the water. Of course, she preferred swimming without a bathing suit.'

'Really?'

This is hard to imagine; Nana was always so dressed, everything matching.

'Sure,' says Grampy. 'One day, old Edgar was working on the house, and he went home for lunch, and we thought he'd gone for the day. We were down at the beach, and Nana wanted to go swimming, but she'd left her suit up at the house so she went in naked. Well, she was walking back up to the house in her birthday suit, and suddenly Edgar comes back from lunch.'

Grampy laughs. 'Edgar swore he covered his eyes, but I bet you anything he was peeking.'

Fear of Flying

Kill Devil Hills, NC. If waves are like orgasms, this was a woman's beach – a showy explosion of giant rollers that broke once, spewed and churned and gathered momentum until they broke again, streaming onto the hard sand in a wash of white foam. After the Currituck ferry, I'd driven to the Outer Banks, the string of barrier islands that curves around North Carolina like a parenthesis ending a sentence. On a map, these islands look fragile, as if any self-respecting hurricane could send them flying out to sea, yet man had not treated the islands with a nurturing hand. The Outer Banks are developed, overdeveloped, crudded up with strip malls and delis and miniature golf, paved over with a five-lane highway called the Bypass, where people on vacation speed fifty miles per hour to get to whatever they want to do next.

And yet it was easy to ignore all that from where I sat, on the back porch of the Tan-O-Rama, the motel I'd chosen for the sole reason that it was painted a gaudy shade of blue, like birthday cake frosting you'd fork to the side. On a beach chair, bare feet propped, morning coffee in hand, looking down a wide beach facing east, I breathed in great gobs of salt air. On my right, men in caps dropped their fishing lines into the waves off a long pier that gleamed in the sun like a rich man's brocade. The sign at the pier entrance bragged 'The Most Fun You Can Have Without Viagra,' and that seemed about right. On a beach this glorious, you could forget about ex-boyfriends and skeptical parents and dogs you had dumped and marriages that weren't happening. Here the ocean was alive and in charge.

Below me, an old guy was surf fishing. I watched him for a while, though fishing isn't much of a spectator sport. Suddenly, his line yanked forward, bending toward an invisible weight. The man cranked his reel and out came a fish, which he dragged mouth first across the sand. He leaned down and removed the hook, dropped the fish by his cooler, then quickly baited up again, cast, and stood motionless, staring at the waves once more, as if he wasn't going to let a fish interfere with his fishing.

I decided to go say hello. Somehow, I don't feel as though I've arrived somewhere until I've met somebody. I like the idea that this person might remember me. Not for long, of course. Just an hour or two or maybe until dinner, when he might retell some snippet of our conversation – what I said, what he said – and so our words would linger on, a candle not yet blown out.

Up close, the man looked older, maybe seventy. His jeans hung off what had once been a rear end. His teeth were mustard-colored. Tufts of hairs grew from his ears and knuckles, and yet he was not an ugly man; just an old guy worn down in odd places.

'Morning,' I said with a nod and smile, hoisting my coffee mug. 'Saw you catch that fish. What was it?'

'Drum,' he said, squinting at me behind green sunglasses. His black cap said Sears.

I nodded, as if I knew something about it.

'Are they good eatin'?' I asked.

Ever since Tangier, I seemed to have developed a pseudo-Southern accent, as though the humidity had gotten to my tongue and made everything sag.

'Oh, yes,' he said.

'How big was he?'

'Twenty-four inches. Six pounds.'

'Can I look?'

'Sure,' he said, waving behind him.

The fish was lying on its side, black eye up, gasping. Sand covered its scales like breadcrumbs. Its lips were thick and white as new chalk. There was something pitiful about that mouth, opening and closing, wanting water and finding only air. A pink trickle of blood and water fell from its lips. Why didn't he put the poor thing out of its misery?

I walked back. 'He's quite a fish.'

'Yes, he's real seafood.'

'Don't you want to kill him?'

'Oh, he'll die.'

We are all going to die, but what could I say? It was his fish.

'You live here?' I asked.

'My wife and I have a cottage. We come down during the weeks, then head back to Virginia weekends when it gets crowded. Been coming since 1978 – back when there was just a bunch of cottages, a grocery store. No Bypass.'

He cranked in his line. A sinker and two hooks bobbed awkwardly through the air like a lopsided mobile.

'Crab got my bait.'

He walked back to his gear, and I followed. The drum was still breathing. I wondered if the fish was in pain or merely dazed; maybe it was seeing its life pass before its eyes, a clear white light, or maybe fish saw blue. The old guy picked up his prize by its gill, exposing the crimson ruffles tucked inside the open flap.

'I'm going to put the fish in the truck,' he said. 'Excuse me.'

He took off with his fish, and I felt bad that the noble drum was going to die in a parking lot. I've always had a soft spot for fishes, their wide-eyed dignity, their scales so carefully sewn in place, their quiet domination of 70 percent of the planet, their freedom, breath by bubble, motion by tail, their hippy glide through the rock and weed, hidden current and slack tide. Way back, way way back, people believed fish were wise, sacred beings. Healers of jaundice and whooping cough and bad luck. The footprint of Buddha.

The old man returned and picked up his pole, then reached into the cooler for a shrimp, peeled it, cut it into pieces, stuck a wad of gray meat on each hook, and walked back to the surf. I followed, resolving to make our conversation outlast my coffee.

'Why do people fish off the pier?' I asked. 'Is that some kind of advantage?'

'No, they just like to sit down. But they charge you for that. Six bucks or so. If you catch something over there, all the guys squeeze next to you because they think you know where the fish are at. I'd rather surf cast. I like the quiet.'

I wondered if that was a hint. 'Am I bothering you?'

'Oh, no, company's fine.'

'My name is Lili.'

The old guy looked confused, studying me through his sunglasses, trying to figure out if I wanted something and deciding, ultimately, I didn't.

'Mine's Archie.'

'Nice to meet you. So let me ask you this, how come there are no women on that pier? Don't any women around here like to fish?'

'Oh, no, women like to fish. My wife fished with me until she had a heart problem. She'll still come out sometimes and sit on the porch' – he pointed back to the Tan-O-Rama – 'or we'll go to the bridge in Manteo, and she'll sit with me. But she don't like to come early in the morning. When I leave, she's still sleeping. So I fish until nine. Then I pick her up, and we go out for breakfast at a diner in town.'

I imagined Archie and his wife at breakfast. They probably had a favorite booth. Maybe Archie didn't have to order; the waitress knew what he wanted. This made Archie happy, that someone besides his wife knew how he liked his eggs. New York was hard that way, not much egg recognition.

The rod jerked forward. Archie started cranking, then paused.

'Here,' he said, offering his pole. 'You want to do it?'

I felt silly, like I was a little old for this, but I took the pole anyway. I'd fished before but never actually caught anything. Not that this was *catching* a fish, but I turned the crank around, hoping it was a false alarm. A moment later, a silver striped fish slid up the sand. Archie walked up a few steps and brought back my prize.

'What kind is it?' I asked.

'Sheepfish.'

The poor thing couldn't have been ten inches, tail included.

'It doesn't look like a sheep,' I said stupidly.

'Nah. But they're good eating. No size limit on sheepfish.'

Everything, it seemed, was good eating. Archie laid the fish on a soiled white towel, unhooked the hook, and dumped the dazed creature in his cooler. The fish thrashed, Buddha's footprint trapped in plastic.

'Now you can tell everyone you caught a fish,' Archie said. He grinned, as if he'd done his good deed for the day.

I smiled, trying to convey I was grateful, which I was, although I'd have rather let the fish go free. Then Archie chopped another shrimp, baited his lure, walked back down, and cast. I finished my cold coffee as the two of us stood looking into those wild, crashing waves, imagining the fish that swam beneath them.

The Wright Brothers Memorial was down the road from the Tan-O-Rama, and that afternoon I decided to go. It was on the Outer Banks, right here on the sand dunes of Kill Devil Hills, that the brothers made history when their precarious flyer staggered into the air. You'd think with a last name like Wright, I'd have loved soaring in the great blue beyond, but this Wright sister hates to fly. I hate the tin can of it. The old air of it. The careening down the runway. The desperate yank up. An hour and 35,000 feet into the flight, it would hit me: We had no business being up here. Why were the flight attendants passing out peanuts when we were all going to die? Thighs clenched, ears cocked for rattles, nose twitching for smoke, I'd daydream disaster, the wing breaking – it could break, most things did at some point – and we'd tumble to earth like a one-winged bird.

I was scared of flying, and I was even *more* scared of what being scared of flying *meant*. My father's claustrophobia began as a fear of flying. I worried that if this one fear took hold, others would follow, like smoke under the door. The whole idea of flight made no sense. How could a machine so monstrous defy gravity? A feather, maybe. A spore in the wind. But a 400-ton airplane?

'It makes perfect sense,' Stuart insisted, drawing a picture to prove it. He'd sketch a wing, the wind swooshing under, the wind swooshing over, arrows pointing up. He'd study my face, like a meteorologist waiting for a break in the clouds, wanting me, as he always did, to believe. But I've never been good at believing what I don't understand.

As a kid, I used to research the things that scared me; paranoia disguised as academic pursuit. In second grade, it was lightning, and, after poring through encyclopedic diagrams of proton clouds, I concluded that I could outlive most electrical storms so long as I didn't golf or curl up next to flagpoles. Two years later, it was liquor, a vice so insidious and toxic, I took a vow of temperance, a solemn pledge that lasted well into sixth grade. And now twenty years later, I headed off to the Wright Museum, looking to be reassured about aerodynamics. A comforting statistic or two. A diagram with even bigger arrows pointing up.

It's always bugged me how men celebrate any great human accomplishment by erecting a big phallus on a hill, and the

Wright Brothers National Memorial is a classic example. The giant stone monolith stands atop a ninety-foot sand dune, and I had to laugh when a brochure at the visitor's center referred to it as the 'Wright memorial shaft.' I couldn't resist asking a male guard if the monument's shape was significant. Something, perhaps, to do with thrust?

The guard said why no, it's a replica of a pylon, a three-sided flying marker.

I thanked him and slunk away.

Reading the exhibits, studying the life-size model of the Wrights' first flying machine, I lost myself for an hour or two. It was really quite a story. The Wright brothers were originally from Dayton, Ohio, but each winter, the slow season in their bicycle business, the young inventors traveled to the Outer Banks in search of strong winds and soft landings. This was in 1900, long before the Tan-O-Rama, back when the Outer Banks were nothing but isolated fishing villages accessible only by water. The brothers slept in a tent on the dunes, shivering at night while they listened to a lonely mockingbird. By day, they studied the physics of balance, proportion, and lift, convinced that while others had failed, they could achieve the impossible.

Their inspiration: a German glider named Otto Lilienthal. Before the airplane, gliders and hot air balloons were the only way to fly, and they tended to head in one direction: down. The museum had a photograph of Lilienthal riding his contraption; it looked like a colossal insect with gossamer wings. The inventor sat in the center in a swinglike harness, feet extended in a half pike, like a man in desperate need of a chair. It wasn't the most secure way to travel, to say the least, and Lilienthal died at age forty-eight when his glider made a fatal nosedive in the dirt. The brothers Wright were not dissuaded.

'For some years I have been afflicted with the belief that flight is possible to man,' Wilbur wrote. 'My disease has increased in *severity and I feel that it will soon cost me an increased amount of money if not my life.'*

Each winter, the brothers returned to the Outer Banks, testing gliders, changing wings, adding elevators front and back. The museum had a collection of their notebooks – black ink on old pages – filled with careful equations calculating degrees and tangents and angles of incidence and aspect ratios. Not until their fourth winter, in 1903, did they add a motor and propellers. But they didn't go far. The propeller shafts broke, nuts and sprockets flew loose, the motor konked to a halt. That night, as winds howled over the barrier islands at seventy-five miles per hour, the brothers chattered in the cold, unable to keep warm even with five blankets, two quilts, a fire, and a hot-water jug.

'The wind and rain continued through the night,' Wilbur wrote, *'but we took the advice of the Oberlin coach, "Cheer up, boys, there is no hope."'*

Finally, the Wright flyer was ready. The brothers tossed a coin to see who would pilot. Wilbur won. The brothers called five volunteers from the Kill Devil Hills Life Saving Station to witness the takeoff. But Wilbur steered the plane up too quickly and three seconds after takeoff, it crashed into the sand.

Three days later, after repairs, on December 17, 1903, in a twenty-seven-mile-per-hour north wind, the brothers, dressed in ceremonial coat and tie, again rounded up the lifesavers. Orville, an amateur photographer, set his camera on a tripod and told a volunteer named Daniels to push the button should they have success. The ground was so cold, puddles were covered with ice. The brothers couldn't hear one another over the loud motor, but shook hands.

Orville lay down on the lower wing and let go of the restraining wire. Wilbur ran alongside . . . ten feet . . . twenty feet . . . thirty feet . . . At last, forty feet down the track, the plane lifted off the ground.

Daniels snapped a photograph.

The craft rose ten feet in the air, then dropped a bit, motor chugging, propellers spinning, forward, forward, before the plane landed safely back on the sand.

Total flight time: twelve seconds. Total distance: 120 feet. Not much farther than a run to first base.

'*They have done it!*' a witness cried. '*Damned if they ain't flew!*'

Sixty-six years later, man would walk on the moon.

Before leaving the exhibit, I jotted down a quote I'd read, something Orville had written as an old man recalling his youth: '*I got more thrill out of flying before I had ever been in the air at all – while lying in the bed thinking how exciting it would be.*' I loved that. It was true of many things. Life seldom measured up to expectation. Men seldom did either. And how could they? I don't know why women expected mere mortals to match our dreams, but we did, or at least I did, or had, or still did but tried not to. Love was most delicious when I had none – when I was a thirteen-year-old virgin lying in bed, hugging my pillow, thinking how exciting it would be.

Outside the museum, in the field where the brothers first flew, stone markers measured the distances of their four initial flights, each a breath longer than the previous. I walked the connecting pathway, wind in my ears, trying to figure out why I was so taken with their story. There was a simple elegance to the tale: Two brothers dreamed they could fly; they built an airplane from old bike parts; they teetered and tottered until they took off. The Wright brothers were romantic *and* practical, contrary impulses I'd never been able to balance. Maybe it was possible to be both. Like Grampy, the old Swamp Yankee. He was practical enough to cover his soup in the microwave with a Tupperwave dome, to clothespin his various to-do lists together so they wouldn't run off without him, to keep an ice pick in his car in case he was suddenly trapped inside and had to hack his way out.

266

This was the same man who snuck into Nana's bathroom one morning and took a photograph of her climbing out of the tub, sunlight warm on her back, a picture Nana made him destroy but that he'd tucked in a pocket of memory for safekeeping (she looked like Marilyn Monroe, he told me), the same man who every summer on his way to Maine drove to Nana's burial plot in Worchester, Massachusetts, and laid plastic flowers by her grave, the same man who stopped again in August on his way home to collect his bouquet.

The more I mulled it over, the more certain I became: It was stupid to settle for a Boyfriend or a Husband. The trick was finding a man who was both.

As I walked back to my car, I thought about Grampy and Mom and her coloring books and the Wright brothers and their airplane with cotton wings, and I decided I was playing this trip too safe. I was playing my life too safe. It was time, as Ellen the psychologist would say, to take some risks. It was time I learned how to fly.

Behind the counter at Jockey Ridge State Park stood a man who could have been Superman's double: six foot four and built like a rectangle. His teeth were as white as sugar cubes, a Greek god's ass in blue jeans. If this is what it took to hang glide, I didn't have it.

'I have a reservation. Wright?'

Superman handed me a clipboard. 'We just need you to fill out this form. You can sit in there and watch the video.'

I followed his finger into a small projection room, where a mom and dad and two children in baseball caps were planted in front of a video. On the screen, a guy was standing on the edge of an enormous bridge, arms spread wide, ready to jump. Spidery hero music climaxed as he leaned back into the open air, like a trust exercise gone horribly wrong. Then he fell, in slow motion, limp and lifeless, helpless, hapless, past acres of blurry rock until one moment before catastrophe his parachute burst open and the bungee cord snapped. Cut to a doctor in a white robe talking about spinal injuries, pointing to medical charts with a frown.

Spinal injuries?

I turned to the mom. She looked unfazed. Slumping in my chair, I glanced at a plaque quoting Otto Lilienthal: '*It is a difficult task to convey to one who has never enjoyed aerial flight. The indefinable pleasure . . . experienced in soaring high up in the air, rocking above sunny slopes without jar or noise . . .*'

Otto Lilienthal was the guy who'd crashed.

The release form did not provide much comfort: 'Hang gliding is a physically demanding and inherently dangerous sport and the Parks Department is not responsible for injury regardless of faulty equipment or error on the part . . .'

Eleven sets of initials later, the instructors, Jockey Ridge State Park, the state of North Carolina, everyone was freed of responsibility for me. Even if I pulled an Otto.

Ground school began at nine-thirty with a short documentary describing our first hang-gliding lesson. We were going to start out on sand dunes – a relief. Jockey Ridge State Park has some of the largest dunes in the country, some reaching a hundred feet high, six million dump trucks' worth of sand in all. While I was happy we weren't going to leap off any cliffs, this video did bear a startling resemblance to the opening moments of *A Wide World of Sports*. These hang-gliding students were experiencing some serious agony of defeat: crash landings with 360-degree spins around the center bar, spastic legs scissoring through the air, bodies slamming into the sand.

'*Keep your eyes out ahead and keep your speed up*,' prattled a Mr Rogersesque narrator. '*Always listen to your instructor. Let the glider fly you.*'

By the time the credits rolled, even the terminally klutzy had caught a little air, and a sunset had blossomed, and the glowing students slapped each other on the back while a New Agey singer cooed: '*Your time is now. You'll learn how. You can try. C'mon and spread your wings and fly.*'

A young guy in a ponytail shuffled in and turned off the tape.

'We'll spare you the cheesy music,' he said.

His name was Lincoln, and he was here to tell us 'how this whole hang-gliding thing works.' Lincoln had bare feet.

'This is your first lesson, and we're going to keep it simple,' Lincoln said. 'All you have to do is run down the hill and wait until your feet leave the ground. The wind is blowing thirty miles an hour so you won't have any problem taking off.'

Thirty miles an hour?

That was about twenty-five miles per hour more than I'd hoped for, but I tried not to think about it and instead looked at Lincoln, which wasn't a bad way to pass the time. Lincoln wore his blond dreadlocks in a ponytail. His army shorts hung low on his hips. A tasteful hoop encircled one earlobe. His goatee was flecked with rust. He looked comfortable, as though he'd pulled on his skin this morning, and it fit just right. He reminded me of a subspecies of ski bum I'd encountered in Utah, the earthy adventure types who could seduce a girl in a single evening by talking about snow. Or in this case, wind. I bet Lincoln knew all about the wind. I bet he could smell it and taste it and caress it in the cup of his hand. I could fall for this blue-eyed boy, for a month or two. Until I woke up one morning and told him to get a real job.

'Steer with your weight,' Lincoln said. 'If the glider turns to the right, high side your weight and shift back to the middle. Keep your hands on the front bar. Not a death grip, just a light touch. To speed up, pull in on the bar. To stop, lift up. This sends the nose up into a stall, what's known as a flare. So, if you want to stay in control, is it better to go fast or slow?'

'Slow,' Dad said.

'That's what everyone thinks,' said Lincoln, rocking back his heels. 'But that's *wrong*. You want to keep your momentum. Otherwise, you turn into what we call mush.

Once you reach stall speed, you lose all control. It's kind of like a bike: The only way to ride with no hands is to get up your speed.'

Lincoln explained there are three kinds of speed – air speed, wind speed, ground speed – and that's why if you fly twenty miles per hour in a twenty-mile-per-hour wind you actually don't go anywhere and my eyes glazed over and maybe Lincoln noticed because he looked at me and said, 'We don't want to overload you with too much information, but one more thing. Where do you think most beginners look when they fly?'

'The ground,' Dad said.

'Right,' Lincoln said. 'But actually, that's *wrong*. Wherever you're looking is where you'll land. Your body will follow your eyes. When people's feet leave the ground, their brain tends to go haywire. What you want to do is look where you want to go, not where you are going.'

That one took me a minute: *Look where you want to go, not where you're going.*

'Like the video said,' said Lincoln, 'let the glider fly you.'

We walked outside to the equipment closet. Three other instructors were waiting: a teenage girl, bent at the waist, twirling her long hair like a soft ice cream cone; a shy, pimply kid in tattered corduroy shorts; and a third guy who wore beads in his hair and was bounding around the deck, sinking in wild lunges and punching the air.

'It's like Christmas, man,' he howled. 'It's *soooo* like Christmas.'

His name was Turtle. His hang-gliding license was Velcroed around his ankle. His shades were shaped like lemon wedges, and he had this way of looking through them as if they were 3-D, as if he were seeing all these cool things you couldn't even imagine. He handed me a harness and a shiny red helmet.

'I have a big head,' I said.

'Right,' he said skeptically.

'I do.'

'Try it.'

It fit.

'Guess what size it is?' he taunted.

'Men's extra large?'

'Small.'

Turtle grinned as though he'd just watched me slip into a size-four nightie.

We walked toward the sand dunes. The wind was howling. Mom and Dad didn't look eager to commiserate about the hurricane conditions so I sidled over to Turtle.

'So there must be some pretty hardcore hang gliders?'

When I'm nervous, I revert to being a reporter.

Turtle nodded. 'There are a lot of tech weenies out there who like to talk above your head and all, but it doesn't have to be that way.'

'So how did you get into it?'

'When I was a kid, I used to have these dreams of falling,' said Turtle. 'I'd just fall and fall and fall'

'Did you ever land?'

Turtle stopped in his tracks. 'If you land, you're dead.'

'Oh, right.'

We walked on.

'Then one night,' Turtle continued, 'there I was, falling again, and all of a sudden instead of falling I was flying. Flying, man, like the Silver Surfer.' He held out his arms in a surfboard zoom pose.

'Like who?'

'The Silver Surfer. You've never heard of the Silver Surfer? He was the coolest, a superhero, you know, comic books. Frank? She's never heard of the Silver Surfer.

'The Silver Surfer's great, man,' Corduroy Boy said.

I felt ninety-nine years old.

'So this is your first time?' asked Turtle.

'Uh-huh,' I said. 'I hate flying, but maybe this will be different.'

271

'Oh,' Turtle nodded, 'it is.'

The sand dunes were remarkable, thirty million tons of sand, a rolling horizon that resembled a woman lying on her stomach, full rump easing into shoulder blades, smoothing into outstretched, dozing arms. As we trudged up, the wind kicked sand around my ankles and blew hair in my mouth. Dad looked annoyed; thirty-mile-an-hour winds were not in the brochure. Ahead on a bluff, a half-dozen other students huddled in silhouette, like extras from *The English Patient*.

From the top of the dune, you could see everything, the beach houses, the Bypass, the sea. The wind was raging, and I asked a middle-aged woman with a cigarette voice if I could put my camera in her bag so it didn't get plastered with sand. Her dog, a miniature collie, was barking his head off.

Turtle taunted him. '*Mine's bigger than yours.*'

The dog growled. Turtle growled.

The dog pawed the sand. Turtle dropped to his haunches and pawed the sand.

The dog bared its fangs. Turtle threatened with dull pointers.

The dog whimpered and licked Turtle on the mouth. Turtle howled. The dog howled. Man and beast wrestled across the sand in a mad embrace.

This man was our instructor.

Lincoln coughed, then spoke with a minister's calm. 'Can you all gather around so I don't have to shout? Well, it's kind of rowdy out. In fact, on a scale of one to ten of rowdiness, this is a ten.'

A deck chair blew over.

Lincoln continued, 'On a day like this, you can get kicked way off track, so we're going to just hold on to the glider and give you each a chance to feel what it's like. Then we'll talk about our options. Now, in such a heavy wind, you want to pretty much just lay there. When we yell "Flare," don't pull up too hard on the bar or you'll turn into a human sand dart.'

A human sand dart, uh-huh. *Cheer up, boys, there is no hope.*

I fastened my crash helmet tight around my chin, then stepped into the harness, a cross between an astronaut suit and a diaper. When I couldn't figure out how to attach the bib, the cigarette woman helped me, looking under my crotch for a hook. The two of us were ducking and bending when Lincoln strolled over.

'I think I can help,' he said. 'Step out.'

I stepped out. He turned the harness upside down. 'Try it this way.'

Dad being Dad volunteered to go first. The girl and Turtle faced the glider down a long gradual slope, and Dad clipped his harness to the glider and hung like a pendulum, body parallel to the ground. Corduroy Boy held one wing. Lincoln held the other. The rest of us stood a respectful distance back, unable to hear Lincoln impart the last rites. Finally, Dad stood up, glider overhead. Gripping the front bar, he ran down the hill.

He hadn't gotten more than six long steps before the wings filled with air and he took off and yet, for one brief moment, his legs, unaware they'd left ground, kept running, swimming impotently through the air, like a cartoon character who hasn't realized he's run off a cliff. The glider bobbed awkwardly down the slope, clumsy and resentful, as if it knew the pilot hadn't a clue. The two instructors held each wing and ran alongside, shouting instructions, until, in a final huff of disgust, the weary craft collapsed on the sand, dropping Dad back to earth with a gut-slamming stomach plant.

'Awwwww,' the cigarette woman groaned. 'Tough landing.'

All at once, I wasn't nervous anymore. This wasn't hang gliding; this was a grown-up version of *One-Two-Three-Whee*. The entire time Dad had been airborne, Lincoln and the boy had never let go of the glider.

So much for taking risks.

I collapsed on the sand, relieved and disappointed. Once

you muster the nerve to be courageous, it's a shame not to put it to use. And yet I couldn't stop watching as each student ran down the hill. It wasn't the flight that fascinated me but the takeoff. The transition between running and flying, the moment when wind overcame gravity only the flyer hadn't realized it, and so his legs raced comically on. It reminded me of sex – everything seemed to these last couple days – how sex had been for me for so many years, how I'd been so busy running, I'd never noticed the lift.

I suppose most women glide into sex, but it wasn't the way I was hardwired. My body didn't soar. I was a jury-rigged Wright flyer held together with pulleys and bike grease, a dreamer's contraption with a log book of failed flights and crash landings, a spit-and-glue flying machine that only after much tinkering and many repairs would finally manage a measly twelve seconds of flight. It was an act of will. The will to unwill. But over time, each flight built on the last – until I went to the places my partners had flown off to all those years. Or so I'd like to think.

Looking back, I'm not exactly sure what I'd been doing wrong. It wasn't some Catholic guilt trip thing. An I-hate-my-vagina thing. I guess you can want something so badly it's bound to elude you. You're so focused on *making* it happen, you don't *let* it happen. The harder you try, the faster it runs away, like a small boy fleeing a grandmother's kiss. Perhaps I underestimated the power of chemistry. (*Why do we turn to science to describe something closer to art?*) The chemistry of love. The chemistry of sex. The inexplicable, irrational spark that cinches the deal. The part you can't plan or argue or hurry along, even if you are thirty-one . . . thirty-two . . . thirty-three. All I know is sex turned the corner when I learned to harness my imagination, to travel both sides of a breeze, to become, as the Wright brothers once said, 'intimate with the wind.'

If I was smarter, I'd have applied what worked with sex to the rest of my life. If I was smarter, I'd have realized a

274

seventy-five-dollar hang-gliding lesson with Lincoln could teach me most everything I needed to know about sex and marriage and love: *Relax. Hold the bar lightly. Look not where you're going but where you want to go. Let the glider fly you.*

When it was my turn to go, I felt sort of stupid, as if the instructors were doing this lame exercise to humor the tourists, which, of course, they were. I hooked my harness to the center pole and hung like a baby bundle from a stork. I practiced shifting my weight side to side to steer, then stood up and ran.

One two three four steps and I was flying, gazing down the hill and off to sea, soaring . . . okay, to be honest . . . soaring six feet off the ground. When I pulled in the bar, the glider rose. When I pushed it out, I dropped. Lincoln told me to relax, to steer with only two fingers, and he was right about that, two fingers on the bar was all I needed to make this buggy go. It was sort of like sailing, how you could play with the wind. I felt light up there, light and lithe. It was all very cool, although at times, with Lincoln and Corduroy Boy running alongside me, it didn't feel like I was moving at all: ground speed, air speed, something like that. When I landed – feetfirst in a squat – and looked back up the slope, I'd gone at least as far as Orville had that first day. It was a beginning. A New Beginning of sorts.

One by one, the students took their turns, and then Lincoln gave us 'wind checks' for a free lesson; 'We want you all to be jonesing to come back.' I was taking off the next morning but kept the voucher anyway. It felt good to have a free flying lesson tucked in my pocket.

I walked back to the park office with Turtle. We skidded down the dunes, wind in our hair. I had one more question I'd been meaning to ask.

'So who are better hang gliders, men or women?'

Turtle didn't hesitate. 'Women.'

'Really?' I said. 'Why?'

Turtle looked at me through his lemon wedges, grinning

saucily at whatever he saw. 'Well, for some reason, women find it easier to let go.'

I woke before sunrise, pulled back my curtain, and could just make out Archie fishing on the beach. For a brief moment, I considered watching the sunrise but fell back to sleep instead. An hour later, I made coffee and walked down to the beach. Archie was standing in the same place, wearing the same jeans, same cap, pole in hand, waiting for a bite.

'I had one but he got away,' he said. 'Brought him right up to the sand.'

'Well,' I said, 'I guess if there wasn't a little competition, it wouldn't be as much fun.'

Archie nodded dubiously. As he got ready to cast again, I stepped out of hook range. The shrimp chunks sizzled through the air into the sea. Then we waited. I tried to fix the sounds of the waves into memory. It seemed incredible the ocean kept doing this fancy dance day and night, even when there was no one around to listen or see.

I told Archie I was leaving today. For a while, he didn't say anything, but then he spoke, as if he felt obligated to impart some old-man wisdom.

'To be a fisherman you have to be patient,' he said. 'You never know if you're going to catch anything. Some days, you might catch a shark. Other days, you might catch a toadfish.'

I nodded, drawing an arc in the sand with my toe.

'You're right,' I said. 'And when you quit, you never know whether if you'd stayed longer, you might have caught a really big fish. But at some point, you just have to go.'

The old guy squinted at me, perplexed, then politely said, 'Right. Can't ever tell.'

Back in my room, I started feeling wistful about leaving. Though I hardly knew Archie, I liked what I knew: that he met his wife for breakfast, his wife who used to fish until her heart wore out but would still go, now and again, so long as it wasn't too early. Archie had his routine; it wasn't exciting,

276

but it wasn't a rut. He'd just whittled down his life to the things he enjoyed most. I wondered if the next person to stay in my room would go talk to Archie. I wondered if I came back next year whether Archie would remember me. Then I decided it didn't matter if he remembered me or not. What was important was that he was there. In the same place. Fishing.

When I dragged my bag out to the car, one of the managers was hosing down his Chevy in the parking lot. He waved.

'You want to do mine?' I called out with a grin.

'Sure.'

I shook my head, smiling, embarrassed. 'Oh, sorry, I was just kidding.'

The manager was nice looking, about forty-five, with a crew cut and a small, tight build. He looked like a guy who took care of difficult things and didn't complain.

'You checking out?' he asked.

'Unfortunately.'

'You really should wash down your car. Salt air is terrible for the paint. Wheel it over and I'll give it a spray down.'

'Oh, no,' I said. 'I was just joking.'

'I know, but wheel it over. Just take a minute.'

'That's awfully nice of you. Thanks.'

So I wheeled over and the manager sprayed the salt and dead bugs off my Mazda and I sat on a step in the sun and we chatted and I couldn't help feeling like we were in some 1950s' date movie where the boy washes the girl's car and the girl pretends to be shy. Maybe it was the hose. There's something romantic (and of course phallic) about a green hose in summertime, sunlight filling the spray with rainbows, water splat-splooshing against the hood. I really wasn't flirting, just being friendly. But when someone is doing you a favor and that someone is a man, especially a Southern man, and there's all that chivalry stuff happening, it ends up being a kind of flirtation. You can't get out of that box. And for the

277

moment, I didn't particularly want to. Let the man deal with the car.

'You from here?' I asked.

'No, but I've been coming here for thirty years.'

'I bet it's changed a lot. What was it like here when you were a kid?'

'There wasn't much,' he said. 'Corolla and Duck didn't exist. We used to shoot wild pigs out there. You know, you really ought to clean your car more often. Nothing kills paint like bird crap.'

'You're probably right. I drove up to Corolla yesterday. What's the deal with all those huge houses?'

It had been a grim ride. These weren't just beach houses, they were dream houses: enormous pastel birthday cakes squeezed together in a sugary row. I'd stopped in an Open House at a turreted castle called something like Ambrosia or Jubilee. A woman with a phony real estate smile told me how most people bought these homes as investments. What could be better? A dream house that turned a profit. For a brief moment, I fantasized about being an arsonist in the Monkey Wrench Gang, setting a hundred birthday cakes ablaze.

But if I was indignant, my new friend took it in stride.

'All that land was owned by this developer,' he explained, scrubbing a stubborn stain on my door. 'Made some deal with the Audubon Society and gave them a bunch of land as a preserve and then he built those mansions. They sell for a couple million a pop. Tom Cruise has one.' That sounded about right. Hollywood proportions and *Top Gun* prices. 'I've thought about getting out my binoculars and sneaking a peek at Nicole.'

I laughed. He stopped and looked at me. 'You want some butter beans?'

'Butter beans? I've never had them.'

'They're good.'

'Well, sure, I'll try some.'

I followed the manager into the motel's kitchen. A large

woman sat by the stove. She looked like a fisherwoman in a Grimm's fairy tale.

'Help yourself,' he said, handing me a plastic bowl.

The broth was a sickly yellow with gray chunks of pork bobbing on top, but there was no way to refuse it now. I fished past the pork to the giant beans, smiling like crazy to show my appreciation in case the woman had made them. I said thank you, and she nodded, and I wondered if she thought the manager was using her beans to cozy up to me, and so I smiled some more to show her I wasn't the kind of woman who took butter beans for granted.

Back outside, the manager started in with soap. I jumped up and said I could do that. He shooed me away and told me to eat my beans. They're good, I said, and they were. Creamy, warm, buttery. Then a couple of guys from the office started giving the manager shit, asking when he was going to clean *their* cars. He waved them off, blushing just a little.

When he was done, I thanked him and handed him my empty bowl. I couldn't tell if he expected something to happen next, like we'd go out for a drink, but I'd made up my mind to go. I felt bad, not giving anything back, but all I could come up with was to say something corny.

'Well, thank you. Not many people are this nice in New York.'

'I bet,' he said. 'You drive safely.'

It was such a pleasant way to leave a place – clean car, full stomach – and yet I couldn't help wondering if I had inadvertently led him on. Butter bean etiquette, always a hard call. Maybe I should have turned down the beans so he didn't get the wrong idea. Then again, if I had, he might just assume I was being coy because men supposedly like women who play hard to get. But what if you were interested in the man but not the beans? Should you accept the beans to be agreeable or fess up that you're not a butter beans kind of girl because it's always important to be who you are?

Shit. Who knew? There were so many ways to send the wrong the signal. You might as well just enjoy the beans.

On the way out of town, I popped in a tape that Peter had made for me to take on the road. At first, this gift had seemed kind of high school – this boy I know made me this tape – but I'd played the damn thing so many times I was surprised it still worked. It was the closest thing I had to conversation, to company. The songs all seemed to be about us, in one funny way or another. Elvis Costello's 'Every Day I Write the Book.' Leonard Cohen's 'I'm Your Man.' And Iris DeMent, singing in that lonesome twang of hers, 'Easy's Getting Harder Every Day.' And then there was 'I Am Superman' by REM, a song I'd never taken the time to listen to but now did, over and over again.

> You don't really love that guy you make it with now do you
> I know you don't love that guy 'cause I can see right
>   through you

Then came the I-am-Superman chorus, which made me smile. I imagined Peter roostering around his apartment, enjoying his musical bravado, laughing at himself.

It was a subtle sort of seduction, wooing by proxy, wooing with humor. But I had to admit, it was working.

Late that afternoon, I drove for miles along the coast, unable to find a room. It was Friday night, at the height of the summer season. As it got dark, I fought off panic as I traipsed from hotel to motel to campground. I debated sleeping in my car but couldn't decide which was safer, a giant supermarket parking lot or a remote side street, and the more I considered both possibilities, the faster I drove and the tighter I clutched the wheel.

Finally, in the small manufacturing town of Georgetown, South Carolina, past the overbooked Budget Inn and Days Inn and Hampton Inn, up turned a cinderblock motel with a blinking ACANCY sign. My room at the Ache and See cost thirty-seven dollars, and I got what I paid for. Cigarette burns pockmarked the bedspread and the shower curtain drooped and the chain lock hung broken and the air smelled like sulfur from the local paper plant. I asked the effeminate man at the check-in desk whether the place was safe, and he told me not to worry. He had a baseball bat. He'd come if I called. He didn't look like the kind of man who was going to protect my virginity, but I thanked him anyway. All evening, I tried not to touch anything: the sink, the toilet, the sheets. And it was here of all places, in the dirty pink of my room, I first dreamed I could fly.

The dream started in the dark; something evil was chasing me, grabbing my shirt as I ran down the street. In a panic, I fluttered my arms and hands until, somehow, miraculously, I floated into the air, past tree branches, past windows and chimneys. The landscape was black and white, smudged like a charcoal sketch. In the glow of a street lamp, I made out the city below, the treetops and rooftops, the careful lattice of sidewalk and road. Gradually, the sky filled with light, as if morning had arrived early that day. I didn't fly like a super-hero, no bold swoop and red cape; I was deliberate, cautious, slightly giddy, slowly experimenting with this new way to be. It was like adding a third dimension, a dull square rising into a glorious cube. I could fly now. This was part of my life.

In the months to come, I kept dreaming the same dream, though it never got old or mundane. Each night I was thrilled to discover that my wings still worked, and that I still had the moxie to leave ground.

Swimming with Grandmother

It was high tide in Greenwich, and the four of us – Grandmother, Grandfather, Chip, and I – padded past the cedar tree, down the grassy slope toward Long Island Sound. I must have been about seven.

Connecticut in the summer is hot and humid. Day after day, a pale gray haze lathers up the sky, and all you can do is lie around in a stupor and hope an afternoon lightning storm clears out the gunk. This was one of those days, too hot to think, too hot for grand ambition, and we were thrilled by the simple prospect of getting wet.

Grandmother led the way. I stared at her feet, bulbous with bunions that popped out between the straps of her plastic sandals. The giant purple flowers on her skirted swimsuit made the dandelions in the lawn look meek. Grandfather marched tall and straight in his navy trunks, like an aging lifeguard reporting to work. Chip was still wearing his glasses, because without them, he saw almost nothing at all. I swaggered ever so slightly in my new yellow suit, proud of the decorative daisy that hung over my belly like a misplaced broach.

When we reached the seawall and the dock propped on

pilings, Chip and I threw down our towels, peered over the edge to look for fish, then made our way down the shallow children's steps to dip our toes in the water. At the dock's far end, Grandmother lowered her stout body down the fireman's ladder and slipped into the ocean without a sound. In a minute or two, we looked up to see her white bathing cap floating away like a beach ball making a grand escape. She swam the breaststroke – head high, face forward – making smooth arcs that barely ruffled the water, as if the ocean were a dear friend she didn't want to disturb. Farther and farther she went, until her cap was just another bobbing buoy, until she was out of earshot, out of range or reach.

Grandfather wasn't much of a swimmer. He approached the task as duty, not pleasure. Climbing down the fire ladder until the water reached his knees, he pivoted, made a short half dive, swam a dozen brisk crawl strokes out, turned and chopped a dozen strokes back, as if this were a military drill, as if he were under orders. Back on the dock, he sat on the wooden bench, water dripping off taut limbs, thin chest panting ever so slightly as he surveyed his wife's leisurely peregrination past the harbor boats.

'Do you think she's all right out there?' he asked.

I sat on the dock, legs crossed Indian-style, careful not to get a splinter, and gazed up at Grandfather, who always seemed tall and wise and inaccessible. I could tell he didn't like Grandmother's straying beyond his watch. He shook his head with a mix of worry and admiration, silently marveling at how his wife, with so little effort, kept herself aloft.

'Do you think if she ran into trouble, I would have time to blow up that rubber rowboat and go out and get her?' he asked, pointing to an inflatable boat back up the hill. 'I tell her not to go out so far, and she says "you're right" and then next time swims farther. There's not much I can do. Maybe I should keep that boat inflated and tie it up down here.'

Maybe he should, I thought. By the time he ran up the hill and blew up the boat and rowed into the Sound,

Grandmother would have drowned. I tried to picture Grandfather rowing panicked strokes in a small rubber boat, but it was too scary to consider for long. Besides, Grandmother would *always* float. She was a magical being, a grand porpoise at home in her native sea. Though I could never have summoned the words, I knew swimming was a way for Grandmother to put distance between herself and the things she knew best, a way to leave the familiar behind. If she couldn't travel, she could swim. If she couldn't swim, she would read or tell stories. Water, words – either one could keep a body afloat.

After a good half hour, Grandmother returned, refreshed and content. Up the fireman's ladder she climbed, pulling off her swim cap, smiling at us, shaking her head to empty the salt water from her ears.

'Was it nice out there?' I asked.

'Just great,' Grandmother said. 'Delicious.'

That afternoon I vowed to become a grandmother as soon as I could manage. Then I'd swim out to sea where no one could catch me. Far from shore, I'd float alone, listening to the seagulls squawk and the *grubgrubgrub* of a Boston Whaler starting its engine, the quick flip of a fish fin breaking the surface and the clink of a sailboat's sheets slapping against the mast while my arms stroked back half circles of water, like a painter retracing a beloved shape. Then, finally, having ventured as far as I wished, I'd turn and look back to shore and admire my husband's silhouette, an integral part of the landscape of home, waiting for me to return.

Grampy walks out onto the deck in Maine and drags a director's chair into the sun. I am eating a tunafish sandwich with Hellmann's Mayonnaise. Grampy has just microwaved a small serving of cod.

'So, Grampy, what do you think it takes to make a good marriage?' I ask.

Grampy puts his fish down and considers.

'Well,' he begins cautiously. 'Compromise. Both people have to want to compromise. If either person is a me-first ego kind of person, it's not going to work. But if you love someone, you want them to be happy more than you want yourself to be happy, so you don't mind doing things for them.'

Compromise. Selflessness. It seems like Grampy had done most of the heavy lifting on that front.

'Then you have to pick someone you're compatible with,' he adds, 'someone who likes to do what you want to do.'

'How did you know you wanted to marry Nana?'

'Goodness,' says Grampy, as if the answer were hopelessly obvious. 'Well, when I was with her, I just felt so marvelous. And when I wasn't with her, I always wanted to be. So I figured the way I could always be with her was to marry her. I guess that was it.'

Therapeutic

Edisto Beach, SC. In South Carolina, waiting in line for a campsite at Edisto Beach, I started talking to a pair of women who were dangling out the front seat of a red truck, fishing for a breeze. We commiserated about what a pain in the ass this was – the waiting, the heat. They were smoking cigarettes and had a plastic cooler that I figured was stocked with cold beer. They looked about my age, and I hoped we might hit it off and throw back a few cold ones that night. The brunette on my side had a blurry tattoo on her shoulder that looked like a bruise. She was telling me how great Edisto was and how there was a beautiful shell beach you could walk to at low tide. The squinty blonde on the passenger side mentioned her husband, and I thought it was cool she had taken a road trip with her girlfriend, just the two of them. A minute later, a man popped his head through the blonde's open window and caressed her forearm with his thumb.

That's when I realized they had brought their men along.

It was silly to feel rejected, but I did. I was in the mood for female company, but the women I saw traveling were always dragging along boyfriends or husbands or kids with runny noses or in need of boo-boo Band-Aids. They were so un-approachable, so bogged down with people pulling at them, needing their attention. Didn't they know that *I* needed their attention?

I walked back to my car. Behind me in line was an old beige sedan with a silver motorboat on a trailer. A small man stood beside the car, smoking. He wore wrinkled green shorts and a mussed T-shirt that read: 'When I use up my sick days, I'm calling in dead.'

He nodded.

'Hot out here,' I said, rubbing sweat off my neck.

'Not too bad.'

'Ever been to Hunting Island State Park?'

The man shook his head and smiled. 'I always come to Edisto. Everything you could want is right here.'

He told me his name was Troy. He was in Edisto to meet friends and go fishing. He had a slow Southern accent, ocean blue eyes, a set of teeth chipped as broken shingles. He looked about fifty. Heavy wrinkles fell across his face. A giant scar spread across one knee. Another broke over his nose like a star.

Troy asked if I was a writer. I asked how he knew. He said he'd been watching me take notes and that his daughter was a writer in Washington for an advertising company so he knew all about the profession and what exactly was I writing? I said I wasn't sure, a travel piece maybe. He said I should write a book about Edisto because there were all these great places, like this secret shell beach. He said he was going shrimping that afternoon when his friends arrived and I was welcome to come along and he'd take me out on the water and I would love it. I must have looked skeptical because he said I should come and not worry, which I gathered was his way of reassuring me he wasn't a lech or something, just a man with a boat.

His offer was tempting. I was dying to get out on the water. After all this time at the beach, the only boats I'd ridden were ferries, which didn't really count. Besides that, I was disappointed with myself for playing things so safe. My hang-gliding foray had hardly been a high-risk venture, and only one state remained between me and Florida. It was time to put something on the line. And yet . . . and yet there was the distinct possibility this guy was a wacko. Cruising for sex, mildly deranged, pathologically dangerous. But he'd said there would be these friends along, so at least it wouldn't be the two of us, a couple, alone.

Troy lit another cigarette, crossed his arms, stretched his jaw, used his pocketed hands to hike up his shorts.

'How long do you think you'd go for?' I asked.

'We'd get you back by dinner,' Troy said. 'Why, you have plans?'

'Not really,' I said, too proud to admit I had absolutely nowhere to be.

'Then come find me when you get settled,' he said. 'I'll be around.'

In a few minutes, the guard waved me forward and offered me lot #3. A red-haired fellow, waiting his turn, said lot #3 was one of the best: on the beach, on high ground. It wouldn't flood in a storm.

'What storm?' I asked.

The man shrugged and looked away.

I drove the car over the sand road and parked on the incline leading up to the campsite. While the beaches in North Carolina are windswept and pristine, Edisto is tropical, a lush jungle of palmettos and ferns. As I unpacked my gear in the clearing, the first mosquitoes attacked. Big fat mosquitoes, aristocratic mosquitoes with bejeweled wings and full gullets; with all the cursing and swatting, it was all I could do to wiggle the stakes into the sand.

When the pup tent was once again standing, I strolled up and over the bluff. The beach was scrappy, short and littered with broken shells. Couples strolled through the white scallops of water that fanned up and slithered back with the break of each gray wave. Mothers lay long on candy-colored towels, watching their children play. You could tell they loved this stubborn stretch of shore, that no one was taking this summer day for granted.

When I walked back to my tent, Troy was waiting for me, eager as a puppy. His brown hair was tousled, as if he'd just lost his hat.

'You coming?' he asked. 'Now, Jimmy's girlfriend didn't come after all so it's just us two guys, but we're good people and all.'

Two guys. Hardly a bus tour, but a group, of sorts. Though it did worry me how Troy kept saying I didn't need to worry.

'I'm coming,' I said.

As I walked toward the car, a big-gutted man I took to be Jimmy climbed out of the front seat. He was naked but for skimpy jean cutoffs and a gold chain round his neck. His hairless belly was as round and tight as a well-stuffed pillow. He looked about my age, give or take. He looked Italian, a mama's boy raised on cannolis.

'Jimmy, niiiicesta meetcha.' His voice was pure Southern cream. I shook his hand, which fell limp in mine.

When I headed for the backseat, Jimmy insisted I sit up front. The car was one of those heavy American rides, a garage sale couch on wheels. The backseat was stacked to the ceiling with gear: clothes precariously piled in a plastic laundry basket, a guitar, a briefcase patched with duct tape. Apparently, Troy was one of those guys who lives out of his car – a breed I recognized, having become one myself.

Troy lit a cigarette and poked his elbow out the window as we bumped along the potholes. 'I want to get me some shrimp,' he said, talking to the sagging roof so his words would float back to Jimmy.

'If I get me some clams,' Jimmy said, 'I am going to make clams casino.'

'You got a pot?' Troy asked.

'Yeah, I got a pot.'

'You got spices?'

'I got salt.'

Troy pulled into the corner store. Jimmy asked me what I wanted to drink. I asked for an iced tea, please. Troy said he wanted grape juice, a drink I'd forgotten existed. A moment later, Jimmy reappeared, and we were off again, shuffling down Route 174 looking for some turnoff that kept not being where it used to be, forcing us to turn around, no easy feat when you're towing a boat.

'You are going to love this, Leee-Leee,' said Troy, stretching each syllable of my name like a tire swing, looping up and back. 'This is going to be the best chapter of your book.'

When we finally found the turnoff, we chugged along until the land ran out, and there was a small launching dock on the edge of a saltwater marsh. I could see why they called this Low Country. Long banks of chartreuse grass spread along the water like a feathery mattress. In the distance, a line of dark trees. Above that, nothing but sky.

Now we had to get the boat in the water. I got out. Jimmy got out, Troy backed the car a dozen yards from the water's edge. Jimmy unhitched the boat from the trailer, and then Troy gunned the car in reverse, crashing into the marsh. Just as water threatened to pour in the open back window, Troy slammed the brakes. The silver motorboat slid off the trailer in a sloppy rush. Jimmy lurched through the water to grab it.

'Jesus, Troy,' he howled. 'Did you have to do it that hard?'

Troy shot back up the incline and parked the car under a tree. I walked over and asked Troy if he had a sweater I could borrow because it had started to drizzle. He produced a sweatshirt from his laundry basket.

'It's clean,' he assured me. He hauled out a plastic cooler and nets and then bounced toward the dock. 'I may live like a hobo,' he said, 'but I have *fun* doing it.'

At the ramp down to the dock, Troy paused to let me go first.

'*Apray voo sea voo play.*'

Jimmy sat waiting in the boat alongside the dock. Just then Troy remembered he hadn't brought life preservers. As he talked over this quandary with Jimmy, Troy held the motor boat against the dock with his bare foot while the current pulled his legs apart in an ever widening split. Troy was saying if we got caught without life jackets, we'd be fined, but most likely we wouldn't get caught, when the boat gave a definitive tug, and Troy fell into the water with an unflattering splash.

Troy bubbled to the surface, all gee-whiz grins. Near the bow, he threw over one leg, then another, landing on deck with a flop. When he stood, his shorts sagged off his flat behind. Water rushed off his chest like rain.

'Ready?' he asked.

This is going to be entertaining, I thought. No life preservers. Capsized captain. Beer-bellied first mate. Vagrant girl vaguely searching for the meaning of life, or at least the meaning of her life. It was all so absurd – so Three Stooges – I pretty much forgot my fears of being abducted with a serrated fish knife. Opting for the middle seat, I squeezed my feet between an old battery, a knot of twine, and several sections of a plastic pole. Troy started the motor, and we took off. Jimmy perched in the prow, face in the wind like a retriever poking his snout out a car window in search of fresh air.

It felt glorious to leave land behind. We skimmed so low along the water that the grass blocked out the horizon. Every so often, a narrow channel beckoned, like an entrance to a maze. I had no idea where we were going and didn't really care. Miles above us, the sky was silent and gray. Troy nudged the boat up an inlet and cut the motor. A fishy funk rose from the mud banks. Then the men went to work.

I'd never seen anyone shrimp before, but I could see there's an art to it. A shrimper's throw net looks like a giant lace doily with weights around its circumference and a cord in the center. The fisherman casts his net overboard, trying to make it land flat and open on the water. As the weights sink, he pulls in the net by the center cord. The weights hug together, capturing whatever is caught up inside.

Troy said he was trying a new net, twice the size of his old one. He grabbed one section in his teeth and held up other portions with his hands, like a matador with a cape. He flung the net overboard. It landed in a clotted heap. Troy cursed, apologized to me, hauled in the soggy mesh, untangled it – this took a few minutes – threw it again, and watched it land in a snarl.

'I am not practiced in this,' he muttered. 'It would take two Philadelphia lawyers to see this through.'

The boat was gaining water but no one seemed to notice. I rearranged my feet, propping them on a pile of rope in the bottom of the boat. Up in the bow, Jimmy was having slightly better luck. Each throw, he caught a couple of shrimp, which he chucked into a white bucket.

'Woowooo,' Troy howled. 'You scare me to death with your talent.'

'Look, Troy,' Jimmy said. 'These shrimp are popping.'

'Well, why don't you do something about it, son?' said Troy, sifting through his net. 'I got an entanglement here.'

Jimmy held up a silvery, four-inch fish by its tail. 'Troy, you call this a toadfish or an oyster crusher?'

'Throw it here.'

Jimmy tossed the fish. Troy caught it. I flinched.

'Toadfish,' Troy said.

'Well, now, some people call them oyster crushers . . .'

'Boy, that is a toadfish.' Troy pointed to a low-flying gull. 'Jimmy boy, lookee there. That bird is coming to laugh at you.'

We had drifted close to a mud bank. Troy picked up an oar, dug it into the mud, pushing us into deeper water. The oar snapped in two. Troy tumbled overboard. A moment later, up he popped, blinking, hoisting, raining again. Neither Jimmy nor I paid much attention as Troy didn't seem to care much whether he was on the water or in the water, soggy or wet.

I was thirsty but had forgotten my iced tea in the car. Jimmy had asked me to hold his grape juice, and while his back was turned, I took a sip. *Whew*. Vodka. So the boys were secretly tying one on. I stole another sip. It reminded me of a certain fraternity punch called Jonestown Juice. I would have asked for my own, but apparently Carolina cocktails were for men only, and I didn't want to be mistaken for a loose Northern woman.

'How many cigarettes we got left?' Jimmy asked.

'There's a pack floating your way,' I said.

The bottom of the boat was now a modest pond. I moved my feet to still higher ground, this time the tackle box. Jimmy turned to me, speaking in almost a whisper.

'Troy and I work in this big company. I'm a manager of twenty-five employees. It's . . . well, it can be, real stressful. Troy and I always said we'd go fishing, only we never had the chance. Now here we are.'

He smiled as though he'd come to the end of a magical fairy tale.

'Say, Lili,' Troy called out. 'Where did you go to college?'

'Brown,' I said, hoping he hadn't heard of it.

'*Ohhhhhh*,' he trilled in mock respect. 'We are high on the intelligence quotient.'

Jimmy was spinning a shrimp around by its outstretched antennas. 'Troy, you ever eat these raw?'

'Nope. Throw it here.'

The shrimp landed smack in Troy's palm. I wished they would stop throwing the poor creatures. In one fluid motion, Troy popped the live shrimp in his mouth and chewed down hard.

'Not bad,' Troy said. 'Not bad at all. Kind of nutty.'

I couldn't watch. Instead, I peered into the bucket to admire our catch. Sandy gray and translucent, the shrimp floated about the pail like weary ghosts. You could see right through their shells to their black eyes, their oval-shaped guts, and thin intestinal tube. I studied the swarm, trying to figure out which were male and which were female. My seashore book said shrimp change sex as they age. Born male, they mature into females. Oysters are even more versatile, swapping sex every few months.

Now there's an ingenious solution to gender inequities, I thought. Yet how strange change-over day would be, tucking away your lipstick, your skirt, heading to the john for a shave. But what fun to have a penis. I'd have an erection right away. Then masturbate. Then masturbate again. Then go to a public bathroom, unzip my fly, open the handy slit in my boxers, and piss a golden arc into a urinal while chatting about the Bulls, the Lakers, the Knicks. Then I'd make love to a woman. Any woman would do. Hell, I'd probably spend all day playing with my new penis.

I looked up.

Troy was staring at me.

I took out my notebook and pen and tried to look busy.

'What is all that swamp grass called?' I waved my hand at the grass. 'Reeds or something?'

Troy squinted. 'Reeds,' he said. 'Just say the old redneck called them reeds.'

Jimmy shook his head dubiously. 'We're going to have to audit this book.'

'Audit the book?' Troy said.

'Yeah.'

'You mean *edit* the book?'

Jimmy threw his cigarette butt into the muddy water and picked up his net. Troy fussed over an extravagant knot. The two of them were so preoccupied, so utterly content, they hadn't noticed that we were now, indisputably, sinking.

Then, like an apparition from another world, a large sailboat glided toward us. Sails trimmed, motor purring, it slid through the water barely leaving a wake. The boat was called the *Therapeutic*, and behind its silver railing, two men in khaki shorts and golf shirts peered down at us, like plantation owners surveying the little people in the fields. They looked like CEOs, like men who dry-cleaned their shorts. The taller one had a gold belt buckle. I could only imagine how we looked from those swabbed decks. Jimmy, his bare belly speckled with mud. Troy, waterlogged. Me, hunched and bedraggled in a half-sunk dinghy.

'Catching anything?' called out Gold Buckle.

'They're popping,' said Troy, struggling to find solid footing among all the floating junk.

'Big?'

'Yeah. Big.' Troy held his index finger five inches from his thumb. I looked at Jimmy, who giggled, measuring out an inch or two of air. Then Troy started bragging some more to Gold Buckle, who listened pleasantly from the poop deck – I have no idea what a poop deck is, but it made me happy to think Gold Buckle was on one.

These guys bugged me. It took me a minute to figure out why. The sailboat, the CEOs, was the life I lived with Dodge. The Greenwich life. The cruising life, where you admire the local shrimpers with the same curious goodwill you use to smash hard-shell crabs with a mallet or eat your first bowl of grits. I would bet Troy's last cigarette the *Therapeutic* was equipped with life preservers and nautical charts, emergency flares, a fire extinguisher, Loran, cell phone, fax machine, waterproof flashlight, sun block (six and fifteen), two sixes of iced, bottled beer, a round of peppered goat cheese. Everything was secure behind that railing. Controlled and comfortable and calm.

I envied that life, and yet I resented it. Why? I wasn't sure. Maybe it was a class thing, always begrudging people who were more well off, assuming they didn't deserve what they had. But who was I to talk? Blonde, green-eyed, Connecticut, boarding-school brat scorning privilege. I knew I was making sweeping judgments about the Ralph Lauren sailors, but dismissing them as snobs made me feel I had been right to walk away from Dodge and from Greenwich and that now, this afternoon, I was on the right boat, even if it was a dinghy that leaked.

Lifting my sodden sneaker, I let the brown water drain.

We'd drifted near a mud flat that reeked of low tide. Nuzzling my nose into Troy's sweatshirt, I breathed in a familiar laundry detergent, then pulled the cotton sleeves over my chilled hands.

The yachtsmen wished us well and eased on their way.

'You see that,' Troy said, when the boat was barely out of earshot. 'I wish I had my guitar. All we got to do is start playing a little and singing and pretty soon they'd invite us on and we'd be eating lobster, *yes-sir-eee*. You see, one side don't know what the other side is like. They don't know rednecks like us. That's why we need the guitar. They want to meet *the people*. They got the money, but they can't sing.'

With that, Troy turned back to the water. Balancing his yellowed toenails on the boat's lip, he stared into the dark water, net above his shoulders, debating where the big shrimp might be hiding.

'Where you at?' he whispered like a mad witch. 'Where you at?'

He threw his net; it landed round and flat. Troy sighed with something like bliss.

'When I die and go to heaven, I hope God has a throw net for me. I could waste my life away doing this.'

And so the three of us wasted our lives away together for another hour or so until Troy announced it was time to drain the boat. Besides, he said, it was getting dark, and we should head back to the campsite and fix dinner. From the looks of the bucket, they'd caught enough shrimp for a few appetizers, but I wasn't about to say anything. Troy turned the motor on full throttle, and off we sped.

Gradually, the bilge water drained through the automatic bailer, a one-way valve that opened only when the boat was in motion. We are alike, this boat and me, I thought: both trying to move fast enough to let the dirty water drain.

We shot through the canals, past acres of lovely tall grass, past the pearl-colored shells embedded in the mud banks. Humid wind hung thick against our skin. The sun pushed through the gray and, for a few moments, Troy's face shone yellow in the light.

Back at the car, I made for the backseat, but Troy told me to 'sit up front with the "white folks."' I winced. The boys were all puffed up about the great grub they were going to make. Troy said he would strum guitar, and we'd have a campground singalong because people love that stuff, and I should come, and we'd grill fish and have a good time. I agreed to stop by, happy to let our adventure roll on.

Night fell. I rode my bike over to Troy's campsite, balancing a box of crackers and a bar of cheddar cheese. My tan legs were glazed with bug spray, and a flashlight bulged in my front pocket like, well, you can imagine. I found the campsite easily. The picnic table was covered with gear, coolers, potato chip bags, and camping junk. They had a fire going.

It didn't take me long to realize Troy was stone drunk. Sweet fumes leapt from his mouth, and his blue eyes leered wildly in the orange flickering light. His limbs hung loose, a puppet in waiting. As soon as I got there, I wanted to leave.

'There she is,' Troy slurred, half singing. 'Miss Lili. Miss Lili. Miss Lili.'

'Hi,' I said weakly. 'I brought hors d'oeuvres.'

'Whore's durvies.' Troy's smile ran down his face.

'Hey, Jimmy,' I said, hoping he was sober.

'Hey,' he said softly. A paisley shirt, unbuttoned, framed his belly like a cheap set of drapes. 'Want something to drink?'

Jimmy didn't seem drunk, but he looked different than he had that afternoon. Was I being paranoid, or was he trying to hold my gaze? His soft face looked even softer, and he had this silly smile.

'What do you have?' I asked.

'We got soda or beer or vodka with, well, grape juice.'

I considered the implications of each choice. Soda (good girl). Beer (fun girl). Vodka (bad girl). Oh, screw it.

'Vodka and grape juice.'

'*Really?*' Jimmy looked impressed.

My cocktail arrived, strong and purple. I sat on the wooden picnic table, opened crackers, cut cheese. The men hung over me, amazed, as if I had whipped up cucumber sandwiches in the Sahara. There was no fish or potatoes or clams casino or anything that could be mistaken for dinner, except perhaps oatmeal cream pies and a box of Cheezits.

Troy grabbed his guitar.

'Don't you worry, Lili,' said Troy, lifting his leg on the wooden bench. 'We're just having a good time. People are going to stop by and sing and we are going to *PAR-TEE!*'

He howled to the moon. Jimmy looked embarrassed.

'I have something for you,' Jimmy said. He disappeared into his tent and came back with his palm closed. He opened his hand slowly. A sand dollar. A perfect white circle, a coin angels might use. He handed it to me with a shy smile. The shell fit in my palm and weighed nothing at all.

'Some people say they're religious,' Jimmy said, 'because if you break them open, there are all these little crosses inside.'

I looked up. Jimmy tilted his head coyly.

I was in trouble.

'It's beautiful,' I said, peering into my hand. 'Where did you get it?'

Jimmy told me some story that I didn't listen to because I was trying to figure out how I was going to gracefully survive this evening without bruising Jimmy's feelings or having a park ranger arrest Troy for public intoxication. I should have realized nighttime changes everything. The benign becomes threatening. Inhibitions fade. I just wanted to escape without either man making a pass at me. Not because I couldn't handle it physically – it wouldn't come to that – but I'd hate to see a fine day of fishing go to hell.

Troy staggered over, steering toward my ear with a hand. He whispered with a splatter of spit.

'Ain't Jimmy handsome? If I were a woman, I'd go for

298

him, but I ain't no *HO-MO-SEX-UAL*. Lili, you have a boy-friend?'

I nodded enthusiastically.

'You married, Troy?' I figured he wasn't but I wanted him to think I assumed he was.

'Divorced.'

'You?' I asked Jimmy.

'Divorced.'

That got Jimmy talking about his ex-wife, how she'd fooled around with his boss, who happened to be his best friend. When Jimmy found out, he quit his job and his marriage. 'Can't work for someone like that,' he said. 'Can't live with someone like that.'

Jimmy slouched on the bench, looking wounded, as if he might cry. Fire danced across his face.

Troy was indignant. 'Can you imagine someone doing that to a big guy like Jimmy?'

I didn't answer, and instead looked around the camp-ground. Through the darkness, I could make out dads grilling burgers and kids sipping punch. Wholesome Americana in every direction. In the center of it all, the three of us – two divorced men, one single, undivorced woman – hunkered together in the shadows, tottering on sadness, sipping spiked grape juice for courage. We pretended we were proud to be traveling light, but the carefree loner routine didn't hold up to scrutiny. This was the losers' corner, no doubt about it. I tried not to think about it. No grand confessions tonight. No big Jimmy tears. No Troy breakdown. No Lili making long-distance phone calls she'd regret in the morning. Just a little shrimp talk, then bed.

'Give me a song, brother, give me a song,' Troy said. '*If I had a haaaaaammer, I'd hammer in the mooooorning. I'd* (bungled chord) *I'd* (bungled chord) *hammer in the eeeeeevening, all over this land.*'

Jimmy perked up with this distraction, tapped his foot and sang. I joined in, clinging to the familiar lyrics like old friends. Troy tipped his head back, serenading the treetops, then suddenly stopped.

'Where is everybody? I thought they would come join us.'

I didn't have the heart to say if I were a parent, I would tell my kids not to go near the drunk man with the guitar.

'Where are those shrimp, Jimmy boy?' Troy asked.

Yes, where *are* they? I wondered. Jimmy got up and boiled water, cooked a couple dozen shrimp, and divided the catch onto three paper plates. The shrimp came in two varieties: small and microscopic.

'Did we catch these?' I asked Jimmy, holding up a larger specimen.

He looked sheepish. 'The little ones. The others I got at the store.'

We peeled the shells and ate to the smell of campfire smoke. Troy strummed the guitar and crooned, '*There was a pretty girl and Lili was her name. She came to Edisto and we've never been the same. Oh, Lili. Oh, Lili. Oh, Lili.*'

Jimmy winced. '*Man.*'

I gave a theatrical yawn and said I really had to get some sleep.

Jimmy said I should wait awhile. He leaned into me, like he didn't want to be alone, like he wanted to curl around me tonight and not think about anything except how my soft body was different from hers. But I put on a face like I had no idea what he was getting at and thanked them both for dinner.

'We'll go to the shell beach tomorrow,' Troy said.

'I'm not sure,' I said. 'I'm going to church in the morning.'

'Church? What church?'

'This black Baptist church I read about.' Though the service on Tangier had been a bust, I'd generously decided to give God a second chance.

'*Jesus, BROTHER.*' Troy howled like a Holy Roller. '*SAVE MY SOUL.*'

Slipping into the darkness, I rode back to my campsite, half wondering if Troy and Jimmy would call after me or follow me back to the tent, but they didn't. I crawled on top of my clammy sleeping bag, lay on my back, and closed my tired eyes.

But I couldn't sleep.

What if Troy and Jimmy showed up? Troy was drunk and Jimmy was lonely, but neither one was planning a midnight rendezvous, were they? Not a chance. Not a single chance. Besides, there was a park ranger somewhere and everything had gone fine this afternoon until the drinking started and even then it hadn't gotten ugly, just depressing, right?

Right.

I closed my eyes and listened to tree frogs chant a murky song. The air smelled like warm earth, as if rain were on its way. I was sick and tired of being sick and tired, sick and tired of being alone. Rolling into a ball on my sleeping bag, I cursed the women in the truck with their damned husbands. I cursed myself for being a grape-juice kind of a girl, for hanging out with Troy in the first place. I cursed men, individually, collectively, the ones with sailboats and the ones who can sing. When this toxic riff finally played itself out, I drifted off to sleep.

Around 3:00 a.m., I woke up. It was raining, gently at first, then mad as exclamation points. Harder and harder, it pounded my tent. The roof was dry, so far. Shining the flashlight on the screened window at my feet, I saw rain was seeping in. Zipping the cover would kill the cross ventilation, but I did it anyway. Lightning flashed, then a shudder of thunder. I starting thinking about flagpoles and five irons, wondering whether tent poles were efficient conductors of electricity.

What the hell was I doing out here?

It was pouring. Stuart swore his tent was waterproof, but it didn't seem possible it could be this waterproof. If the storm got really bad, I could make a break for the car. Just as I'd begun to calculate how wet I would get sprinting across the campsite, a truck pulled up the incline.

Jesus Christ. Who the hell is this?

It was just like a horror movie, the classic lightning storm scene at the opening when some seemingly innocent woman is murdered so the brainy detective has a mystery to solve. The dead actress doesn't even have a speaking part. She's gone that quickly.

The truck door opened, slammed shut.

I peered through the tent mesh, body locked. *Will anyone hear me if I scream?* It seemed unlikely. Light from a flashlight wobbled toward me. Footprints pressed into wet sand. I was utterly defenseless, naked in a nightshirt, nylon for walls. *I hate camping. I hate this trip.*

'Lili,' the voice hissed. 'Lili, it's Troy.'

Jesus Christ, it was Troy. Drunk Troy, *I ain't no homo-sexual* Troy. He shined his light in my tent, looking for my face.

'Yes?' I said, trying to sound casual and polite, a hostess at the front door greeting an unexpected guest.

'Just wanted to make sure you're not getting too wet in the storm.'

Some voice came out of me. I am quite sure it wasn't mine.

'No, no. I'm fine. Not wet at all.' Rain had formed a puddle at my feet.

'Okay,' said Troy. 'Just checking.'

He paused, as if he had something more to say but didn't know how to say it. Then he hobbled through the downpour to his truck. The engine started. His headlights danced across the dripping brush as he drove off.

I exhaled. Everything was okay. Everything was just fine. Troy was being paternal, chivalrous. Hadn't he realized he would scare the shit out of me? I flopped back down on my sleeping bag, breathing slowly, steadily, pretended I was safe in my bed in New York. When that didn't work, I told myself the rain was New Age music pumped into the tropics just for me. When that didn't work, I lay on my back and waited.

And waited.

Eventually, the rain slowed to a wistful dripdrop. Then finally, I stopped thinking, and stopped thinking about how I should stop thinking, buried my head in my sweater, waited for sleep to come.

'Lili. Lili. Wake up.'

Morning. Almost morning. My eyes jolted open. *Oh my God, it was Troy again.* He was staring at me through the mosquito netting, hands on kneecaps, like a bear peering into a cave. His face looked as wrinkled as a used Kleenex. For a minute, I couldn't remember what was going on, why Troy seemed to be everywhere at once.

Propping myself on elbows, I tried to look alert.

'It's a nice morning for sleeping,' Troy began. 'But I'm putting the boat in the water.'

This took me a minute. 'I'm going to church, remember?'

'*Oh, geez*,' said Troy. 'I forgot. Sorry. Okay . . . Well . . . Sorry. See you later then.'

I wanted a room with a lock and I didn't care if it was that Bates Motel back in Georgetown. It was only seven o'clock but there was no way to sleep. Carrying a clump of clothes into the communal bathroom, I tried to clear my head with a stiff hairbrush and splashes of cold water. The face in the mirror didn't look like mine. It occurred to me that my trip might be working: maybe I was someone else by now.

Later that morning, I parked in back of the New First Baptist Church. This was the reason I'd come to Edisto in the first place. One of my guidebooks claimed this was the first church in America built by a woman. Her name was Hepzibah Jenkins Townsend, and she was a white woman raised by slaves. Born in South Carolina in 1780, Hepzibah was just a baby when her mother died and her father was imprisoned during the Revolutionary War. The slaves who worked the indigo plantations took in the little girl and raised her as their

303

own. Years later, she married a wealthy indigo farmer, though she wasn't the kind of wife who was cowed by her man. When her husband refused to include his daughters in his will, Hepzibah moved out in protest. Mr Townsend relented. Later, she wanted to build a Baptist church for the slaves who'd raised her, but again her husband opposed her plan. Undaunted, Hepzibah built a tabby oven (tabby is a cement-like material made from crushed oyster shells) and opened a bakery that sold bread and cookies from a roadside stand. Dollar by dollar, the nest egg grew until, in 1818, a church was erected which Hepzibah deeded to the black Baptists of Edisto. Years later, when she died, she was buried in the old church cemetery.

I liked the story and decided to go to a service at the church. It wasn't much of a plan, but it felt right. I was trying to trust these instincts, to steer my glider with only two fingers on the bar.

The old church was white clapboard with four skinny columns and a steeple like a top hat. Someone had told me regular Sunday services were held in the church's addition, and sure enough, people were filing into a white block building. Too bad. I'd wanted to sit in Hepzibah's church. Walking through the wet grass, I searched for Hepzibah's grave, wishing the sun would come out, but a gray haze covered Edisto tight as a terrarium. Even after last night's downpour, the sky was mustering the energy to rain.

The cemetery looked forlorn. Old grave markers, square slabs of white stained stone, tilted this way and that, as if overpowered by ancient winds. One obelisk-shaped marker was particularly tall and encircled by a rusty iron fence. Weeds clamored at its feet. Sure enough, it was hers.

Hepzibah Jenkins (1780–1847) . . . Her character was so strongly cast, and her impulses were so generous, that she was an object of indifference to no one. From early life, she professed the Gospel of Jesus Christ, and her faith continued firm and constant to the end. With this, she blended so much humility that her most frequent religious confession was 'I am a sinner saved by grace.'

I am a sinner saved by grace. I love the word 'grace.' The way it always looks better capitalized, Grace, the way Gr stands as solid as a column or a good idea, and then *ace* sails on forever, a bird over water. My first brush with grace was in grade school when we were made to say it every lunchtime before opening our paper sacks.

God is great.
God is good.
Let us thank him for our food.
Ahhhhh-men.

My little mouth repeated this grace without thought or feeling, holding the *Ah* in Amen with bratty ridicule. Then there was a short silence until some smart aleck would pop a potato chip bag or, even better, fart.

Years later, I fell in love with the secular connotations of Grace. It reminded me of a wisp of tall grass bending to the wind or a pregnant woman, her stomach round as the moon, or a clean dive into clear water. I wanted to move through the world with Grace but instead cut a bedraggled figure, dropping things, losing my way, swearing, late, always late, latching onto love only to bail out, leaving ragged ends, like a dull knife trying to cut rope.

All around the churchyard, families tumbled out of American cars. Men in dark suits. Mothers and little girls in pastel finery – lace dresses and freshly ironed gloves, black umbrellas tucked under their arms. Feeling underdressed in my khaki shorts, I ducked behind the church to put on lipstick, fluff my hair, scrape sand out of my ears.

This was my first black church service. I wondered if I was intruding. Surely I wasn't their first white guest. Still, in the foyer, timidity overcame me. I pretended to read some plaque about Hepzibah and tried to muster my nerve.

'You coming in?' asked a voice at the door.

'I would like to.'

'Well, you're welcome.'

A large woman in a bleached white dress handed me a program. I slid into a pew toward the back and tried to blend in, which was pretty much impossible. Women with long sparkly nails and full bosoms bent this way and that, pecking cheeks and hugging and asking their *how-yous* and *how's so-and-so?* And the hats – I have never seen such hats: a rombus-shaped hat and a wedding-cake hat and a figure-eight hat and a dinner-plate hat and a hat that looked like Mickey Mouse ears and one that spiraled around like the Guggenheim museum. Some had brims and others lace. Many hats were bigger than the faces they shaded and defied all laws of gravity. Amid such pageantry, I felt plain, desexed, a flat-chested stick doll in hand-me-down clothes.

The church itself was modest, ten rows of pews in two sections, a tile floor, five gold-colored chandeliers. Above the pulpit hung a cross outlined with light bulbs, which reminded me of Atlantic City. This didn't feel like a particularly holy place, more like a vessel ready to be filled.

Then the singing started. Not all at once, but gradually, as if an urge had welled up and now needed to be expressed. Up at the pulpit, a man with an electric guitar strummed a few chords. The chorus, ten beaming ladies in white dresses, sang and clapped their way down the center aisle to join him up front. The song had four lines, which the chorus repeated in ever-widening circles of sound.

Oh, *what a mighty God we serve*
Woke me up this morning
Got me on my way
Oh, *what a mighty God we serve*

I kept waiting for the next stanza, for the piece to end or progress, but they sang the same four lines again and again.

With each verse, the sound grew richer and the words meant more. Sweat clung to the back of my neck, to the creases behind my knees. An usher handed me a paper fan. I turned it over, read the funeral home ad on the back, then waved sticky air past my face and wondered, as I always do when I fan myself, whether the exertion of fanning actually made me hotter. It didn't matter, I suppose, it felt good.

Everybody was letting loose now, like corn kernels sizzling in oil preparing to pop. People stood and clapped and swayed, rocking elbows, tilting chins toward heaven until the only ones left seated were the elderly, infirm, mothers balancing babies, and me. I couldn't decide whether to stand. I wondered if I looked aloof, not joining in, and yet I didn't want to seem presumptuous or phony. After all, I was a guest, a white guest, the *only* white guest, the worst kind of religious tourist, an agnostic hoping to find God on her summer vacation. The presumptuousness of this desire made me cringe.

> Oh, *what a mighty God we serve*
> *Woke me up this morning*
> *Got me on my way*
> Oh, *what a mighty God we serve*

I stared at the backs of people's heads. Hair so different from mine. Cornrows and tidy Afros and straightened hair and straightened curled hair and little plastic barrettes and the short squiggles of men's hair cut close to the scalp. Then I glanced up to the church windows, stubbly, opaque glass, the kind that doesn't let you see out. It felt as though this church were the only thing alive, as if the rest of South Carolina had shut down, waiting for us to be done.

> *Woke me up this morning*
> *Got me on my way*

307

I thought about Troy, waking me up, getting me on my way. I thought about his yellow headlights pulling up last night, and the old redneck bending over and checking in on me. I tried to think about God but didn't know where to start. *God is Pooh Bear. The Fat Lady is Jesus Christ Himself. The Father, the Son, the Holy Spirit. God is great, God is good, Let us thank him for our food. Woke me up this morning, Got me on my way, Oh what a mighty God we serve.*

Whom did I serve?

Myself most of the time. Sometimes, I wished I had been raised religious. It seemed a lot easier to be born into religion than adopt one later. What comfort to believe God is watching over you, that there's a master plan, that there's *some* plan, that you're part of something larger, a piece of a whole. Spiritual . . . *ha*. I was a lost satellite circling in the dark.

When the chorus finally stopped, it wasn't like those Episcopalian hymns that end with a decisive major chord. Rather the hymn trailed off with hoots and claps like an old car coughing and sputtering to a halt. Up front, a man in a double-breasted suit started preaching about Jesus. I couldn't hear him very well, but it sounded like a testimonial. The man worked himself into a trance with his chanting. Eyes closed, he built on his rhythm. The woman next to me in a toothpaste-green dress started yelling out *that's right* or *Amen*. Her hands were weighed down with heavy gold rings, like someone loved her a lot and wanted to show it. She lifted them to clap and fist the air, doing her part to cheer the good sinner on.

When the man wore himself out, the reverend took to the pulpit. I was expecting some showy preacher, but this man was no caricature. In his black robe and billowy sleeves, he looked serious, ageless, like he could look inside you and figure things out. When he started preaching, people were still hollering and praying and paying him no mind, but he didn't take offense. After announcements about invalids in hospitals and Bible study and people we should pray for, he told us the message of the morning: '*It is examination time.*' His cadence reminded me of fly fishing. He cast out his line and then, with a quick wrist, snapped back the fly.

'Now, when you go to the doctor, he looks you over, up one side and down the other; they call that *preventive medicine*. Well, you need to look into your heart. You need to look into your heart and do some *preventive maintenance*. Because right now, *it's examination time*. When you done wrong, you got to go back and reconcile. Then it will be all right. But you must look at yourself. And it will be all right. If you look at yourself. Because only *you* can judge *you*, and *when* you judge you, then *everything* is going to be all right.'

Now he was chanting, sweat beading up, glasses fogging.

'*It'll be all right. If I examine myself. It will be all right.*'

Up came the tambourines and the guitar and the preacher chanted louder and louder until I felt like we were broken sticks swept up in his cyclone. The preacher cajoled and exhorted and demanded that we look into our hearts, deep into our souls, and take stock of what we saw, take stock of where we were, make changes, follow the righteous path of *Jeeeeeesus*.

Then it was communion time. I stayed in my pew. I'd once made the mistake of taking communion. The summer I was thirteen and working as an au pair, my family took me to Easter service, and when it came time for the Eucharist, I shuffled up to the pulpit because I was too embarrassed to let everyone know I didn't believe in God. Terrified I'd be fingered as a fraud, I kneeled when the person in front of me kneeled, ate the wafer, sipped the syrupy wine. It seemed to go okay. Back at home, we devoured a carton of donuts, and all I could think was that Christ was slurping around with all that powdered sugar and jelly. It was one of the few times I felt God was watching me. And he wasn't pleased.

After communion, the chorus started up again.

Sometimes you have to pray to get along
Sometimes you have to pray to get along
Sometimes you have to pray to get along
Just can't hardly get along

Sometimes you have to shout to get along
Sometimes you have to shout to get along
Sometimes you have to shout to get along
Just can't hardly get along

Sometimes you have to . . .

As the voices grew stronger, everyone stood back up and the church rocked on its heels as if it couldn't contain all the sound, as if the music would punch open the windows, throw back the doors, burst onto Route 174 to call forth the people of Edisto. I sat in my pew and watched, feeling like a white girl, a white girl who didn't believe.

'Oh, yes *indeeeeeeeed.*'

The woman next to me in the pale-green dress was letting loose. She punctuated the melody with '*Oooohh yes*' and '*My Lord*' or sometimes, a musical holler. Everything inside her was coming out, a catharsis, a purge. I liked the way these Baptists just flat out said that life was hard, instead of maintaining a Yankee stiff upper lip. They just dumped it all on Jesus, a fine idea in my book. There was just one problem: I didn't believe in God. I couldn't *imagine* believing in God. I mean really *believing*, not just *pretending* to believe, or *trying* to believe. So many things didn't add up. The same old unanswered questions: How could one being, no matter how divine, create a world? And if he had, why hadn't he done a better job of it? How could anyone remember so many people let alone love them? Why didn't he put in an appearance every now and then, for the fans back home? It made no sense. But I suppose it wasn't supposed to. You weren't supposed to *think* God, you were supposed to *feel* God. Like

310

love. *And what the hell did I know about love?* My version of love was so stingy. Two minutes after I met a man, out came the abacus to figure out what was in it for me. No wonder I didn't walk through the world with Grace. Grace, the marriage of strength and surrender. Grace that night diver, trusting the cold water to open for her shoulders, waist, feet, then shutting tight again, erasing all trace of the fall. Surrender. Believe. I didn't know how to do either.

That's when I stood.

I didn't deserve to stand, but I stood anyway. I stood and leaned against the pew in front of me, moving my lips silently to the mesmerizing words, which having been repeated so many times, had lost all meaning or, rather, seemed to mean everything, as if all other words were superfluous, because these four phrases embodied everything that needed to be said.

Sometimes you have to sing to get along
Sometimes you have to sing to get along
Sometimes you have to sing to get along
Just can't hardly get along

That's when I realized if I let this music go any deeper I was going to cry. Standing in this roaring congregation, I felt utterly alone. They had God, and I didn't. Maybe I never would. I bit my cheek and set my jaw and yawned one of Stuart's fake yawns and dug my nail into the cuticle of my thumb and tried to pretend I was somewhere else, but there was no escaping the singing Baptists, the wooden pew, the cardboard fan with the tongue depressor stick. As the thunderous chorus called forth the Savior, I stared hard into the church's cloudy windows, wondering if, on the other side, it had finally started to rain.

When the service ended, the woman next to me held out her hand. It felt soft and worn as she bounced our hands about, then she looked at me over her bifocals, then *through* her bifocals, as if to make a thorough study.

'Thank you for coming,' she said.

'No,' I said. 'Thank you.'

I walked to the entrance. It was pouring rain. Women huddled in the foyer. Husbands raced to bring the cars around. I still wanted to see the inside of the old church and so darted across the grass and pulled on the side door. Inside, the church felt solid and welcoming. The ceiling was high, the walls the color of cream. Four tall windows on each side let in a gentle light. A dozen columns marched through the pews, six in each row. A second-story balcony wrapped around overhead; I envisioned children's faces peering down, waving, dropping wads of paper on a lady's extravagant hat.

I sat in the fourth pew. The noise outside – the rain and car horns and women calling out good-byes – seemed miles away. With one thumb, I rubbed dried sweat off my palm, twisted my neck until it cracked, smoothed the wrinkles in my cotton shorts, then looked up at the altar, cluttered up with an old refrigerator, a card table, a file cabinet, a couple storage boxes. This was Hepzibah's church. Her spirit had nailed the boards and cut the windows. It was here I tried to pray.

I've never known exactly how to pray, but I did the best I could. Leaning on the pew before me, I thought carefully of the people I loved: Mom and Dad, Chip and Sue, my nieces, Grampy, Grandmother, my close friends, the exes; I wished them health and happiness and a few moments of peace. I promised to give more and expect less. That's when I realized I was *thinking* this prayer, not *feeling* it, and I tried to shift the prayer from my head to my heart and then finally nudge it into my soul. I had no idea where my soul was, but imagined it as an inner-body, outer-body, all-body sort of thing, like a woman levitating in a magician's trick. Then I tried to send the prayer to God, which felt as futile as mailing a letter without an address, the kind of botched correspondence that winds up in the post office slush pile. I don't know whether the prayer worked. But I tried.

When I was done, I slid back in the pew, hands empty and open in my lap. As my eyes ran up and down a string of Christmas lights knotted on the card table, I thought about all the time I'd wasted, wondering and worrying, afraid to give myself to anyone, afraid to let anyone give himself to me. I thought about the fishermen in Gloucester falling off the greasy pole as they reached for the flag. I thought about Grandmother wanting to travel but swimming instead and how she'd always float back to us, sticky with salt. I thought about Dad eating out that first time and how he wasn't sure where to put the tip on the credit card slip and how Mom leaned in close to show him how. I thought about Jimmy giving me a sand dollar, about all the tiny crosses hidden inside, and how you could only find them if the sand dollar broke.

And that's when, finally, I wept.

I hadn't been back at the campground ten minutes before up walked Troy. If the old boozer was hung over, he hid it well.

'How's church?'

'Good.'

'You the only white girl?'

I nodded.

'Did they say "*Praise Jesus I AM FOUND*"?' Troy did his evangelistic routine, staggering back from the knees, chin to the sky.

'More or less,' I said.

'You still want to go to the shell island?'

'I don't know. I guess it's still sort of raining.'

'It don't matter to me,' Troy said. 'I'm going out in the boat regardless. If you want to go, I'll take you. If you don't, that's fine, too.'

'Where's Jimmy?'

'I *knew* you had a thing for him.' Troy grinned as wide as a boy with a secret. 'Girls just *love* him. He left early this morning. Had to go see his sweetheart. They live together. He don't love her though. She bosses his ass all around. *"Jimmy, whatchu doing down in Edisto with that no-good Troy?"'*

What was I doing in Edisto with this no-good Troy? At this point, I was beyond caring. I'd already paid for another night at the campsite and had no plan for the day.

'You leaving today?' I said, trying not to sound hopeful. I didn't want this outing to spill into a cozy evening for two.

'Yeah, as late as I can. Got to work tomorrow.'

'Well, I'd like to go to the island, if you're sure you don't mind.'

'No, course not,' Troy said, cheering right up. 'Bring your camera. I got to show you something. *You're gonna go crazy.*'

I gathered a few things together and climbed into the passenger seat of his wide American ride. Troy was all grins, saying how much he admired my spirit because I just *did* things and I didn't let anybody get under my skin. Troy swore he was going to show me a stretch of road I'd never forget in all my life because it was so beautiful and I would absolutely have to take a picture to show everybody back home. We drove back up Route 174 and turned off down a small side road.

'Lili,' he said. 'Now, don't be scared when you get down here. You are going to think you are at the end of the earth.'

Through the windshield, I could see what what he meant. A line of enormous live oaks formed a majestic archway over the road. Before this trip, I had never seen live oaks, but I'd fallen hard for their charms. The day before arriving in Edisto, I stopped at Angel Oak, the oldest oak in South Carolina, some fourteen hundred years old. Its trunk was twenty-five feet in circumference and its limbs were gray and heavy as an elephant's trunk. Some branches were so enormous they dragged along the ground until, in an act of defiance, they rose again, reaching for the sun.

These Edisto oaks were dramatic in a different way. Limbs

314

stretched high over the road as if reaching for a lover on the opposite side. Each branch was covered with feathery Spanish moss, like an elegant woman dripping in boas. The trees were so entangled you couldn't tell where one tree began and another ended. It radiated the hushed awe of a cathedral.

'If I die, I want to die right here,' Troy said, slapping the steering wheel. 'I'm for real. You can bury me right here.'

'It's beautiful,' I said. 'Let me take a picture.'

I got out and tried to cram all those trees into my viewfinder, but it was hopeless. I snapped anyway, then got back in the car and sighed.

'Now don't worry, but I always drive real fast through here,' Troy said. 'It's just something I do.'

The car lurched forward down the single-lane sand road. Faster. Faster again. Troy wasn't kidding. Perhaps this was his way of assuring he *would* die here. Stones flew, pinging furiously against the wheel well. The engine moaned as we raced twenty . . . thirty . . . forty miles per hour. The road kept curving, making it impossible to see what was coming around the bend. As the car raced on, I felt like we were riding Chitty Chitty Bang Bang and the old jalopy was getting ready for liftoff. I wondered if Troy had been drinking.

We passed a yellow caution sign: CHILD AT PLAY.

Troy sped up.

'Ooowooo,' he whooped, looking over at me, taking his eyes completely off the road, taking his hands completely off the wheel. 'They've seen me. Child at play.'

Bracing my hand against the dashboard, I imagined the accident, the scene at the hospital: me, a bandaged mummy in a Charleston hospital, Troy in the next bunk, bottle under the sheets, serenading me with his guitar. *Oh, Lili, Oh, Lili, Oh, Lili.*

Just then, I saw the end of the road. Troy let up the accelerator. The car slowed down. In front of us stood a rundown house, a small dock, and a colossal man with a bearded face and black waders. In one hand, he held the collar of a large growling dog.

'There's a *real* redneck,' said Troy, sounding protective. 'Don't worry. I talk their talk.'

Troy got out and shot the breeze with the man in waders and paid him a five-dollar docking fee, keeping one eye on the dog and its fangs, and soon we were back on the water. The boat was gunked up with yesterday's mud and smelled like yesterday's fish.

My sense of direction is so lousy I never did figure out where we were or where we went but about ten minutes later we motored up to shell beach. It didn't look like anything special. Just a stretch of barren shore, flat ocean on one side, grasses on the other. The cross current made getting to shore dicey, but Troy managed. A few feet from the beach, he hopped into the water, hauling in the boat so I could stroll onto the sand without getting my feet wet.

The beach was empty, not a person, not a boat. Just Troy and me, a light breeze and a scurrying tide. It felt as though Troy had brought me to the first beach on earth, or maybe the last, like we were the sole survivors in an apocalyptic movie. Man and Woman. Sucking on seaweed, fretting about the continuation of the species.

Damn. I was out there now. If Troy was going to pull something, this would be the place to do it. No one knew where I was. *I* didn't know where I was. Well, it wouldn't do to look scared. I put on my everything's-okay face and announced: 'I'm going to go for a walk.'

Troy nodded.

'All up and down here are shells,' he said, pointing. 'Tons of 'em.'

I headed down the beach, waiting to feel a hand on my shoulder. I turned. Troy was messing with the boat. I headed down the beach again, waiting to feel a hand on my shoulder. I turned. Troy was *still* messing with the boat.

Then it occurred to me that I was being a complete jerk.

316

Here was a guy who had offered me exactly what I wanted, a boat ride to the shell beach, the beach the girls in the red truck told me was remarkable. Not only that, he wasn't one of those clingy, needy guys who wants to *share* every moment, puffing along at your elbow, making lame-o chitchat. No, this guy let me walk the beach alone. And isn't that what we all wanted? A man who lets us walk the beach alone. Or better yet: A man who lets us walk the beach alone and takes care of the boat.

And how do you treat him in return?

Doubt him. Take him for a creep.

You would think after spending three hours with the Baptists, I'd have learned a thing or two about faith, but no. I felt so ashamed it was like I *was* in church, listening to the kind of sermon I like best, the kind that makes you feel low and mealy and determined to do better next time, the kind that makes it such a pleasure to walk outside afterward and see the world waiting for you, as if you deserved to be part of it all, as if you'd been redeemed.

I looked down at my feet and started paying attention to the shells on shell beach. Giant bunches of them clustered together at the high-tide mark. Clam shells, cockle shells, razor clams, dosinia shells, silvery jingle shells, moon shells, bits of coral. Here and there a giant conch, which I pressed against my ear, listening to its windy breath. I wandered back up the beach toward land. Yards of grass, as tall as me, grew along the beach's edge. Beyond it, clumps of green undergrowth, fields of marsh grass and pockets of swamp. And quiet. The breezy quiet of open space, echoey and vast, the sort of expanse that makes you feel small and yet at peace. Nothing moved. It's strange how little life you can see in such spaces. Creatures crawl and burrow and swim and buzz and plod, and we look out and see only a gull or two. So much goes on beneath the surface.

I walked for a half hour or so, filling my pockets with shells. As I was about to turn around, I spied an enormous sand dollar, bigger than the one Jimmy had given me. It had five thin slits, narrow as keyholes, and a delicate five-petaled flower engraved by a loving, steady hand. Its lavender underside had a nubbly texture like a fingerprint, and there was another flower, this one fuller, like a poinsettia. Troy would love it. I walked back down the beach to show him what I'd found.

When I got back, Troy was sitting on the sand feeding Cheezits to the gulls, trying unsuccessfully to get a fat bird to eat out of his hand. A thin layer of sand covered his entire body, as if he were a clam dunked in batter. I emptied my pockets and arranged my booty like a still life.

'Wow,' he said. 'You did great.'

'Check this out.' I passed him the sand dollar.

'You found one. That's a beauty.'

'What kind of shell is this?' I asked, holding up a shell that bore a startling resemblance to Troy's toenails.

'A mollusk?' offered Troy. 'I don't know. What do I look like? A marine biologist? You hungry?' He passed me the Cheezits.

'Thanks.' I threw back a few and felt my teeth squeak.

'Might be a little sandy,' Troy said.

I nodded, forcing a swallow.

Troy sighed happily. 'You are such a trusting person, Lili.' I gazed out to sea, wondering where this line of conversation was heading. 'Not many people would come out here with me. You just trust *everybody*. Wait till I tell people back in the office about the nice person I met this weekend. They are not going to believe it. I wish I had a video of you I could show them.'

I felt like a trophy bride.

'You're cute as pie,' Troy said. 'Now, I'm not flirting with you. I am just saying you are cute as pie.'

I didn't know what to say. Perhaps I should have chimed in about how nice *he* was, which was true, or how cute as pie *he* was, which was sort of true; Troy was charming in his own way, but I didn't want to tip the balance of our fragile arrangement.

'What's the name of your boat?' I asked, trying to nudge the conversation along.

'Well, it don't have a name, but I think I'll name it *Lili*, because I am awfully fond of you. *The Lili*. You know if I was lucky, I'd get stranded here with you.'

'You, me, and a box of Cheezits.'

'Wouldn't need nothing else.'

We sat for a few moments and my head felt thick and heavy and I realized I was absolutely exhausted. The fitful night in the pup tent, the three hours in church, the heat, my endless musings over the precise circumference of my stupidity, the million and one wonderings about whether I was playing things too safe or not safe enough, the pondering over who had God and who didn't, the worry over whether I'd ever find love that would last, all of it had left me worn thin.

I needed to put my head down and rest.

'I might have to take a quick nap,' I said.

'*Oh, man*,' Troy said giddily, as if I'd proposed we go out for pizza. 'That sounds good to me.'

He propped his head on his tackle box, then curled his torso like a shrimp. I lay on my side, facing away from him, rested my head on my arms, and closed my eyes.

Troy called out in his best girly falsetto: '*And then the old redneck lay down on the shell beach and fell asleep . . .*'

I laughed, too tired to reply. The sand softened into a mattress. The sky dropped over me like a blanket. In the haze of sleep, I decided I didn't have to watch out for Troy; Troy was watching out for me. A moment later, when Troy tugged my arm, I didn't cry out. He stood over me, holding a yellow life preserver.

'Use this as a pillow,' he said. 'Wake me up if you want to get going.'

I thanked him and pressed my cheek against the soft rubber

and closed my eyes and once again felt the beach close in tight around me. The ocean streamed in and the ocean streamed out, whispering something I couldn't quite hear.

In an hour or so, I woke up. Troy opened his eyes a few minutes later. We sat up on the sand, side by side, a bit dazed, staring out at the horizon, that long line that cuts the world in two. Though I didn't think it possible, Troy looked even more sandy. He stretched his right arm toward me like half a drawbridge.

'Take my hand,' he said.

'What?'

'Take my hand.'

I took it, lacing my fingers in his, our arms forming a steeple over the sand. Troy beamed, squinted, like he was fixing this moment in his mind.

Lazily, we motored back to the landing and secured the boat to the trailer. Troy said he wanted a grape juice and I said me, too. The ice in the cooler had melted. The half-frozen bait was swirling around the water with the grape juice and vodka. Troy found a plastic cup, cleaned it with fish water, then poured me a drink. Half juice. Half vodka. No ice. It tasted like a melted Popsicle, only better.

As we drove back to town, the sun came out. I leaned out my window into the light, feeling triumphant. Shell beach was warming into a fine memory. Troy and I didn't talk much, just sipped and drove past the low houses, the low land.

'Take a drive round town?' he asked.

I nodded. And so we toured around Edisto on a Sunday drive. Troy showed me the house he used to rent and one he wanted to buy. I picked out my dream house, a two-story white cottage with a wide porch. Troy insisted on buying me a bag of ice. Finally, we pulled into the campground.

'I have some of those cheese and crackers,' I said.

Troy nodded. I guess neither of us was quite ready for him

to leave. So we sat before a chorus of mosquitoes, and I cut slices of cheddar cheese.

'So you love this boyfriend?' Troy asked. Somehow his question didn't surprise me.

'I think so,' I said. I was thinking of Peter.

'Well, make sure you do,' he said. My eyes followed the curve of his shoulders, the wrinkled armpits of his T-shirt, the lines weighing down his eyes, his cheeks. Suddenly, he looked older. As though he'd made most of life's hard choices and now was living with them, for better or worse.

'You got to be sure you're in love,' he said. 'I have been in love, real love, but not with my wife. I thought I loved her, but I didn't. We were married, but we weren't in love.'

He paused, rearranged his mouth. 'Well, I wish you well. I hope you learn what you need to learn because you are a nice person. If I were twenty or thirty years younger, I'd ask you to marry me.'

Troy smiled, his face downturned, sea eyes imagining how it would be.

For the first time, I put our age difference aside and wondered if Troy and I could ever have worked, when Troy was younger, when I was younger, before he'd started to lean so heavy on the booze. I pictured us on the shell beach, taking hits off a bottle of Chianti, singing Peter, Paul and Mary, off kilter, off key. Troy would have tried to find me a shark's tooth and come up empty. I would have buried his feet. We would have had great fun until the whole thing blew up and went to hell. Which it would have. No doubt.

When Troy finished his daydream – I wondered if his was like mine – he got up. I got up. Troy gave me a hug. We held each other and blinked. Troy pulled away, and I watched his bare feet cross the campsite until he paused and turned around.

'Some lucky guy is going to get you one day.'

'I hope so,' I said, swatting a mosquito, missing. Troy climbed into the seat of his overstuffed car, tooted the horn, and drove down the sandy road, boat wobbling through the potholes, hand waving out the open window.

I let go a long sigh.

Troy was a good man. No sooner had I decided this – definitively – than I missed him. I cut myself a slice of cheese and opened a beer and traveled back into my daydream, letting myself picture the two of us together. Hell, it all starts with imagination. The bottom line is there's just no telling with men and women. Not really. Not ever. Even when everything's settled, it's not. Even when there's no way, it's all still possible.

In Bed

We stopped short of making love. After three months of false starts, Peter and I were getting used to all that heat having nowhere to go. Peter was an idealist; I was learning to be. It would be right or it wouldn't be, and so we pulled apart, lay on our backs, cooling down, slowing our breath, settling into the warm sweat of our bed.

Spring in New York, a time for romance and all that, and I was in the thick of it now, like some dumb movie, a love story no one quite dares believe. Except this version was messy, shiny and mottled as a bower bird's nest. I looked out my window to the water towers on Broadway and felt worry inch in close. Peter tugged the hair on my forearm, quick pulses, the ticking of a secondhand.

'When's he coming?' Peter asked.

'Next week,' I said. My thumb circled the meat of his palm. I thought about Stuart in Utah, packing up his things, his bungee cords, his duct tape, his dog, getting ready to drive east to come live with me. 'What am I going to do?'

Peter spoke slowly. Each sentence was its own idea. 'I don't know. I can't answer that for you. I don't like this situation.'

I turned my head away and studied the wall. 'Believe me, I don't like it either. I didn't want this.'

'Tell him not to come.'

'I can't do that.'

'Tell him to get his own place. This is New York. People need space. Nobody shares a studio.'

'He's moving to New York to be with me.'

'Tell him things have changed.'

'He still needs a place to live.'

'This isn't the right way to start.'

'For us?'

Peter didn't say anything. He meant for us.

'Of course, it's not the right way to start,' I said. 'The right way to start is to be twenty-five and carefree and innocent, but it's a little late for that.'

'Have you ever had someone put their finger in your ear?'

'*What?*'

'Have you ever had someone put his finger in your ear. It feels good. When I was a kid, I used to stick pencils in my ear. The eraser side. I love that. Watch.'

Peter put his finger in my ear, pressed against the walls, his nail biting the skin, crescents of hurt. He folded the ear in half, swam through the channels, then reentered the canal, opening up places that weren't there before. It felt like sex. It sounded like sex. Or water. Or a shell at the beach.

When I started to cry, Peter drew me close. My nose pressed into his neck. His fingertips circled my scalp, a tender scratch looping south. Eyes closed, I drifted in the darkness, while Peter whispered *I'm sorry, I'm sorry, I'm sorry.*

This didn't seem right.

'It's not your fault.'

'I know it's not my fault but I'm sorry. I'm sorry you're sad. My dad used to say that when we were upset. It was almost like a wail. *I'm sorry, I'm sorry.*'

He was right. Where had these words been hiding? Why hadn't I said them? I was sorry for the way I had treated Stuart and sorry that I started things with Peter this way and sorry I hadn't known my own heart. Had I told Stuart I was sorry?

I couldn't remember. Probably not. Maybe once, a passing remark, some cheap defense, a hurried transition to the next said thing, when what I needed was an echo, a chorus, a ululation that would build and grow.

I'm sorry, I'm sorry, I'm sorry.

It was time for a joke, some kind of recovery.

'*Daaaaarling*,' I said, pulling back to look at Peter, running my finger down the length of his nose. 'You know I could never leave you. You'll just have to think for the both of us.'

'Tell him not to come.'

'I can't.'

Peter sat up, cross-legged. I sat up to meet him, blew my nose. I studied his long arms, pale with freckles, the way his stomach relaxed in a slight pouch. His toenails were purple, some sort of fungus. He watched me watch him. He smiled.

'Do you like what you see?'

'I do.'

'Lie down.'

'I've got to get going.'

'Lie down.'

We lay down, face to face, close enough that his nose went double and his eyes spun like two blue saucers on a juggler's stick. This was love. Or hypnosis. No, perhaps archeology because he was digging for answers and coming up short. Frustrated, Peter rolled on his back and asked the ceiling his questions.

'*Why do we fall in love? Why do we fall out of love? Why do we have to die?*'

Grampy walks out onto the deck in Maine and drags a director's chair into the sun. I am watching a distant sailboat make its way past the island.

'Well, Lili, shall we get out the Ouija board tonight?' Grampy asks, chuckling at his own joke.

'You still have that thing?'

'Of course,' Grampy says, pretending to be shocked by the question. 'It's in the front hall closet. You know Nanny and I predicted your brother was going to be a boy? Of course, I guess we had a fifty-fifty shot at it.'

'Nana really believed in all that stuff?' I ask.

'Sure.' Grampy nods. 'Nana believed in astrology and reincarnation. She always said she had lived other lives.'

'Who had she been?' I ask.

'Well, she wasn't sure exactly, but she knew she'd lived in a castle.'

I try not to laugh. 'So she was royalty?'

Grampy smiles. 'Naturally.'

Learning the Principle of Creativity in the Realm of Eternal Change

Key West, FL. Any fool knows that when a woman completes a journey of self-discovery, she's supposed to marry the man of her dreams. Or, at the very least, get engaged. Particularly if the woman is as old as Jane Tarbox. And particularly if the woman has already let a high school sweetheart, a Nantucket waiter, a French tennis clown, a college boy, a Wall Street banker, a house painter, a Washington spin doctor, a botanist, a veterinarian, and quite possibly a dreamy writer from Manhattan slip through her fingers. By now the adventuring woman is supposed to have company in her car. By now, *the man is supposed to be driving.*

Yet here I was – alone – roaring through Florida trying not to lose my mind in the heat. For all my predeparture bravado about taking a road trip to sort out my love life, my *real* life, two thousand miles later I hadn't come up with any brilliant solutions. At least nothing pithy enough to sum up in a sentence.

The funny thing was: That was all right. I was all right. Everything was pretty much all right.

Did I feel different? My dad asks me this question every birthday as a joke, and I always say no, but this time the answer was yes, a little. Bolder. More optimistic. I had this blind faith that things would settle down in their own way in their own time.

Somehow.

Of course, hanging your hopes and dreams on Somehow is a pretty shaky bet, but what choice do we have? Besides, Somehow is a big step above *Dream On* or *Fat Chance*. You could do a lot with Somehow, if you didn't try too hard.

The final push south through Florida was long and tedious and unbelievably hot. Florida in August – I must be out of my mind. In Fort Lauderdale, I stayed the night with parents of a college friend. We spent the afternoon watching Max, the family dog, swan dive into the swimming pool to retrieve his chew toy, while my hostess, Sophie, a former actress bubbling with theatrical gush, grilled me with personal questions.

'So do you have a boyfriend? . . . Two? . . . Well, what fun for you! I hope my son finds a nice girl some day, only he likes *Asian* girls. Imagine! *Asian* girls. Don't ask me why.'

Dinner with wineglasses. A bed with ironed sheets. It was so nice to be mothered, I wanted to curl up in the guest bedroom and never leave. But early the next morning, I dragged myself out to the Mazda, which had taken on the cacophonous smell of stale muffin, chardonnay, and dank tent. Sophie packed me a picnic of string beans and crackers – 'What else do vegetarians eat?' – and I headed south through hellish Miami to the Keys, my mind buzzing with images of what was to come.

Plantation Key, Fiesta Key, Long Key, Conch Key, Duck Key, Crawl Key, Boot Key, Pigeon Key, Ramrod Key, Summerland Key, Boca Chica Key, and, get this one, No Name Key. I'd never realized there were so many keys, that this string of islands stretches more than a hundred miles. My back was sweaty against the seat, my butt numb. Every twenty minutes or so, I crossed a bridge, caught a peek of blue water, a tease of beauty, but then another pink stucco shopping center, another billboard reminding us it was only twenty-five miles to Key West's Ripley's Believe It or Not.

It was my first trip to Key West, but I could see it already. There'd be simple, proud hotels, where twenty-five bucks bought you a faded yellow room with rusted screens, a ceiling fan, a rope hammock out back. There'd be limpid beaches, cockatoos, parakeets, and cranes stooped in wetlands. (Somehow I'd morphed the Everglades into the Keys.) As for the famous sunset, a handful of sun-stoned villagers would gather at the town beach to dip a ceremonial toe. And there I'd be . . . tan, barefoot, braless in a black sundress, the proud traveler at journey's end. Around me, a corona, a glow so palpable that rum-warmed couples would shake their heads in admiration. It was a rapturous, almost holy vision. A symphonic final chapter written in purple prose.

They send you off to college to try and gain a little knowledge,
But all you want to do is learn how to score.

I'd been saving this Jimmy Buffett tape for just this moment. Drumming the steering wheel, I sang along with a head bob and shoulder shimmy. At a red light, a goateed guy in a beat-up sedan stared at me and I just smiled.

Fifteen miles . . . six miles . . . Entering Key West.

Here. *Here.* Two thousand miles and finally here. But wait, wait just one minute . . . this town is a mess, *the same old tourist clusterfuck.* Howard Johnson's. Quality Inn. Day's Inn. Alamo. Domino's. White sun frozen in chrome. Cars circling like condors. Cars pulling in, cars pulling out. I almost started to cry.

By the light of the moon
He's a Frenchman for the night . . .

329

Oh, shut up, Jimmy.

Then a sign for Old Town. The road narrowed. And suddenly . . . I was on a tranquil street of brightly colored houses with gingerbread trim and rocking chairs and gay rainbow flags and pastel porches, single porches and double-decker porches that tilted or hunched or curled, like dottering old people set in their ways. Palmettos burst from the sandy soil. Bougainvillea dangled shocking pink blooms. Someone had chucked a pair of sneakers over the telephone wire. You could feel eccentricity pressing against the front doors waiting to be let out, as if the party had started years ago but it was never too late to join.

Parking under an enormous blossoming poinciana tree, I pedaled my bike around until I landed at the Red Rooster Inn, a yellow Victorian with a cock head (pun intended) the size of a dishwasher perched on its second-floor porch.

Inside, the concierge, a sweating gay man with a diamond chip in one ear, graciously let me haggle him down five bucks a night. Then I hit him up for traveling suggestions.

'It all depends on what you want to do,' said the concierge, who reminded me of Sting, only pudgy and rumpled. 'You should probably start with the Conch Train.'

'The Conch Train?'

'It's this red tourist train where they toot-toot round the island and tell you about all the houses.' His hand circled the air.

I rolled my eyes.

'*Uh-huh*. You got it. Well, there's the Hemingway House and Southernmost Point.' He sounded totally bored, or maybe it was too hot to be helpful. 'You will probably spend a lot of time in the bars.'

'I suppose,' I said, not wanting to appear unadventurous.

The phone rang. 'Excuse me.' He daintily plucked the phone with his index finger and thumb. 'What now, Princess?'

'How do *I* know if she's straight?' The concierge rolled his eyes for my benefit.

'*Ask her?* Only for you, Precious.'

He turned to me. 'Our chambermaid wants to know if you're straight.'

I nodded, sliding onto a stool, elbow on the bar, chin in my palm.

'Yes, Francis, you randy boy. Our lovely guest is heterosexual. Good-bye now. And don't call back.'

He hung up the phone, paused. 'And, of course, you'll go down to the sunset so you can say you've been. It's a nightmare, but sacrifices must be . . . And the cemetery . . .'

'The cemetery?'

'*Oh, yeees.* Our cemetery is quite unique. People used to be buried there, but now, well, the water table is so high, the highest elevation on the island is six feet, and I guess the bodies kept floating to the surface so they dug everybody up and put them in crypts. Some of the inscriptions are quite clever.'

'Like?'

'"Wish you were here." Or "I told you I was sick." My favorite is "At least I know where you're sleeping tonight." I haven't seen it for myself, mind you' – he clapped his hand to his heart – 'but that's what I've been *told*. It could be just a story.'

'Wait, it's true or not true?'

'I really can't be sure. There are lots of *stories* about Key West. Some of them *are* true. Don't forget, Key West is an end-of-the-road place. People here are running away, from the law, from life. No one gives a fuck about who you *are* or who you *sleep* with. It's not like all those horrible places like *Iowa* or *Indiana*. I mean, here, when you wake up in the morning, you still know you are gay, but at least you don't have to *hide* it. If people can't deal with faggots, they shouldn't come. *Period.*' He sounded almost petulant now, as if remembering some old slight, but he quickly cheered again. 'That's refreshing for straights, too. No one is peeking under the sheets to see what you're *up* to. The bad part is that no one will *commit* to anything.'

'You mean relationships?'

'Relationships. Jobs. Plans. Tomorrow. They're all running. Forget pinning anyone down. They're drug addicts or artists or gamblers or they're terribly rich or terribly poor or some kind of *criminal* with a record. This island has a long weird history. Key West was settled by pirates and wreckers and scavengers. People come here to escape. Listen, lovely, how many places can you go to an A.A. meeting seven days a week and N.A.—'

'N.A.?'

'Narcotics Anonymous . . . N.A. twice a week.'

I nodded.

'Listen, this island used to be wild, really wild. No laws at all. It was all drugs, and the jail was bursting. Busts every weekend. Now we have *families* and *Disney* and the *Hard Rock Café* and—'

The phone rang again. 'Yes, my hunka burning.'

Pause.

'Listen, straight boy. Hold on to your pants. I'm talking to our lovely guest . . . How do *I* know?'

He looked at me. 'The chambermaid wants to know if you're available?'

I shook my head.

My new friend nodded approvingly. 'I didn't think so. A great girl like you.'

Putting his mouth back to the phone, he snapped, 'No, she's not available. Now go dust or primp or something and stop nagging me with your pathetic fantasy life.'

He slammed down the phone with his thumb and index, pinkie raised. I would have said this was impossible, but I saw it myself.

You might think it tricky to stay lost on a two-by-three-mile island, but I managed admirably. Landmarks disappeared like Brigadoon. My first foray around town, I stumbled on Fort Zachary Taylor, the naval base. The next day, after being told the fort was actually a park with a beach, old Zachary was nowhere to be found. Another morning before breakfast, I went jogging, studying my paper map before heading into the heat, only to end up lost in the projects. Yes, there are projects in Key West where poor folk live in tumbledown shanties with chickens clucking about and couches propped up on front stoops and long stretches of eerie early-morning silence.

All roads lead back to Duval, the island's main commercial drag, an overbuilt strip of restaurants and Jimmy Buffett knickknack stores and cafés serving key lime pie and, according to one guidebook, forty-five T-shirt shops, whose messages rival Atlantic City's for lewdness: '*If You're Not Into Oral Sex, Keep Your Mouth Shut.*'

In a *Paris Review* interview, Hemingway, one of Key West's more illustrious residents, is famously quoted as saying: 'The most essential gift for a good writer is a built-in, shock-proof, shit detector.' The same seemed to hold true for Key West. Apparently, the Southernmost House isn't *really* the southernmost house; it only *used* to be. And Key West's Oldest House may not *actually* be the oldest house, it just says it is. The tour guide at the Hemingway House museum told us that Papa and his third wife, Pauline, were the proud owners of fifty-one six-toed cats. My guidebook insisted the cat colony actually lived in Cuba, not Key West. After a while, I realized it didn't much matter what was fact and what was fiction, we'd all come to Key West for the myth. Like the stories Nana used to tell, the tales about Key West weren't always true, but they sounded good.

That night, I went to a gay nightclub that people insisted was the *real* Key West. There was a drag show by the pool. I squeezed past handsome boys in clingy shorts and leaned against a white picket fence. Infused with light, the pool water glowed a sensual David Hockney blue, and the evening breeze brushed across its surface like the rustling of desire. I watched it, remembering Peter running his finger along the underside of my arm. It felt like half a lifetime since we had touched.

The M.C. told us to give a warm welcome to Googie Gomez.

Googie strutted out in a hot pink minidress and platform go-go boots with rhinestone sparkles, lip-synching the Top 40 song, 'Barbie Girl.' Though Googie had invested some serious hours in her getup, I have to say Page and I did better back in the rodeo Barbie days. Googie looked like Barbie dumped into radioactive waste, especially as she vamped past a pair of sturdy lesbians with buzz cuts, their hands splaying their pockets like men with nothing to say. Googie certainly had Page and me beat on the sexual moves. She humped a tent pole, slithering a feather boa between her legs like dental floss between teeth, pumped her buttocks to the gods. '*Come on, Barbie, let's go party! Ah, ah, ah, yea.*'

Other drag queens came and went, preening to Elvis songs and Donna Summer, and I confess I found the whole spectacle a bit dull. Key West may pride itself on being risqué, but hell, you could see the same camp in Salt Lake City. And in Utah, there was the added excitement of defying the Mormons. With so few taboos in Key West, Googie Gomez wasn't blasphemy. He was just another girl.

The next morning, I visited Nancy Forrester's Secret Garden, an acre of woman-made rain forest packed with rare botanical ferns, orchids, and mile-high palms, supposedly the country's only frost-free public garden. Nancy was in her fifties, bohemian in her distraction. When I started asking questions, she offered me hot coffee and I asked for water and we parked ourselves on her porch – her house sat in the center of the garden – and talked, or, rather, she talked and I listened.

Nancy told me how she didn't view her garden as horticulture but art, how she could sell this land to a developer and make a killing but she would never leave because she was turning her life over to the spiritual power of green spaces.

She talked so long my hand got sweaty, my notepaper moist. Her story had begun to remind me of the plants in her garden, stretching and entangled, no end or beginning, until I'd long since forgotten my initial question and it was all I could do not to fold my hands over my growling stomach, close my eyes, and doze.

'People feel something special when they come to the garden,' Nancy was saying. 'An energy, you know. We've had weddings here, commitment ceremonies. One woman married herself.'

'*What?*' I perked up from my slump. 'Some woman married herself?'

'Her name's Allison, a beautiful girl. She's a nurse, works with AIDS patients, and last month, she invited all her girlfriends and they had a ceremony here in the garden and she married herself. I mean, not legally, of course. A commitment ceremony. And her dress was—'

'Why did she want to marry herself?' I interrupted.

'You should ask her. She works at the hospital.'

'How did she do it?'

'Well, she wrote her own vows. They were quite beautiful.'

'Until death do us part?'

'Something like that.'

'And the honeymoon?'

Nancy looked at me sternly, trying to decide if I was poking fun. 'You'd have to ask her.'

Marrying myself . . . why, the option had never occurred to me. Finally, the solution I'd been looking for all these miles.

I tried to imagine breaking the news to my parents.

'Mom. Dad. I have something I want to tell you . . . Uh, well . . . I know you've been waiting for me to get married, and I've got some good news: I've decided to marry myself.'

Dad's terry cloth hat falls off his head.

'Now, I know I'm not the in-law you expected . . . but in time I'm sure you'll come to accept me as part of the family.'

335

What a wedding it would be! I'd rent out a Third World island, float in on a boat at sunset, hire native boys to blow trumpets into the night. All my friends would come and we'd dance and I'd feed myself cake and everyone would celebrate my happy future . . . with me! In her tearful toast, my maid of honor would declare it had been love at first sight: She'd explain how, after so many near misses, I'd finally found a soul mate.

After the celebration, when the last guest stumbled home and I'd finally got myself alone in my honeymoon suite and it was time to consummate the vows . . . well, I guess I'd know what to do.

But what if, after the wedding, the Prince finally rode into town on a stallion named Jake? I couldn't marry him, *too*, that would be polygamy. I'd have to divorce myself, dump the old ball and chain. (Roger had always said I'd make a lovely first wife.) But I had such a hard time ending relationships. Seeing love fritter away to nothing, saying good-bye for a lifetime, it was all too tragic.

What would I do without me?

Oh, the heartache, the loss. I'd have to break the news to myself slowly. I'd do it over the phone. Over e-mail. No, no, too lowbrow. I'd do it in person, look myself straight in the eye, hold my hand in mine.

'Lili, you know I still care for you,' I'd tell myself. 'It's me, not you. I just need a little space and time to sort things out, think things through. It's just not fair for you, to go on pretending like this. But don't worry. You'll find someone some day, someone better than me. I wish you only the best. You deserve it. No one deserves it more than you. And you know . . . maybe . . . *we could still be friends.*'

The girl who married herself agreed to meet me for a drink.

She'd been friendly on the phone, flattered to share her story. We met at an outdoor bar, a glorified shack with plastic tables and chairs. As I walked in, a young woman, my age, waved me over. She was pretty, boyish yet girlish, with short brown hair, straight white teeth, and perfect skin. She looked athletic, as if she could hit a softball deep into right field, as if she could run quick enough to catch it.

'How you doing?' she asked, putting down her beer to sit up and shake my hand.

'Great,' I said. 'It's nice of you to meet me.'

'Sure,' she said. 'Just got back from the beach. Get yourself a beer.'

I'd been expecting someone a little crazy, but Allison was not so easy to dismiss. Propping her bare feet on the circular table, she began to tell me about herself. She was thirty-five, divorced, not from herself but from her first husband. Born and raised in Kentucky, she'd gotten married in a Baptist church with a big gown, seven bridesmaids and seven grooms-men, the whole shebang. The marriage hadn't lasted two years.

Of course, I played coroner. 'So what went wrong?'

'I guess I jumped too soon,' she began. 'My husband *looked* like a dream. He had everything I always wanted in someone, except unconditional love, acceptance of who I am. I thought when you got married the man is supposed to love you for who you are, but I was sorely mistaken.'

'What didn't he accept?'

'He just knew how to pick the scabs off old wounds. He was jealous of my past. He made me feel bad about old relationships. He'd ask questions and then hold the answers against me.'

I looked into my beer. Old No. 42 had done a little of that herself.

'After the divorce, I came to Key West for vacation, then realized I had to stay. I've found great space here. I've got this incredible apartment that looks out into trees. You should come see it. It's like a nest, like a treetop cabin. When I first came here, I was a wreck. I didn't know what I felt anymore. I didn't know what was *me*. You really don't have to be you when you're with someone else.'

Ah yes, I thought, the old crab-shell game.

'I knew it was time for me to live alone, but God it was hard at first. I was so lonely and sad. I'd read and write and listen to jazz and write in my journal everyday and watch myself struggle with being alone. But eventually, I found my own place and grew to like me for the first time in my life, to like being in my skin.'

She was so right. This is exactly what I needed to do. I kept *meaning* to be alone, but there had always been so many, well, *interesting men*. Holing up in Key West, breathing in the flowery breeze, losing yourself in a saxophone riff, it sounded so peaceful. Of course, pain often sounds romantic when it isn't your own.

'My women's circle helped a lot,' Allison added.

'*Your what?*'

'Women's circle. Have you heard of these?'

I shook my head.

'We're a bunch of women who get together, people who are looking for community. We meet once a week. They are not bitch sessions or group therapy – well, sometimes they are – but we talk and laugh and do group meditation. We are all just struggling to figure out who we really are and be okay with that. You know, who am I and what is my Truth?'

Who am I? I wondered. *What is my Truth?* Maybe I wasn't deep enough to have a Truth. Maybe I needed to focus on simpler questions, like *Where am I? What is for lunch?* As if to confirm this, I studied Allison's brilliant red toenails, wondering if I could pull off such a shade. *Had I ever had a Truth? If I had, where had I left it?*

'But tell me something about *you*,' Allison said. 'What brought you to Key West?'

'Just traveling,' I said vaguely, implying there was no story worth telling. The last thing I wanted was to talk about me. 'So where did you come up with the wedding idea?'

A book, Allison said. This great book about how to be a luscious, wild woman, and one of the suggestions was to

338

throw yourself a wedding. As soon as Allison read this, she started composing her guest list.

'I've fallen in love with *me*,' she said. 'So I decided to scream it to the world. I'm not perfect; I'm imperfect, but I'm here on earth to be the best Allison I can be.'

'But why marriage?'

'I finally made a commitment to myself, since I had dodged it for thirty-five years. It was a way to honor myself. A marriage of my masculine and feminine sides, my yin and yang, uniting the strong, athletic me with the more yielding, compassionate me. I want to rejoice in my Allison-ness.'

I squirmed. Anything remotely New Agey makes me feel like a Yankee, stoic, more than a little repressed. And yet the Girl Who Married Herself seemed so calm, *so normal*. But honoring myself? Rejoicing in my Lili-ness? Good God, I was trying to overcome my Lili-ness, become someone better. I looked down at the stack of silver bracelets on my wrist, the ripped thumb cuticle, the white spots on my nails, my big knees marked up with old scars.

I looked up, thought of something, and grinned. 'How did you propose?'

Allison got the joke but answered seriously. 'I said something like "You are my running partner, my scuba partner, and my friend and I'd like you to be my wife."'

'Or husband?'

'Husband *and* wife.'

The wedding itself was an intimate affair. Thirteen women – a coven, as Allison put it – gathered at night in Nancy's rustic cottage with wine and bread and cheese and fruit and wedding cake. The bride wore a pale-green dress with a long V in back, a crown of flowers, and dragonfly earrings. She walked down the aisle in bare feet, then read the vows she'd written.

'*I vow to nourish my body and soul with laughter, exercise, nutritious food, positive thoughts and words about myself and others . . . to forever dance to the music of my soul . . .*'

I squirmed again. Dance to the music of my soul? I could barely find my soul, let alone make it play music.

'But what did it *feel* like?' I asked.

Allison considered for a moment.

'Great,' she said. 'I show people the pictures and they say, "Oh, you look so beautiful." And you know, I *felt* beautiful. Oh, and after the vows, I told the guests they could all kiss the bride.'

I laughed. 'So it was better than your first wedding?'

'Better?' Allison frowned. 'No, *different* . . . yes, *better* because with my first wedding, the excitement was outside of me. It was a performance, for my parents, for other people. This one was centered in me, for me.'

It all sounded so me-ish. So me-centric. Me-opic. I couldn't decide if this was a good thing – tending one's own garden, think globally, act locally, that kind of thing – or terribly narcissistic, solipsistic, the plague of our shallow age and times, so self-absorbed, so self-help. Then again, Allison was a nurse, *an AIDS nurse*. She cared for sick people; she gave of herself.

'So are you dating anyone now?' I asked.

The question slipped out. Clearly, if I had been the kind of woman who knew her own Truth, this question would be beside the point, but I didn't and it wasn't.

Allison smiled. 'I've been seeing this wonderful man. He's a former Navy SEAL, of all things. I didn't invite him to the wedding, and his feelings were a little hurt, but he knew, on some level, I only wanted women.'

Emily Post rule #355: Never invite your boyfriend to your wedding. Never invite your husband.

'Do you think you'll ever get married?' I asked. 'I mean, to someone else?'

She laughed. 'Well, I don't know. Old fairy tales die hard. If I did, it would be completely different. I'm not going to lose myself in someone else again. I'd have to be with someone who encourages me to grow, someone who was cocreating with me.'

It sounded like a New Yorker cartoon. One thin woman at a cocktail party whispers to another: '*I used to be codependent, but now I'm cocreative.*'

'So you're happy now?' I asked. 'Happily Ever After?'

Allison wiggled her toes. 'Let's just say the joys are more simple now.'

As we paid the bill and got up to go, I mulled over what Allison had said. Marrying yourself – it was pretty ridiculous. And yet, maybe Allison had a point. Making a commitment to yourself, to your happiness and well-being, knowing what you felt, having some idea why, creating something, being creative with someone, alone but together – they were ideals worth shooting for.

Maybe I *should* marry myself. Though if I did, it would have to be a secret ceremony. No guests, no church, no coven or china. No, if I ever got the nerve to ask for my hand in marriage – and I accepted – I'd definitely have to elope with myself.

Then it occurred to me: Maybe I already had.

As Allison and I walked back to town, a young man rolled his bike toward us, carrying a towheaded toddler in a backpack.

'Leon,' Allison called out, turning to me. 'Now *here's* someone you should meet.'

The stranger gave Allison a hug. His hair fell to his shoulders in long lightning bolts. His T-shirt was fashionably ripped to expose hard-earned muscles. He looked like a cross between a personal trainer, a Nordic god, and Fabio.

'Heeeey, Allison,' he said softly. 'What's up?'

'Leon, this is Lili,' said Allison, rubbing the little boy's cheek. 'And this angel is Atlas. I've been telling Lili all about my wedding. Lili, if I have one piece of advice for you before you leave Key West, it would be to get Leon to read your chart. This man has changed my life.'

Now, I've never held much stock in astrology, but I believe in the power of accident. And if an astrologer rolls his bike into your path on a sunny afternoon in Key West and he's been known to change lives and you've spent the last two months searching, scrounging, for a little spiritual guidance, well, only a fool would ignore that sign. Or perhaps only a fool would fall for it.

Leon was living on some friend's sailboat, but he could read my chart the next evening if I met him at the bookstore where he worked. I should come around nine; by then Atlas would be asleep. Leon usually charged $100 a reading, but since I was a traveler, I could pay him whatever I could. Throughout these negotiations, Allison beamed up at Leon like a little sister in awe.

The next night, I rode my bike to the bookstore and rang the bell. Leon unlocked the door with a smile. We had two small problems. Atlas was not asleep, not in the least, and Leon had forgotten his chart on the boat.

'The best thing to do is to go out to the boat and do the reading,' he said.

'Where is the boat exactly?' I asked, wondering if this were some kind of ruse, looking at Atlas, debating if he was old enough to play chaperone.

'In the bay,' Leon said. 'We can take a water taxi. They run until one.'

God. This was going to be a long night. I paused, until the old Ken Kesey line came to mind: *You're either on the bus or off the bus*. For a few more days, I was still on the bus.

'I can definitely get back?' I asked.

Leon nodded.

'Let's go.'

As we walked to the docks, I tried to make small talk. 'So do you read charts full time?'

'And write fantasy books,' Leon said. 'This little guy is named for the hero of my fantasy series, Atlas Astroworld. I picked out the name twelve years ago. I am also self-publishing an astrology book. In the first half, I dissect

342

Jungian archetypes. Then I map Jesus' chart. Check out that moon.'

The moon was full and bright as a headbeam. The sheer wonder of it made Leon pause.

'My moon is in Aquarius,' he started up again as I locked my bike to the pier. 'That's how you get a weirdo like me. I have the soul of a humanitarian. But my sign is Aquarius, the mad scientist. Are you getting all this, Atlas?' He peered back at the boy who was fiddling with Leon's hair. 'He's going to know so much by the time he grows up. He's a vegan. I'm thinking I'm going to move soon. Key West is a good place to get your vision started, but my chart says I'm in the process of a major transformation. I'm just leaving it open to the Universe . . .'

Leon struck a pose like a Shakespearean actor, arms imploring the heavens. 'I say "Universe, do with me what you will."'

This was the guy who changed Allison's life? Just as I was wondering how I could politely extricate myself from this chart-reading venture, a boy in a skiff motored up to the dock.

'Here's the water taxi,' Leon said.

There didn't seem a politic way to escape, so I took the young skipper's hand and stepped onto the boat. Leon gave directions and we spun into the bay, weaving between sailboats. The moon fell upon us with so much light, objects held onto their hues, like black-and-white photographs colored by hand. It felt magical to be on the water, free and a bit wild, like racing through Manhattan in a taxi at night. I smiled at Atlas, snug in his pack, his curls flattened by wind. I could have spent hours cruising the bay, but the skiff pulled alongside a good-size sailboat. Leon climbed over the railing.

'How late do you run?' I asked the boy.

'Until one,' he said.

'I definitely need a ride back.'

The boy nodded. 'If you don't call, I'll just come.'

The boat spun around, shot into the night. Leon opened the hatch and climbed down the ladder. I waited on the deck, looking up, taking in the night. Maybe the stars did hold the secret to who we were, who we would be. Every one of us – the fat lady, the drug dealer, the transvestite, the cop. Maybe it wasn't God but the stars who were in charge. Maybe—

'Watch your head coming down the ladder,' Leon called out.

Belowdeck, Leon was arranging a bed for Atlas, pulling out books and a tape recorder, opening a tub of hummus and a bag of organic tortilla chips, telling Atlas it was time for night-night.

'Whose boat is this?' I asked, taking a seat at the galley bench.

'She's a friend of mine, a client, an artist. She lives on the boat but had to leave on sudden notice. Her boyfriend – he's an Aquarius, good guy – is in prison in El Paso for dealing. So she went up there to bail him out. Offered to let me stay here rent-free. So I said, "Hey, Atlas, we're moving to a boat."'

What kind of life was this for a toddler? I looked into Atlas's round blue eyes for signs of distress, but came up empty.

'And his mother?' I asked.

'Louisa lives in Key West. We had a couple good years. I never checked Louisa's chart when I met her. That was my mistake. I should tell you that I am pretty sure in a previous life I was the poet Percy Shelley. Now, he eloped with his first wife, just like Louisa and me. Later Shelley fell in love with another woman, Mary Shelley, the one who wrote *Frankenstein*, and his first wife was so jealous she committed suicide. Now, Louisa's not too happy, but she hasn't tried to kill herself. Anyway, me, I am supposed to be remarried in six months, just like Shelley. I told the universe last night, "Universe, I am ready." Do you like hummus?'

I nodded, speechless, still back on Louisa's not killing herself.

'Now, back in the Renaissance, I am pretty positive I was the German astronomer Johannes Kepler.' Leon waited for my reaction and, sensing skepticism, quickly added, 'Or his apprentice.'

'*Really?*' I said.

Leon plopped Atlas on the bench next to him, facing me.

'Okay,' he said, rubbing his hands together. Leon dipped a chip for Atlas, gave him a pen to hold in his sticky fist and paper for doodling. Then he arranged a piece of cardboard, markers, a compass, and astrologic papers before him and pushed RECORD on the tape recorder.

'Now when were you born?'

'November 22, 1963, at 9:34 a.m. in Hartford, Connecticut.'

Most people pick up on the significance of this date, but Leon made no comment. Instead, he began drawing an astrological chart, describing various parts as he went. Two minutes into it, I was lost.

'Here we have a map of the sky when you were born. These are the Houses. I called them Realms of Experience. The Signs are around here. They are Styles of Archetypal Expression. The DNA is encoded in us. Like in every society since the beginning of time, there has always been a warrior, a leader, a messenger, a little reporter . . .'

He giggled warmly.

I worked up a smile.

'Look here, you've got Capricorn rising. That means you are here to redefine community. You are wearing the mask of the elder, the wise old woman. Your approach to the world – *who you are* – your experience of yourself is Capricorn, which is like going deep within yourself to find the truth, like a hermit, and then bringing it out to the world. You want to achieve something, but you are very cautious and practical.'

Leaning forward, I waited impatiently for the good stuff, something about love.

'Now, you have Libra on the midheaven. But Libra is governed by Venus. And Venus is in Sagittarius. So your

345

career in life has something to do with teaching, philosophy, and expanding horizons. But your motivation is Mars, exploring the spirit. Now, your spirit vision is in the twelfth house, the House of the Subconscious. You've got Venus in there, too. It's like, *whoa*, relationships.'

I perked up. My relationships were very, like, *whoa*.

'And Mars is also there. Now, this house also tells us how you experienced the womb. Yours was in conflict.'

Already in the womb, I was in conflict. It was all starting to make sense.

'On one side, you had Mars, the Warrior. The other, Venus, or Love. So you had the push-pull. That might carry into relationships.'

Relationship push-pull. Yes, yes, that was me.

'I guess I am a little confused,' I began.

'Well, overall, you are learning the principle of creativity in the realm of eternal change,' Leon said. 'It's a deep statement.'

Leon paused, giving me time to absorb this wisdom. Great gobs of hummus dribbled down Atlas's cheeks.

'So you have the soul of a genius,' Leon continued, 'a little inhibited, but it's going to shine more over time. You are following the path of the sorcerer, the gypsy, the scholar. Now, Venus is the significator of your midheaven in your twelfth House of Images and Illusions. This is a very romantic place. You are in love with love.'

In love with love – well, that was true.

Leon picked up an astrology text. 'You're searching for the perfect, idealistic experience. Some people will search forever for Prince Charming only to discover the person they desire is human and fallible after all.'

After all this – no prince?

'Now, your Jupiter is in Aries . . . This means you value self-expression, action, belief based on personal experience, doing your own thing . . . you're probably going to write about some weird things . . . weird things . . . weird things.'

I tried to pay attention but felt myself drifting off into the twelfth House of Daydreams and Exhaustion. It was too much to take in at once. I sat straight as a mannequin and pretended to listen, but let my thoughts wander where they would. Going to an astrologer was like seeing a shrink. You pay someone money to tell you nice things, to make life's chaos understandable, to reassure you your fuck-ups weren't entirely your fault. Hell, even the best astrologers never got it *all* right. They talked and talked and you picked out the parts that fit you, like hunting for your clean clothes in the family laundry basket. If you didn't know it coming in, you wouldn't believe it going out.

Atlas's eyes were getting heavier, and so were mine. The boat cradled us and Leon's words soothed like white noise. He was saying something about Jesus having three signs in Scorpio, or maybe I did, or maybe he did, I'm not sure; I wasn't listening.

'You are in the process of a slow, powerful transformation . . . digging and probing to find the truth . . . Wisdom often comes from the soothsayer, the genius, the fool . . .'

So I had journeyed two thousand miles to end up on a borrowed sailboat with an astrologer who thought he was Johannes Kepler reincarnated. He was forecasting my destiny, but I couldn't even listen. We all had to run our own circles, I guess, relearn what the last generation had learned and *told* you and you *knew*, but didn't *really* know, because it hadn't happened to you. Hardly an efficient way for a species to operate. Darwin would not be pleased. (Of course, anything that displeased Darwin pleased me immensely.) I guess there weren't any real answers until you made them real. It reminded me of a news story I'd once read. A preacher in North Carolina had performed a mass baptism, saving two thousand souls in a single morning. The job was so Herculean, he'd done the Lord's work with a fire hose.

'It's not the water,' the preacher had explained. *'It's the belief you have in it.'*

347

Maybe the same held true for husbands. It wasn't so much the man, but the faith you had in him. Maybe there wasn't a right man until you chose one, until you let yourself believe.

'*You are a perpetual traveler. You are physically restless. Independence is the breath of life for you. Your many adventures can interfere with your ability to form close relationships. You trust logic over emotion . . . but you are working to effectively combine your heart and your mind.*'

Leon consulted another book, eyes jumpy, chin gleaming. Leon had all the answers, but I was ready to settle for a few decent questions. *Where did love go?* I had no idea, but this much seemed clear: It was stupid to make a list of requirements about love. *Everything was negotiable.* Even if you chose the dowdiest Husband, your fate wasn't secure. Everything love touched turned risky. It was all knife and fish.

Come to think of it, this whole happy-ending business was silly. Love might be happy; but it was never an ending. Why? Because love wasn't *one* thing; it was many. Love shifted, evolved. *It got old.* Either you learned to live with old love – appreciate the rhythm of its tides, cherish the occasional rogue wave – or you spent your life chasing new love, like some bombed-out groupie forever on tour. Choosing the rowdy road show meant missing out on other things, quieter pleasures – *the joys are more simple now* – like watching your kid toddle around naked in one of those cheap plastic baby pools and her pointing to the *wawa* like she invented the stuff herself and your explaining that this water was like the water in the ocean and the water that was rain and the water that was ice. Water was all these things; like love was all these things: pool and ocean and rain and ice.

'*You are learning a triple dose of surrender. Letting things go, moving on.* Render *means to melt.* Sur *means to the highest. So it's like melting to God.*'

Who wanted all the answers to love anyway? Having the perfect road map would make romance as deadly as the Conch Train, as tedious as painting by numbers. Better to stumble along. *Anything worth doing was worth doing badly.* Besides, love that ended badly had its own sort of grace; it was worth celebrating; it was real at the time. Maybe I'd misjudged Grace in that way. Maybe Grace wasn't always calm and composed, a wooden boat patiently rowing to shore. Maybe Grace slopped along in Troy's motorboat, maybe it schlepped through the mud flats in a sinking whaler, with tackle boxes and knotted throw nets and dead bait, not a life preserver in sight. Maybe the struggle to Grace *was* Grace; maybe the struggle to love *was* love. Maybe you didn't have to get anywhere, you just had to go.

I stirred this around a good while, as the boat swung on its mooring, as the sheets clanked against the mast, as the sea slopped against the hull, as the astrologer rattled on about rising suns, as the moon whispered iridescent light through the open hatch. And I thought, *I am ready to go home now. It's time to drive in the other direction.*

Atlas had fallen asleep, his cheek resting on a cushion. Just as I was wishing that Leon would pick him up and tuck him into bed, I heard the purr of a motor.

'I think I hear the boat,' I said, trying not to sound overly eager.

'*Oh, no.*' Leon grabbed his hair with his hands. 'I'm not done. I'm . . . I'm . . . I am going to have to send this to you.'

'I could send you a check,' I offered.

Leon nodded. 'Leave me your address.'

I scribbled my address, thanked Leon, gave a silent goodbye to Atlas, and crawled up the wood ladder into the night, breathing in all that freedom and air. The skipper with the boyish face was waiting for me.

'How did it go?' he asked, as I stepped over the railing.

'Nice enough,' I said. 'Although I don't think I learned much.'

The boy nodded, as if he wasn't surprised.

On the ride back, the taxi guy and I got to talking and he told me he'd been in Key West for two years now and it was time to find a 'land job.' I'd never heard that expression, a land job. He said a lot of people in Key West live on boats so they didn't have to pay taxes, so they didn't really exist. They collect welfare or disability. They drink or deal or hide out, drifting.

Drifting, I'd had enough of that for a while. The way I see it, Key West is a good place to get your vision started, but I was ready to move on, ready to call Peter and see what would happen next, ready to open myself up to the Universe. And maybe even the power of green spaces.

I looked over at the boy. He reminded me of someone, but I couldn't think whom. This used to happen to me all the time. Strangers would stop me on the street and swear I looked just like their neighbor, cousin, childhood friend. They promised it was a compliment, but it never felt like one. The funny thing was, it didn't happen anymore. Maybe it takes a few decades to be you – enough that no one mistakes you for someone you're not. Maybe *you* need a few decades before you don't mistake *yourself* for someone you're not.

Leaning back, I watched the clouds race past the moon, feeling my automatic bailer drain once again. The dozing boats awoke as we sped past them, then quieted back down, prows to the wind, drifting only as far as their moorings allowed.

'*Universe*,' I whispered, '*do with me what you will.*'

Again the boat ride ended too quickly. Tilting my watch to catch the moon glow, I saw it was past one, though now, for some reason, I didn't feel tired. Just as the boy offered to take me on a ride around the bay, a blond Rasta-looking guy slithered toward us, collapsed against a piling, opened a Styrofoam take-out container, and began scarfing down a hamburger. He sat cross-legged, his thighs as thin as the French fries he folded into his mouth. He told us he was being deported to Cuba in the morning and was looking to sell his boat, a thirty-five-footer.

'How much you want for it?' the taxi guy asked.

The man looked at him, forehead creasing as he figured his odds. 'Twenty thousand, but I'd take ten.'

The taxi guy shook his head. Out of his league.

'I paid twenty, two years ago,' Rasta man said, scratching his calf with a thumbnail. 'But I gotta unload it. They're going to ship my ass out of here.'

He gestured at me with his greasy chin.

'You want to get married?' he asked, through bits of churning hamburger. 'You get the boat. I get the marriage license.'

'Sounds like a deal,' I said. 'Nice boat?'

'Great boat.' He took another bite. 'Of course, I'd have to get divorced first.'

Another marriage proposal. Some girls have all the luck. And as indisputable proof of the success of my journey, this time I knew just what to say.

The next day, I drifted around town, saying good-bye to the sights, staggering over the prickly coral at Fort Taylor beach, trying to wade deep enough to swim. That evening, I went to Mallory Square to watch the sun go down.

It was, as the concierge had warned me, a 'scene.' Hundreds, maybe thousands, of tourists cram onto a wharf, milling and mingling among skeevy palm readers and come-hither portrait artists and jugglers on unicycles, playing with fire, passing the hat. Even though watching the sunset in Key West is a famous attraction, what tourists are *supposed* to do, you still feel like a chump, as though anyone with an iota of imagination would have taken one look and bailed. Forget bare feet, not with all the fallen candy and bird crap, and when it's time for a libation, one meager Myers and OJ sets you back seven bucks, and then you realize just how bad your timing is; not only are you thirty years too late for the hippies, but in August, the sun doesn't fall into the sea but disappears behind an island owned by drug kingpins and captains of industry. Not that it matters much because there's nothing even vaguely poetic about this particular descent into evening, not with the muscle-bound juggler one toss away from self-immolation and the sunset cruises slopping through the bay and the tongue-studded waif asking you to take her picture with a disposable camera.

'How do you focus?' I asked, staring into the yellow cardboard box.

'Don't focus,' she said. 'Just push the button.'

If this was the last spit of sand in America, we needed to think about landfill. This wasn't the picturesque ending I'd imagined for myself; surely, I hadn't traveled all this way to wind up in a tourist cliché. But even when a place is pretty much ruined, you can usually salvage something decent if you get in the right frame of mind. Squeezing under an out-of-bounds cord, I claimed a spot on the edge of the pier, slipped off my sandals, dangling my toes over the water, thought about how far I'd come. Two months ago, I'd stood on top of Cadillac Mountain, with Stuart and Brando, watching the cold solstice sun rise from the east. I was so scared back then, confused and edgy. And here I was – sitting on the proverbial dock of the bay, in my linen dress with shell buttons, smoking a bummed cigarette, sucking ice cubes from an empty cocktail. Uncoiled, that's how I felt. Like a snarl of string patiently untangled, ready to serve some worthy purpose.

Tomorrow it would be time to head home, but wait, not so fast. Right now, I was sat in this moment, rubbing dirt off one ankle, waiting for the crowd to move on. The sun, heavy now and low in the sky, was trapped behind the rich people and their houses, though slivers of orange light periodically shot out, as if to insist it ain't over. Not yet.

This land, this country, it waits patiently for us. Like some lopsided love affair, the traveler takes and takes and gives almost nothing back. In your time of need, you can throw yourself against it and see what happens. Your journey, your nebulous need to lose yourself for a while, doesn't have to make sense. Intuition will do, a hunch or an itch, and when the duffel bag is zipped, you're good to go.

And so we begin anew. Accelerating into the shyness of morning, hugging the middle lane until we make up our minds. These questions of loneliness, togetherness – you can only go so far in those old shoes. As best as I could make out, the only way to be alone is to keep moving, and even then it isn't easy; and the only way to live with someone is to keep moving, and even then it isn't easy. Perhaps relationships were not so much a question of bravery as practice. Practice in the nimble art of reinvention.

It was dark now. Mallory Square had emptied except for a few couples whispering secrets, sharing a last cigarette. I walked to Duval Street, bought a slice of pizza, and sat back to watch the tourists float downstream.

Dad

Before heading north, I called a few friends and then my parents. Dad answered the phone and after some where-are-you-how's-the-car-when-are-you-coming-home small talk, he relaxed and I told him the fresh gossip I'd just learned through the grapevine: Dodge Dominguez was rich, off-the-charts rich.

He was building a house in Silicon Valley that was big enough for his cold cereal wife and their two kids, all of whom, it seemed, needed a lot of space. To juice up the story, I embellished with a few fictional details: It was a two-million-dollar house. Most of it glass. There was a sunken tub. A gazebo. A Bernese mountain dog. One hell of a shower.

Dad heard my sarcasm, a petty brand of envy. It pissed him off to hear his only daughter whine, and he sputtered: 'But you don't care about money. You care about writing and Mexico and love.'

I nearly dropped the phone.

Only a few people love me enough to remind me who I am.

I reached for a pen and scribbled his quote on a Post-it. Later, I tucked the yellow paper in my wallet for safekeeping, next to my other forms of identification. They were words I could lean on, my own wooden cane, should one day I feel boxed in or lost or be stuck in the canned soup aisle, unable to move.

Grampy walks out onto the deck in Maine and drags a director's chair into the sun. I am daydreaming about things that have happened and things that might be.

Grampy takes a long sip of his favorite summer beverage: cold coffee mixed with prune juice. I look at his hands, his freckles, his gold ring.

'So, Grampy, what was your wedding like?' I ask.

Grampy studies the ocean, the islands, looking deep into memory, trying to bring back the day.

'Well, I don't know,' he says. 'Not too big. There were a bunch of people there, I guess. I was so excited I didn't pay much attention. The day I married Nanny, my feet didn't touch the ground. Have you ever felt like that?'

I nod. Just recently, in fact.

'Well, that's the way it was with me,' he says. 'I just floated into church, and there she was.'

Floating

Little St Simons Island, GA. There was just one more thing I wanted to do.

A couple of weeks earlier in South Carolina, while walking down the beach on Kiawah Island, I met this guy named Dean who insisted the place I *really* needed to go was Little St Simons, a private island off the coast of Georgia. A businessman named Philip Berolzheimer bought the island in 1908 to harvest lumber to make pencils, but then fell in love with the land and established a nature preserve. Except for a few dirt roads, a lodge, and a handful of guest houses, the barrier island was pure wilderness, ten thousand acres of maritime woods and tidal marsh, habited by deer and alligators and diamondback rattlesnakes.

For most of the year, the Berolzheimer family rented out their place, often for corporate retreats. Rooms were exorbitant, but artists were occasionally invited to stay for free. Dean, a friend of the great-grandson of Philip Berolzheimer, said he'd make a phone call and see if he could swing me a room. After he laid the groundwork, I called the resort's manager, Lucy, and said I was a writer, writing something about something. She asked me to check back in a week. When I called again from Key West, Lucy invited me to spend one night, gratis.

The whole time this was happening, I kept thinking this pencil story sounded awfully familiar. So did the name Berolzheimer. Finally, I put two and two together. Six years after breaking up with Dodge, I was heading off to the private island owned by his parents' closest friends, a place Dodge and I had always meant to visit, to ride horses on the beach.

At first, I felt triumphant, even smug. I didn't need Dodge to bring me to paradise, I could get there on my own. There were, of course, a few minor differences. Dodge's family visited at Thanksgiving, when the air is brisk and the bugs minimal; I was arriving in the dead of August, when the Georgian shoreline turns into a second Mosquito Coast. When Dodge came, he was a guest of honor invited to stay as long as his busy schedule allowed. I was a passing acquaintance of a friend of the great-grandson of the original owner; my welcome expired in twenty-four hours.

I rode to the island on a small shuttle boat with a naturalist and a cook. When we arrived at a dock near the central lodge, I saw we were back in the land of live oaks and palmettos. Lucy, a gentle woman with a tanned face, met me at the dock and showed me to a guest house. The island reminded me of a Southern version of Sundance, Robert Redford's resort in Utah, where, for a pretty price, you could admire the quiet wonder of nature while being pampered in a most understated way. The bed was large and firm with thick cotton sheets. Each room came equipped with a bathrobe, a flashlight, bug spray, just like the *Therapeutic*. The lodge was decorated with buck heads and antique family portraits. On a sideboard outside the kitchen sat Thermoses of cold drinks and a plate of homemade sugar cookies.

Little St Simons has no paved roads and only a handful of staff vehicles. Guests navigate the island by foot, horse, or bike. I opted for a bike, grabbing a blue no-speed bicycle from the communal fleet and heading down the two-mile path through the woods to the beach. The forest was magical. In a marshy clearing, a pair of deer nibbled the sweet grass.

Bleach-white egrets stood motionless, their necks a wisp of an S, as if a calligrapher had drawn them by hand. I saw my first armadillo, a little old lady hunched under a round, lacquered shell, tiny feet pinching dainty steps as if she were afraid to soil her shoes, tail swaying like a parasol she'd forgotten she was holding.

I was a happy, sweaty mess; so much beauty waiting for me to roll up and see. Eventually, the forest opened onto a field of beach grass. At the path's end stood a gazebo. I threw down my bike on the sand and walked to the edge of the grass.

And there was the beach. A spectacular beach, all to myself. Gray, hard-packed sand stretched for seven miles. After so much honky-tonk development, it felt miraculous to find a shore utterly barren. The horizon was a single, uncluttered line, with nothing but water between me and Africa. I swam and walked and found myself singing.

That night, we gathered for dinner in the main lodge. The island's dozen guests sat together family-style, passing platters of meat, bowls of mashed potatoes and steamed cauliflower.

'How's Claudia doing?' a Canadian woman asked.

'Better,' said a man I took to be Claudia's husband. 'But we had quite a scare.'

'What happened?' I asked.

'My wife was bitten by a stingray,' the husband said. 'She was wading at the beach, felt something slimy and tried to jump away but it was too late. She was in terrible pain, couldn't walk. I had to carry her to the truck. She's spent the day in bed with a fever and was really dizzy.'

'That sounds terrible,' I said.

Terrible, and yet not terrible enough to dissuade me from fulfilling one final plan I'd hatched. All these weeks of driving along the beach, and I still hadn't gone swimming at night. After dinner, I wanted to ride back to the beach and skinny dip. I wanted to stroll down the beach naked in the moonlight. It was time to dance to the rhythm of my soul.

* * *

Back in my room, dinner caught up with me. Wavering at the door, I looked longingly at the crisp sheets, the feather pillows, then let out a sigh. On went the bug repellent, the borrowed headlamp, and off I stole into the night.

Somewhere past the lodge, I lost my bearings. It was dark, really dark. I followed one white fence until a pair of bulging eyes jumped into my headlamp. I nearly screamed. A horse, of course. For a brief, irrational moment, I wondered if it would attack. But the mare sneezed contemptuously, and I headed down the dirt path into the woods, my headlamp emitting a meager, hazy glow. It hadn't occurred to me the forest would be spooky. Palmettos cast wild spiked shadows. Heat lightning, brittle flashes of white light, snapped in the distance. Insects darted in close, on the back of my neck. *Buzz, click, tart chirp, wing flap, chewchew, creak, snap, trip, lip, ahhhhhhh, flip, chirp, guzzleguzzle, huzza, snip, flip.* It made the mosquitoes seem friendly, their *zzzz* familiar as family.

My tire skidded out in a sand patch. I got off, slogged through the sand, anxious to get my feet back on the pedals. Rattlesnakes. Alligators. Did they come out at night? Of course they did. Alligators left the swamp at night to forage for food. They had to *cross the road to get to the food.* Sweat trickled underneath my pant legs. Swatting my cheek, shifting my sagging headlamp, I imagined myself as the last human being on planet Earth, an epic figure laboring through the night, the hopes of mankind resting on her shifting lap as she pushed onward, onward to the sea.

Finally, I made out the silhouette of the gazebo. I dropped my bike, walked to the edge of the knee-high grass, looked, and gasped. The beach had disappeared. All of it, gone. The tide had rolled up to within a foot of the grass line. The blue water had blackened to stain. Forget the Aphrodite routine; I'd landed at the river Styx.

The last thing I wanted to do was swim, but *by God, I was going to swim.* I lifted my sweaty shirt over my head, unzipped my khakis, stepped through the leg holes of my cotton underwear, dropping my belongings in a pile on the grass. My clothing suddenly seemed precious, pieces of me I didn't want to leave behind.

I took a baby step forward, felt my toes sink into the sand. The waves rushed forward in looping, mesmerizing swirls, pulling back sand, pulling under bits of shell, whatever its greedy arms could grasp. The heat lightning lit the horizon with staccato pulses; a clot of purple clouds brooded low in the sky. Not a light or window or warm voice, just the hungry murmurings of the tide and hot flashes of electricity gone mad. What is the first rule of swimming? Never swim alone. Who was I kidding?

We spend our whole lives swimming alone.

I marched defiantly forward.

The water reached my knees. The grade of the beach was so gradual, it was going to take forever to wade out deep enough to swim. I imagined stingrays darting under the surface, their diamond-shaped bodies cutting figure-eights between my legs. Who would find me here if one bit? I'd have to slither onto the sand, a fish come to land, all white lips and yellow belly, hoping someone had the good sense to miss me.

But who?

I walked up to my waist. A gooey something slithered past my calf, followed by the familiar prickle of a fresh jellyfish sting. My hands stirred up phosphorescence, tiny silver beads that had lost their chain. Their beauty seemed like a trap, an evil enchantment designed to lure me into deeper water.

There I stood. Half wet. Half dry.

Then the voices rose, the Greeks, the chorus. *You are so pathetic. Alligators and rattlesnakes and riptide and stingrays — only you could turn a midnight swim into a death march.*

I chopped the water with the edge of my hand. Phosphorescence flew. I remembered that day at the beach on the Cape, the first time I saw waves. I guess, in some ways, I would always be the same timid girl. The key was to motor through fear, swim around it, carry on, imagine the pleasures waiting on the far side of the waves. *This was my life*, a story I wrote as I went, and maybe I didn't believe in God and maybe I only knew a few things about love, but I knew something about storytelling and this *particular* chapter of this *particular* story ended with me swimming naked. It was the natural rhythm of the tale – it might have even been my Truth. Or maybe it just sounded good.

I stretched my arms into the water and felt my bare feet lift off the sand.

And there I was, floating.

One woman on the edge of the Atlantic, letting the ocean take her where it would. When the tide swooped in, so did I. When it pulled back, I drifted from shore. My breathing slowed to meet its cadence, and I paddled, not to go anywhere in particular but merely to wallow, one sea creature among many, a mermaid without the tail. I reached down to scratch my jellyfish bite, felt the lightning shake through me. Then I had a thought that made me happy: I was living up to the story I wanted to write.

When I started to get cold, I stood, dipping my hair back into the water, smoothing it against my scalp.

And then, slowly, serenely, I walked out of the sea.

Acknowledgments

I would like to thank all my friends and fellow writers who waded through pages of this manuscript and offered me insight and encouragement. They include Barbara Bean, Tom Chiarella, Barney Collier, Gail Greiner, Lis Harris, Sally Hurst, Robert Issacs, Richard Locke, Jeff McMahon, Julie Nichols, Michael Scammell, Sarah Shey, Thomas Roma, Craig Wolff, and Jim Zug. Many thanks to Alex Boyden, Liz O'Connor, John McEvoy, and Charlotte and Ozzie Sherman for putting me up on the road, and Margaret Traub-Aguirre and Penny Britell for giving me work at home. Also, I am sincerely grateful to my agent, Elizabeth Sheinkman, and my editors, Becky Cole, Suzanne Oaks and Claire Johnson at Broadway Books. I would also like to thank the men and women in this story – the people, not the characters – who helped me find my way. And finally, most of all, I would like to thank my husband, Peter Graham, who gave me the courage to write something that mattered.

INSTRUCTIONS FOR VISITORS
LIFE AND LOVE IN A FRENCH TOWN

Helen Stevenson

'THE MOST AUTHENTIC, ENJOYABLE AND EVOCATIVE BOOK ON
FRENCH LIFE THAT I HAVE READ IN YEARS'
Joanne Harris

'WHAT BEGINS AS A SUPERIOR LYRICAL TRAVEL GUIDE
TRANSFORMS INTO A TENDER LOVE STORY AND A VERY
PERSONAL MEMOIR OF A DISASTROUS AFFAIR'
Good Housekeeping, Book of the Month

Le village is a small town at the southwesternmost tip of France. Here a young
Englishwoman fell in love with France, the French and one Frenchman in
particular. In her seductive, lyrical and witty memoir Helen Stevenson writes
not as an expat but as someone adopted by villagers as one of their own. By
Stefan, the Maoist tennis fanatic, who lives off his lover in solidarity with
the unemployed; by Gigi, the chic boutique owner who dresses her ex-lovers'
girlfriends; and by Luc, the crumpled cowboy painter and part-time dentist,
who comes to embody both the joys and the difficulties of transplanting
oneself into someone else's country, culture and heart.

'IN HELEN STEVENSON'S MEMOIR OF AN ILL-FATED LOVE AFFAIR
. . . SEX AND GOSSIP HELP PASS THE TIME. THERE ARE AFFAIRS,
BUT ALSO HISTRIONIC JEALOUSY, MELODRAMATIC BUST-UPS
AND ANY AMOUNT OF UNREQUITED LUST . . . A PLAUSIBLE AND
SOMETIMES AFFECTIONATE PORTRAYAL OF ONE SLICE OF
FRENCH LIFE'
Independent on Sunday

'AS BEGUILING AND AS ENIGMATICALLY SEDUCTIVE A PIECE OF
WRITING AS YOU COULD ASK FOR . . . A BEAUTIFULLY TACTILE
AND REFLECTIVE MEDITATION ON THE OUTSIDER'S EXPERIENCE
OF A COMMUNITY'
The Times

'A STARTLINGLY ORIGINAL WORK'
Harpers & Queen, Book of the Month

'CLEVER, GRIPPING AND ELEGANTLY WRITTEN'
Independent

0 552 99928 8

BLACK SWAN

BEST FOOT FORWARD
From La Rochelle to Lake Geneva – the Misadventures of a Walking Woman
by Susie Kelly

Why would an unfit, fifty-something Englishwoman embark on a solo walk cross France from La Rochelle on the west coast to Lake Geneva over the Swiss border?

And why would a total stranger from San Antonio, Texas come to live in her crumbling French farmhouse to house-sit for a multitude of boisterous and unpredictable animals?

With no experience of hiking or camping, not to mention using a compass, Susie Kelly found out the hard way that it is possible to be overloaded and ill-prepared at the same time. Scorching days, glacial nights, perpetual blisters, inaccurate maps, a leaking tent and an inappropriate sleeping bag were daily vexations, but as she hobbled eastwards, the glory of the French landscape revealed its magic and the kindness of strangers repaid her discomfort in spades.

Best Foot Forward is an hilarious and heart-warming tale of English eccentricity, the American pioneering spirit, and two women old enough to know better.

A Bantam Paperback
0 553 81490 7

FOUR CORNERS
A Journey into the Heart of Papua New Guinea
by Kira Salak

The Beach meets *Heart of Darkness* in an extraordinary travel memoir charting 24-year-old Kira Salak's three-month solo journey across Papua New Guinea.

Following the route taken by British explorer Ivan Champion in 1927, and amid breathtaking landscapes and wildlife, Salak travelled across this remote Pacific island – often called the last frontier of adventure travel – by dugout canoe and on foot. Along the way, she stayed in a village where cannibalism was still practiced behind the backs of the missionaries, met the leader of the OPM – the separatist guerrilla movement opposing the Indonesian occupation of Western New Guinea – and undertook a near-fatal trek through the jungle.

Selected by the *New York Times Book Review* as a Notable Travel Book of the year, *Four Corners* is both a gripping true story and a parallel journey into the author's past, where she revisits the demons that drove her to experience situations most of us can barely imagine.

'Kira Salak is a real-life Lara Croft'
New York Times

'A luminously written, thoughtful account . . . exemplary travel writing'
Kirkus Reviews

'A remarkable work . . . her encounters with fierce-looking men and women are surprisingly accurate and full of charm'
Tobias Schneebaum, author of *Where the Spirits Dwell: An Odyssey in the New Guinea Jungle*

A Bantam Paperback
0 553 81550 4

TAKE ME WITH YOU
A Round-the-World Journey to Invite a Stranger Home
by Brad Newsham

Shortlisted for WHSmith's Travel Book of the Year 2003

'For everyone who believes that travel is mostly about kindness and an open heart . . . Newsham brings back treasures that every wanderer might envy'
Pico Iyer

Someday, when I am rich, I am going to invite someone from my travels to visit me in America.

Brad Newsham was a twenty-two-year-old travelling through Afghanistan when he wrote this in his journal. Fourteen years later, he's a Yellow Taxi driver working in San Francisco. He's not rich, but he has never forgotten his vow.

Take Me With You is the compelling account of his three-month journey through the Philippines, India, Egypt, Kenya, Tanzania, Zimbabwe and South Africa as he searches for the right person – someone who couldn't afford to leave their own country, let alone holiday in the West. Newsham's story will change the way you think about your life and the lives of those you meet when you travel.

Who does he invite home? Read *Take Me With You* and find out . . .

'A terrific travelogue. He is a wonderful guide: observant, curious, witty without being clownish, open-minded without being gullible . . . Newsham offers an abundance of colour and telling detail'
San Francisco Examiner & Chronicle

A Bantam Paperback
0 553 81448 6

A SELECTED LIST OF TRAVEL WRITING
AVAILABLE FROM TRANSWORLD

THE PRICES SHOWN BELOW WERE CORRECT AT THE TIME OF GOING TO PRESS.
HOWEVER TRANSWORLD PUBLISHERS RESERVE THE RIGHT TO SHOW NEW RETAIL
PRICES ON COVERS WHICH MAY DIFFER FROM THOSE PREVIOUSLY ADVERTISED IN THE
TEXT OR ELSEWHERE.

All Transworld titles are available by post from:
Bookpost, PO Box 29, Douglas, Isle of Man IM99 1BQ
Credit cards accepted. Please telephone 01624 836000,
fax 01624 837033, Internet http://www.bookpost.co.uk or
e-mail: bookshop@enterprise.net for details.
Free postage and packing in the UK.
Overseas customers allow £1 per book.